SIMPLE, BRIEF,
AND PRECISE

How to Write with Clarity

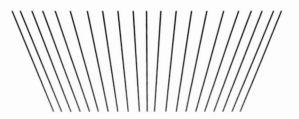

DARREL WALTERS

GiA

GIA Publications Inc.

SIMPLE, BRIEF, AND PRECISE
How to Write with Clarity
DARREL WALTERS

G-10499
ISBN: 978-1-62277-595-8

Copyright © 2021 GIA Publications, Inc.
7404 South Mason Avenue
Chicago, IL 60638
www.giamusic.com

No matter how eloquently a dog may bark, he cannot tell you that his parents were poor but honest.

- Bertrand Russell

Each species has a skill that distinguishes it. Birds fly. Fish swim. People think and use language.

Our species-specific gift makes language indispensable to effective human interaction. Language skills correlate highly with success in creating academic and professional documents, exploring possibilities, promoting ideas, collaborating with others, and—in general—conducting business of any kind. For that reason, any institution or business beset by individual failures to write effectively will be crippled by misunderstandings, errors, senseless inquiries, and wrong turns—and ultimately by the personal and financial losses that those entanglements generate.

TABLE OF CONTENTS

Writing as a Process

LIST OF FIGURES

ACKNOWLEDGEMENTS

I am indebted to friends, colleagues, and students from various businesses and universities with whom I have worked and from whom I have learned, and especially to those who took time to read *Simple, Brief, and Precise* in manuscript form and offer helpful comments. Thanks are due especially to Richard Grunow and Christopher Azzara, and to the faculty and students at Eastman School of Music. Two other persons were invaluable in the final stages of preparation. Kerry Green swept the final manuscript for cleanliness, and Laura Bauder formatted it.

The late Marcella O'Connor, an English teacher from Muskegon, Michigan, has played a greater role in my writing than anyone can know. She insisted long ago that I respect the art of language and perpetually elevate my use of it. The force of her will and the power of her lessons lit my path. During our last conversation, when she was just short of her 101st birthday, she continued to inspire me—as she does even now, more than 20 years after her passing.

For years of support and forbearance, I am especially grateful to the love of my life, Carol Walters, and to my daughters. All large projects have a way of spilling energy and sacrifice into the lives of loved ones—energy and sacrifice that I acknowledge and appreciate.

INTRODUCTION

In a 1970 cartoon, Pogo the Possum looked at a forest strewn with trash that shouldn't have been there. He paraphrased Commander Perry's classic military message: We have met the enemy, and he is us.

Today we struggle through page after page of difficult-to-read writing strewn with material that shouldn't be there. We waste time with its density and lack of clarity. It runs us in circles and raises more questions than it answers. Like the trash in Pogo's forest, the trash strewn throughout pages of writing is not "just there." We put it there. We throw hurdles in each other's way with one writing flaw after another. We have met the enemy, and he is us.

Seldom is the problem laziness, nor is it insensitivity toward readers. Rarely do any of us think "I'll just throw words out there and let the next person worry about what they mean." Still, we find ourselves wasting time with each other's confusing, drudgery-laden writing. Then we spend more time by telephone, e-mail, or text, asking "What did you mean by...?" The only reason two persons who know and use the same language should ever have to ask "what do you mean" is if the language is used less than well.

We've had help getting into this fix. A few generations ago nearly all teachers of all subjects railed against poor uses of English and insisted on well-written papers. Then the rarified air of post-World War II spawned the "cool" generation of the 1960s. Criticism that had been seen as helpful to students was seen by many as hurtful. Whole school systems subscribed to a make-them-feel-good approach. Great numbers of teachers yielded to pressures to be less "uptight"—to protect students' self-esteem. Many good teachers fought the trend (some still are), but eventually most of the old guard retired. The subliminal message to impressionable students was that using language well is not particularly important. Language skills withered.

Inattentiveness to language now has become a habit for many, compounded by impaired skill due to lessons not learned. We torture each other with the fallout. That doesn't have to continue. Much of what's needed to stem the tide is specific and learnable. By becoming more skillful and more attentive in the use of language, students will produce superior work and businesspersons will restore efficiency to communications and momentum to the business day. Two jobs need to be done to make that a reality:

1. Identify specific writing tendencies that make reading difficult.

2. Care passionately about not only *what* is written, but also *how* it is written.

I'll take care of the first job: that is the target of this book. The second job is yours. If you and I join forces, you can begin almost immediately to write with an eye toward efficient reading—toward communicating in a way that lets others take your message in quickly and accurately. That will allow your readers to get on with their work, clear-headed and confident. The efficient reading you make possible for others will raise the level of productivity around you, and your reputation for clarity will serve you well both professionally and personally.

On the cover of this book you saw an overview of the solutions I propose: if writing is to be read quickly and understood thoroughly, it needs to be **simple**, **brief**, and **precise**. Of course that's only a skeleton. The details of how to accomplish those virtues lie within.

I hope you use *Simple, Brief, and Precise* (and one of my writing seminars if you're so inclined) to reduce the prevalence of dense, unclear writing in your environment. I hope also that your business, institution, or school—by having large numbers of writers seeking simplicity, brevity, and precision—will reap the increased productivity that comes with clear written communication.

Darrel Walters
Ft. Washington, Pennsylvania

THOUGHTS ABOUT USING THIS BOOK

Simple, Brief, and Precise is designed to be an accessible writing guide for business professionals and students, with particularly keen appropriateness for graduate students. Chapters are short, principles concise, and examples and figures uncomplicated. Content stems from writing flaws seen in tens of thousands of pages of editing and advising. You'll find it to be a friendly and helpful writing companion exactly as it is, but a few preparatory tips will help you extend and enhance your study.

1. Read Chapter 10 to reinforce the importance of attitude toward language.

2. Think of the book's last section, "Writing as a Process," as The Big Picture. Whether you read that first or last is a matter of personal preference.

3. Scan columns of verbs in Appendix A sparingly to avoid overload.

4. Leaf through Appendix B, beginning on page 154. Mark words that strike you as personally troublesome, and study a few of them periodically when small bits of time permit.

5. To check your progress as you proceed through *Simple, Brief, and Precise*, make use of the *WORKBOOK* housed in Appendix D. It amounts to a collection of writing exercises and solutions designed to seal in learning as you complete corresponding chapters or sections of chapters. **Read the introductory material on page 202 before you begin to use the exercises.**

6. Use the study planner on the next page if you want to proceed through the book systematically in the manner of a self-directed writing course.

The first session in the study planner (longer than the others) **is important to your gaining an overview of the book.** The other 17 sessions are somewhat equivalent in length. The order shown below is as good as any, and it has some merit because of occasional references back to previous chapters. In reality, though, sequence is not critically important after Session 1. Do use exercises from Appendix D as directed throughout the text to inventory and strengthen your learning as you proceed.

Study Planner

Session	Pages	Content
1.	iv–xi, 1–9	Table of Contents, Introduction, Options, Chapter 1
2.	11–16	Chapter 2: Let Simple Words Dominate
3.	17–21	Chapter 3: Highlight Actions and Actors
4.	22–27	Chapter 4: Give Readers a Clear Path
5.	29–35	Chapter 5: Make Words Earn Their Space
6.	36–40	Chapter 6: Monitor Sentence Length
7.	42–48	Chapter 7: Choose Words Precisely
8.	49–57	Chapter 8: Place Words Precisely
9.	59–63	Chapter 9: Learn Basic Grammar (first part)
10.	64–71	Chapter 9: Learn Basic Grammar (second part)
11.	72–77	Chapter 10: Speak Well to Write Well
12.	78–85	Chapter 11: Accommodate Gender Elegantly
13.	87–99	Chapter 12: Use the Common Punctuation Marks Well
14.	100–109	Chapter 13: Expand Your Punctuation World
15.	111–115	Chapter 14: Prepare Yourself
16.	116–125	Chapter 15: Embrace the Act of Writing (first part)
17.	125–132	Chapter 15: Embrace the Act of Writing (second part)
18.	133–139	Chapter 16: Revise and Reflect

CHAPTER 1
SOME PRINCIPLES TO GUIDE YOUR WRITING

This nine-page chapter, a kind of annotated table of contents, offers a quick preview of the book—a feel for its essence. **Read this chapter lightly for now. It is too content-rich for you to digest fully before you read the book itself.** You'll find it most vivid and useful later as a review.

Inside the back cover you'll see a simple list of these principles for handy reference. To make the list still handier, **photocopy that page on card stock and trim the margins.** You'll have a bookmark that keeps the principles in front of your eye at every turn of the page.

These writing principles are numbered and listed in the order you'll read about them. Because the body of the book begins with the issues of simplicity, brevity, and precision, some basic principles (grammar and punctuation) that might be presented up front in a prioritized list appear later in this list.

1. Let simple words dominate (pp. 11–16).

Resist temptations to create intellectual effects with unnecessarily complex words. Complex words will dazzle a few readers: *His pedagogy was fraught with insipidness.* Simple words will communicate with many: *As a teacher, he was a bore.*

2. Use active verbs (pp. 17–19).

Some words are equally strong as a noun or a verb (light; shovel); others are strong only as a noun, but they are commonly pressed into service as a verb (dialogue; impact). Long-term use of nouns as verbs does force legitimate language shifts over time. "Impact," for example, has made substantial movement in that direction (inadvisable as I believe that to be). Your writing will be strongest in the here and now if you choose well-established verbs that describe actions or thoughts specifically. (See Appendix A, *A Collection of Useful Verbs*.) In that same spirit, avoid nominalizing the action of a sentence.

Nominalized (weak):	*He has an understanding of how to proceed.*
Verb-based (strong):	*He understands how to proceed.*

3. Use active voice (pp. 19–20).

Use passive voice sparingly and purposefully. Rare circumstances make passive voice preferable, but generally *X created Y* is stronger than *Y was created by X*. Weakest of all is passive voice with an indefinite actor: *Y has been created.*

4. Keep people visible (pp. 20–21).

Your readers will want to know who is responsible for what. Avoid personification—attributing an action or thought that requires human will to an inanimate object.

No:	*The research investigated four common problems.*
Yes:	*The researchers investigated four common problems.*
Yes:	*Anderson, Knox, and Klein investigated four common problems.*

People like to read about other people—about what they are thinking and doing, and how they are interacting. In addition to avoiding personification, be intentional about referring to people in your writing—individually or in groups, by name or position, with nouns or pronouns—so readers can make a personal connection with them. Quotations add still more people power.

5. Be consistent (p. 22–23).

You risk losing readers when you use multiple terms to refer to a single entity, for example, *employees, workers, colleagues.* Construct a logical system of terms, and then use those terms consistently throughout your document. Also be consistent in format: don't vary the capitalization pattern or font size of section headings, the underlining or italicizing of a particular kind of term, or the sizes of margins and indentations.

6. Avoid overstatement (p. 23).

You endanger your credibility with readers if you write dogma,

> No: *There is no discipline in the public schools.*

> Yes: *Lax discipline has become a problem in many public schools.*

or if you inflate descriptions,

> No: *Our meeting was great—absolutely unbelievable.*

> Yes: *We had a congenial and productive meeting.*

or if you overuse qualifiers,

> No: *She was very composed under extreme fire.*

> Yes: *She was composed under fire.*

7. Avoid understatement (p. 23).

You undermine your own ability to communicate strongly and effectively if you lean on hedge words.

> No: *Excessive tardiness may potentially endanger your good standing.*

> Yes: *Arrive on time, or eventually you may lose your job.*

8. Avoid jargon (pp. 23–24).

Jargon (shoptalk and colloquialisms) alienates readers from outside your immediate environment, especially readers who speak English as a second language. It also reduces the shelf life of your writing. Jargon is fleeting; Standard English lasts.

9. Use positive form (p. 24).

To know what is *not* is a lesser form of knowing than to know what *is*. Negatively written statements, like inside-out socks, become useful only after someone has turned them. Don't give that job to your readers.

No: *He didn't attend as frequently when she was not there.*

Yes: *He attended more frequently when she was there.*

10. Use parallel form (pp. 25–27).

Parallel form—between paragraphs, sentences, parts of sentences, and even words—speeds comprehension. If you were to write the second sentence below rather than the first, you'd smooth the way for your readers.

Not Parallel: *The Anderson party chose to travel by day, but night travel was chosen by the party that Carson led.*

Parallel: *The Anderson party chose to travel by day, the Carson party by night.*

A common byproduct of parallel form is word reduction.

11. Avoid filler (pp. 29–32).

Filler words and phrases such as *in the event that* in place of *if*, or *on a daily basis* in place of *daily*, probably crept into your writing when teachers began assigning papers of prescribed lengths. Your immediate concern was not what to write, but rather how to fill pages with words. To write maturely, you need to adopt the slogan *fewer words* as a beacon that lights your way through each sentence and paragraph. Revise with an eye to brevity, clarity, and overall ease of reading, and believe fervently in this simple truth: skilled writers use fewer words than unskilled writers.

12. Avoid redundancy (pp. 32–35).

Eliminate words that duplicate what you've either written or implied elsewhere. Also eliminate words redundant to common knowledge: *past history* and *improve in the future* are redundancies because all history resides in the past, and the only place one can improve is in the future.

13. Monitor sentence length (pp. 36–40).

Expect readability to suffer proportionally as your average sentence length exceeds 20 words. A good target range for average sentence length is 16–20 words.

14. Vary sentence length (p. 36).

A sea of similar length, similarly constructed sentences dulls the senses of your readers and makes them less alert to what you have to say. Vary sentence length, and give readers an occasional gift—a sentence containing maybe 2–5 words.

15. Choose specific terms over general (pp. 42–45).

General terms give readers hints; specific terms give them information. Unless you have a good reason for limiting your readers to hints, give them information.

No: *We implemented the plan only after we had the benefit of his input.*

Yes: *We started the fundraising campaign only after soliciting his advice.*

16. Respect shades of meaning (pp. 45–47).

Search diligently for the most effective terms. Expand your vocabulary constantly and be sensitive to fine shades of meaning. Little words— conjunctions and prepositions—are no exception. As bridges between words or word groups, they must be precise to convey an accurate sense of the relationship between the words they join.

17. Be wary of word popularity (p. 48).

New words and new word uses pop up periodically and spread quickly among persons easily drawn to fads. Resist them. There's no substitute for Standard English if you want to communicate precisely and effectively.

18. Keep the modifier and the modified together (pp. 49–52).

A modifier is a word that qualifies another word or word group. *I only saw her once* implies that *only* modifies *saw*. In reality, *only* modifies *once*. For maximum strength and minimum confusion, put the modifier next to the modified: *I saw her only once.* (Note: This principle is violated much more frequently than it is observed.)

19. Follow an action phrase with the action's subject (pp. 52–54).

No: *Upon arriving at the office this morning, yesterday's lost contract began to worry Joe.*

Yes: *Upon arriving at the office this morning, Joe began to worry about yesterday's lost contract.*

The contract did not arrive at the office this morning; Joe did. At best, such a misplacement of the subject weakens a sentence. At worst, it misleads readers.

20. Orient readers with word placement (pp. 54–55).

To avoid disorienting readers, even momentarily, provide a context for material to come. This principle applies not only to documents and paragraphs, but also to sentences:

No: *Employee motivation is high, absenteeism is declining, and profits are approaching record heights, according to the latest union newsletter.*

Yes: *According to the latest union newsletter, employee motivation is high, absenteeism is declining, and profits are approaching record heights.*

21. Emphasize material with word placement (pp. 55–57).

Speakers emphasize points by volume, inflection, or gesture. When you write, you must rely on word placement and punctuation. The point of greatest emphasis is at the end of a sentence or paragraph.

No: *You must arrive by 7:00 p.m., regardless of what kind of difficulties you encounter.*

Yes: *Regardless of what kind of difficulties you encounter, you must arrive by 7:00 p.m.*

Note: In many cases, principles 20 and 21 have a symbiotic relationship.

(Your use of punctuation for emphasis will depend on familiarity with the full range of material shown in Chapters 12 and 13.)

22. Use correct grammar (pp. 59–71).

When you use correct grammar, you give consistency to your writing, you ease the reader's job, you reduce chances of being misinterpreted, and you sound intelligent. That kind of power is difficult to ignore.

23. Speak well to write well (pp. 72–77).

Your mind taps a single language reservoir whether you put words into the air or onto a piece of paper. If you speak clearly, precisely, and efficiently you'll improve your chances of writing clearly, precisely, and efficiently. Consider reading Chapter 10 as if it were Chapter 2.

24. Accommodate gender elegantly (pp. 78–85).

For centuries, writers have applied generic-masculine pronouns (*he, him, his*) to circumstances that apply to both male and female. Some modern writers react to that practice by applying generic-feminine pronouns (*she, her, hers*) in the same way. Do neither. Also avoid such awkward impediments to reading as his/her and s/he. The pairing of a plural pronoun with a singular antecedent (If *a person* does X, *they* will regret it) has gained recent acceptance as a solution, but the most effective course may be to avoid generic pronouns altogether wherever possible. Chapter 11 offers specific advice.

25. Use punctuation correctly and to full advantage (pp. 87–109).

Don't let guesswork determine where you place commas and other common punctuation marks. Your readers deserve a better roadmap through your writing than that. Also, expand your use of punctuation to the less-common marks. Punctuation used to its fullest is a dramatically rich writing tool that can help you convey pause, emphasis, tone, and relationships.

26. Identify your audience and your purpose (p. 112).

Give direction and cohesiveness to everything you write by identifying at the outset, and remaining ever conscious of, your intended audience for the document and your precise purpose for writing it.

27. Gather and organize materials (pp. 113–115).

To be sure that your perspective is complete and accurate, prepare yourself with the best supportive material you can find, and with more than you expect to need.

28. Establish a timetable (p. 115).

The most telling statement about your commitment to quality for a writing project is the time you allot for it.

29. Give order to paragraphs and sections (pp. 119–125).

Include in any organizational unit (paragraph, section—even the document as a whole) only material that belongs together. Then present that material in a sequence that eases comprehension. Use transitions (words or sentences) to lead one sentence or paragraph smoothly to the next.

30. Acquire a feel for writing (pp. 125–128).

Recognize the stages involved in a writing project and the relative influence of inspiration and effort. From those realizations, create a comfortable, reliable system tailored to the ways you work best—a system by which you can produce eminently readable documents that serve their purpose clearly, precisely, and completely.

31. Think on your seat (pp. 128–130).

Never put your mind on automatic pilot while writing. Everything you write should stem from thought rather than from imitation or habit.

32. Be sincere (pp. 130–132).

Consider your readers friends toward whom you want to remain genuine, sincere, and forthright.

33. Revise during and after writing (pp. 133–136).

Whenever you put words on paper or on a computer screen, consider those words a first draft. They are tomorrow's trash. To write well is to revise, and then revise again—and still again if the result is not exactly what you want. A common question is, "Should I revise as I write or after I have finished?" My answer is "both." Every sentence and paragraph is fair game for revision at any time you perceive a possible improvement. Still, no amount of revision on the fly relieves you of the need to revise the whole document—probably multiple times—after you have completed the initial draft.

34. Solicit a fresh perspective (p. 137).

Knowing your subject well and working with it intensely tends to create a chasm between your perspective and that of your readers. Arrange a reading partnership with someone whose judgment you trust and who will be forthright with you. Read each other's work and trade frank comments about both content and presentation.

SIMPLICITY

Avoid pretense. Let simple words and simple constructions dominate so the complex words and complex constructions you find indispensable can do their job without distraction.

CHAPTER 2

LET SIMPLE WORDS DOMINATE

Don't let complex words seduce you. If you do, you may write something like this:

> We anticipate implementation of the construction initiative.
> Please facilitate procurement of the required permits.

Put yourself in the reader's place. You'll find that you prefer something like this:

> We expect to break ground soon. Please get the permits we need.

Simple words are strong. They transmit thoughts to readers quickly and vividly. Complex words tangle readers' minds and slow them down. Complex words also damage recall. Think how easy it is to hold onto a mental picture of "expect to break ground soon" as compared to "anticipate implementation of the construction initiative."

Having made a pitch for simple words, I need to make clear that I'm not talking about using simple words exclusively—only about having them dominate your sentences. For example, I opened the paragraph above with four simple words. Then in the second sentence I used *transmit* and *vividly*, two less-simple words that are important to the sentence. They say precisely what I wanted to say, and they constitute only about 15% of the total, allowing simple words to still dominate. If you try to use simple words exclusively, you'll risk making sentences unnecessarily long and cumbersome. Look at how a complex word (*malfunctioned*) streamlines this sentence:

No: There was some kind of breakdown in the electric timer.

Yes: The electric timer malfunctioned.

My primary message is that you should use simple words as a matter of course. Make them the foundation of your sentences. By doing that, you'll create a context that helps readers understand the complex words that you find indispensable. You'll also condition readers to respect your well-chosen complex words, because they'll know that you use them only to be precise, descriptive, and efficient—not to show off your vocabulary.

What prompts so many writers, perhaps you, to overuse complex words? Why do such good, solid words as *use*, *do*, and *help* get pushed aside for *utilize*, *implement*, and *facilitate*? Is it a matter of consciously showing off on paper? I don't think so. The practice may stem from imitation and uncertainty. You read what others write and hear what they say, and you fill your mental files with their words and phrases. Those words and phrases then spill out easily onto your pages. You are blending in with the norm! As commonly used complex words imbue your subconscious with a sense of belonging, sincere personal thought moves to the back seat. You *acquire* or *procure* rather than *get*, and you *possess* rather than *have* or *own*. You recommend that an action be taken *at this juncture* rather than *now*, and you *demonstrate* rather than *show*. In short, you begin to take dictation from the tapes in your head as a substitute for thinking in specifics.

Laying such unnecessary hurdles in front of readers does not make you sound intelligent and impressive. It makes you sound stiff and artificial—lacking in original thought. The only antidote I know for this writing problem is to feel secure in your own ability to think, and confident that your thoughts and ideas have merit without decoration. Be yourself.

I like the term Richard Lanham applies to sentences strewn with unproductive complex words. In *Revising Prose* (1991), he calls it "the official style" (p. 56). The aim of the writer (or speaker) of such a style seems to be to use as many syllables as possible. You've seen and heard it many times. A trooper standing in front of a hospital faces the TV news camera, and then describes the aftermath of a street attack:

> An elderly male individual had just exited his vehicle when the alleged assailant physically accosted him and relieved him of valuables. The victim has been transported via medical emergency vehicle to this treatment facility.

What really happened? An elderly man was mugged and robbed as he got out of his car, and he was taken to the hospital in an ambulance. Everyone will understand that to be the case once they cut through the verbal smokescreen, so why not just say it? Why burden readers with the job of translating?

If you write in "the official style," you'll do damage beyond irritating readers and robbing them of valuable time: you'll sound like someone other than who you are. That's a disservice to everyone—most of all to you.

Also, straining for effect may cause you to write less precisely. In Chapters 7 and 8 I write extensively about imprecision, but here I should touch on a unique threat to precision posed by artificially complex words. For example, writers addicted to extra syllables like to write *anticipate* in place of *expect,* but *anticipate* suggests some kind of preparation for what's expected. When plain old expectation is all that's involved, *anticipate* is imprecise.

I ~~anticipate that~~ the books ~~will~~ arrive by the end of the week.
(expect ... to)

You'll also create imprecision if you enlarge your words with the pretentious suffixes *ly* and *ize.*

More ~~importantly~~, prepare the surface well before you paint.
(important)

~~Firstly~~, prepare the surface well. ~~Secondly,~~ open windows for ventilation.
(First ... Second)

~~Finalize~~ preparations at least one hour before the first scheduled interview.
(Finish)

Be thorough. ~~Utilize~~ every tool available to you.
(Use)

You may intend to tell readers what is "more important," but if you write the adverb *importantly* you imply that the action is done in an important way. Similarly, the adverbs *firstly* and *secondly* technically tell in what manner (*firstly*) rather than in what order (*first*)—and to be consistent you'd have to write such oddities as *fifthly* and *eighthly*. The *ly* affectation is common, but it works against readability, clarity, and precision.

Finalize is merely a pretentious variation of *finish* or *complete*, but *utilize* is both pretentious and imprecise. To *utilize*, according to its fundamental definition, is to make something serve a particular purpose. That's a more specific meaning than the general term *use*. If you tie a hammer to a string to make it function as a counterweight, you might say you've *utilized* the hammer, but if you drive nails with it you've simply *used* it. Unfortunately, *utilize* is used so widely now as a pretentious synonym for *use* that *utilize* itself has virtually lost its usefulness (or utilizationalness!). I've discarded the word altogether.

In short, any effort you make to elevate your vocabulary artificially is likely to stiffen your style, damage precision, lower readability, and distract both you and your readers from your core message. So resist reaching for words that sound impressive or fashionable. Instead, choose words for their function. Sometimes you'll use a complex word because it offers exactly the twist you need. Good. That's an argument for nurturing your vocabulary. To know many useful words is to expand your choices. In general, though, simple, functional words serve you and your readers best, especially for everyday writing: letters, memos, e-mails, minutes, reports, evaluations, and so on.

Shown in Figure 1 are some complex words and expressions followed by simple counterparts. The complex words are useable, and sometimes even preferable. Still, the list provokes thought about the kinds of simplified word choices that save readers time, effort, and confusion. The words on this list, a mere scratching of the surface, come from my observations and from suggestions made long ago by Rudolph Flesch, a 20th Century writer who wrote prolifically about our use of language (1962, 1964).

accomplish	do	initiate	begin; start	provided,	
accordingly	so	institute	start	providing	if
acquire	get	intimate	hint	purchase	buy
alleviate	ease	jeopardize	risk	purported to	were said to
anxiety	fear	[at this] juncture	now	purveyor	supplier
ascertain	find out	laboratory	lab	purview	scope
attempt	try	lengthy	long	rationale	reason; basis
attired	dressed	likewise	also; so	realize	know;
attributable to	due to	locality	place		understand
aver	say	magnitude	size	receive	get
bestow	give	majority	most	reiterate	repeat
cognizant	aware	maximum	most; best	remarked	said
commence	begin	modicum	some	remittance	payment
communicate	talk; write	motivation	drive; reason	remuneration	fee; pay
consequently	so	multitudinous	many	render	make
contribute	give	naught	nothing	require	need
declare	say	necessity	need	requisite	needed
demise	death	nefarious	vicious	reside	live
demonstrate	show	negligible	small; tiny	residence	home; house
derive	get; find	numerous	many	response	answer
devoid of	without;	obligatory	binding	restrict	limit
	lacking	obtain	get	retain	keep
domicile	home	obviate	cancel; prevent;	reveal	show
dwelling	house		forestall	salient	important
educator	teacher	occur	happen	sanguine	hopeful
elapse	pass	oftentimes	often	satisfactory	good; OK
elicit	get; bring	originate	start	secure	get
eminently	highly	palpable	obvious; clear	select	choose
emphasize	stress	paradigm	model	stance	attitude
employ	use	partake of	have; use	subsequently	later; next;
endeavor	try	patently	plainly		after that
espouse	hold; support	paucity	little; few	substantiate	prove
facilitate	help; ease	pending	until	suffice	do; be enough
forthwith	right away	per annum	a year	supersede	replace
frequently	often	per diem	a day	surmise	think; suppose
gasoline	gas	perchance	perhaps; maybe	take place	happen
germane	relevant	permit	let	terminate	end; stop
harbinger	sign; omen	peruse	read	thereafter	after that
harken	listen	phenomenon	idea; event	thereof	of it
heretofore	until now	philosophy	idea; thought	transformation	change
hubris	arrogance	portion	part	transmit	send
identical	same	possibility	chance	transpire	happen
impair	weaken;	precipitous	rash; hasty	transport	move; carry
	damage	predicated	based	ultimately	in the end
impart	tell; give	predominantly	mainly	underprivileged	needy; poor
impede	hinder; stop	prevalent	common; typical	unintentionally	by mistake
inaugurate	start; begin	previous to	before	vaunted	celebrated
inception	beginning	prior to	before	vehicle	car
indeed	truly; in fact	procure	get	vicissitude	change; turn
indicate	hint; suggest	provide	give; offer;	wherewithal	means
inform	tell		supply		
initial	first; early				

Figure 1. Some Examples of Complex Words and Simple Counterparts

You might also read "A Case for Short Words," pages 33–37 of Richard Lederer's *The Miracle of Language* (1991). It demonstrates very effectively the power of short, simple, common words. *The Miracle of Language* is illuminating and entertaining, as Lederer's work tends to be. I recommend it highly.

You will find no better time than right now to face up to an important decision you need to make about your approach to writing. Do you want to dazzle a few readers, or do you want to communicate with many? An important step to communicating with many is to commit yourself to two principles:

(1) Believe firmly that simple words are superior to complex words except where complex words offer unique meaning or a desired flavor.

(2) Monitor your writing and your revisions constantly to be sure that simple words dominate.

Examine Exercise #1 on page 204 (solution on page 215).

CHAPTER 3
HIGHLIGHT ACTIONS AND ACTORS

The questions *what* and *who* are always in the forefront of a reader's mind. If your writing is unclear about actions and actors, you will frustrate readers by failing to answer those most basic questions. Your sentences will strike them as indirect and unnecessary complicated. So keep *what* and *who* in the forefront of your thinking as you write, and answer those questions so plainly and frequently that your readers will never have to ask them.

Use Active Verbs

Verbs are the engines that run your sentences. They should reveal the action clearly. Don't complicate your sentences by replacing active verbs with noun clauses—sometimes referred to as "nominalizing" a sentence.

Don't write this	**Write this**
She will arrive at a decision soon.	She will decide soon.
I have an understanding of it.	I understand it.
There is a difference in our views.	Our views differ.
He was uncooperative when asked to leave.	He refused to leave.

When you cloak the action of a sentence in a noun clause, you give readers empty verbs (arrive, have, is, was) rather than verbs that tell what's happening (decide, understand, differ, refused). Refresh your feeling for descriptive, active verbs periodically by scanning some of the roughly 3,000 verbs listed in Appendix A, *A Collection of Useful Verbs* (pages 141–153).

Noun clauses aren't the only road to nominalization. Sometimes writers neglect active, descriptive verbs in favor of nouns that are neither powerful enough nor specific enough to convey the action effectively. As Calvin and Hobbs point out, "verbing" language impedes understanding.

Calvin and Hobbes   by Bill Watterson

Some words are strong either as a noun or as a verb (shovel, light, bat), but many words that are strong as nouns present weaknesses when pressed into service as verbs (access, address, experience, impact, implement, leverage, result). For details about the inadequacy of those nouns as verbs, read the individual alphabetical entries in Appendix B, *A List of Troublesome Words* and Appendix C, *Four Business Buzzwords Elaborated Upon.* To illustrate my point briefly here, I'll elaborate upon the use of *impact* as a verb.

An impact is a forceful coming together, as in a collision. My guess is that the noun *impact* has become fashionable as a verb because of the strong visceral impression it makes, but its impression of strength only camouflages its actual weakness. It has become a bluster-ridden substitute for verbs in the neutral column below, and an information-deprived substitute for verbs in the positive and negative columns. Ask yourself why you would use *impact* as an all-purpose verb when you have an array of specific verbs (only a few shown below) by which to describe any given effect with precision:

Neutral	Positive	Negative
influence	improve	damage
affect	enhance	abuse
change	boost	impair
	elevate	demoralize
	advance	destroy

Each time you press a noun into service as a verb, you're doing more damage than simply "weirding" language. By neglecting an enormous reservoir of verbs, with all their shades of meaning, you're missing an opportunity to describe the precise nature of a cause-and-effect relationship. **(Examine Exercise #2, page 204.)**

Use Active Voice

Active voice and active verbs are first cousins, so active voice was unavoidably foreshadowed in Exercise #2. Active voice is simply a style of sentence construction that has the subject acting (Anna has written the research results). Passive voice, by contrast, puts the object in the position of subject (The research results have been written by Anna). Sometimes the actor is invisible (The research results have been written). The strength of active voice is that it identifies the actor/action relationship in a direct, unambiguous way.

Readers like active voice for its specificity and clarity. They like having the subject identified early and unmistakably as the actor and followed closely with a descriptive verb that reveals the subject's thought or action. Where a desired emphasis calls for passive voice, use it (The best speech was delivered by a newcomer), but you'll do well to make active voice your default approach to sentence construction.

Don't write this	**Write this**
She was driven downtown by Bill.	Bill drove her downtown.
She was driven downtown.	Bill drove her downtown.
A budget cut has been ordered.	The dean has ordered a budget cut.
A curfew has been imposed.	The police chief imposed a curfew.

As sentences become longer, passive voice becomes a greater enemy of simplicity and clarity. Compare these sentences. Which would you prefer to read?

Passive Voice: We recommend that there be established an ongoing communication between the educational establishment and members of corresponding professions.

Active Voice: We recommend that educators communicate regularly with practitioners whose specialty they share.

You can see the potential of passive voice for evasiveness. If the writer of the four short sentences above wants to keep the spotlight off Bill, the dean, or the police chief, passive voice is the perfect tool. Passive voice, therefore, is a hallmark of bureaucratic writing, designed to keep accountability at arm's length while creating an appearance of having said something significant.

> **Bureaucratese**: The question of who may or may not have been involved in the alleged illegal activities having to do with the establishment of voting precincts will be addressed.

> **Straight Communication**: I have ordered the District Attorney to investigate the establishment of voting precincts, and to report improprieties to me by early May.

Don't write bureaucratese unless you're trying to be evasive. If you write in that style you'll irritate readers with unnecessary reading difficulties. You'll also risk giving the impression that you either lack information or have something to hide.

You may want to check your writing routinely for passive voice. It's a disease that's infected more writers than not. If you find that you write in passive voice much of the time out of habit or imitation, take heed and reform. Use passive voice only for a specific purpose, and use it infrequently. For each passive voice structure in your writing, you should be able to explain why you chose passive voice over active voice. If you can't, chances are the passive voice structure is not a choice, but a blunder. **(Examine Exercise #3, page 205.)**

Keep People Visible

Besides weak verbs and passive voice, another inadvisable stylistic practice that may remove people from the forefront of your writing is personification—the practice of ascribing human attributes to inanimate objects. Avoid implying that studies, theories, literature, departments, and other inanimate objects engage in such human behavior as *examine*, *dispute*, *find*, *strive*, *seek*, and so on. Introduce your readers to the people behind the actions you write about by attributing the actions to them directly.

Don't write this	Write this
<u>A study</u> by Richard Reese (1985) <u>examined</u> four key variables.	In a 1985 study, <u>Richard Reese</u> <u>examined</u> four key variables.
Evening <u>shifts need to contact</u> the division director.	<u>Managers</u> of evening shifts <u>need to contact</u> the division director.
This <u>company finds itself</u> in financial difficulty.	<u>We</u> at P.J. Cooks <u>find ourselves</u> in financial difficulty.
<u>This paper will concern itself</u> with early hydraulic systems.	<u>The subject of this paper is</u> early hydraulic systems.

Human will is required to fulfill each of the verbs in the sentences above: *examined, contact, finds, concern.* Make clear to readers who those human beings are, either by name or by some identifying information such as position or profession. In the case of the last example, the author's name on the paper cited will introduce a real person to readers. The purpose for the change in wording is to avoid implying to readers that the actual paper is "concerning itself" with the information it contains. It is not. The author is. The distinction is slight, and you might think it overly technical, but the value is that readers will make a more immediate and personal connection with the author than with the paper.

Look for every opportunity to help your readers make important personal connections. The ultimate personal connection is to have the actor "speak" to your readers by use of a quotation.

Impersonal: Profits have shown a 12% increase over last quarter.

Personal: According to CEO Harold Dolan, profits have increased 12% over the last quarter.

More Personal: CEO Harold Dolan said, "I'm pleased and heartened by the dramatic 12% upturn in profits over the last quarter."

The more you make clear who is doing and thinking what, the less you force readers to dig for information by inference. You put solid ground beneath their feet. That increases their chance of reading efficiently and cheerfully.

(Examine Exercises #4 and #5, page 205.)

CHAPTER 4
GIVE READERS A CLEAR PATH

In this chapter I'll show several stylistic choices you can make to avoid putting unnecessary hurdles in your reader's path: be consistent, avoid overstatement, avoid understatement, avoid jargon, use positive form, and use parallel form. Like the choices I recommended in Chapters 2 and 3—use simple words and highlight actions and actors—these stylistic choices will declutter your writing to give it the simple, easy flow that readers appreciate.

Be Consistent

Readers want consistent terminology. It orients them and keeps them firmly grounded. Varied word choice can be a legitimate tool for adding interest to writing, but generally it complicates non-fiction writing unnecessarily. Especially if content is technical or complex, readers will gladly accept repeated terms in exchange for knowing precisely what you are saying.

Don't write this	Write this
Each <u>class</u> met for instruction twice weekly. One <u>level</u> met on Mondays and Wednesdays and the other on Tuesdays and Thursdays. The same teacher taught both <u>groups</u>.	Each of the two instruction <u>groups</u> met twice weekly, the E1 <u>group</u> on Mondays and Wednesdays and the E2 <u>group</u> on Tuesdays and Thursdays. The same teacher taught both <u>groups</u>.

Consistency in content is also important. In a recent article, an author comparing pitchers on two baseball teams gave the ages of two pitchers on one team and one pitcher on the other, but he ignored the ages of all the other pitchers. Such inconsistencies infuriate readers. **(Examine Exercise #6, page 206.)**

The next three sections are a matter of monitoring the tone of your writing. If you overstate or understate, or if you use jargon that shuts out some readers, your writing will lose the simplicity and innocence it needs for easy reading and quick comprehension.

Avoid Overstatement

Overstatement raises eyebrows. Don't describe as *essential* something that is merely *helpful* or *important*. Don't describe a very successful event as *great* or *unbelievable*. It may be exceptional, even extraordinary, but true greatness and unbelievability are extremely rare. Lincoln was *great*, and seeing him alive now would be *unbelievable*: few people or events you encounter will deserve such superlatives. Also, use elevating adjectives sparingly (*very*; *extremely*), and refrain from applying them to dichotomous terms. For example, *typical* and *atypical* are opposing conditions: there are no degrees of typicality. The same is true for *unique* (one of a kind) and *not unique* (not one of a kind). Don't twist your readers' minds by writing "very typical" or "extremely unique." **(Examine Exercise #7, page 206.)**

Avoid Understatement

Understatement drains strength from your writing. To write "I believe X *may* happen" is weak: almost anything *may* happen. To say something substantial, write "I believe X will happen," or at least "I believe X is likely to happen." Understatements can become downright falsehoods, as in commercial claims that "results may vary." The truth is that results *will* vary. Not only do understatements weaken writing, but they may prompt readers to think of you as less than forthright. **(Examine Exercise #8, page 206.)**

Avoid Jargon

Jargon—offhanded daily language that readers from outside your sphere will not understand—shrinks the audience for your writing. Your jargon may come from shoptalk ("leverage the optics" in place of "take advantage of appearances") or from colloquialisms ("He wasn't totally on board" in place of

"He was less than enthusiastic"). Use Standard English. It enables a broad range of persons to understand fully and immediately what you are writing. It's particularly helpful to readers for whom English is a second language. Also, Standard English gives your writing shelf life. The jargon you write today may disappear altogether in a generation, leaving your statement unintelligible to many readers.

In e-mails and text messages, jargon tends to reach an all-time low. If you and your close friends exchange personal communication in some kind of shorthand, be careful not to use that shorthand in formal communication. If instead of "I called Mr. Cage for you," you write "I buzzed cage 4 u," you'll appear immature and unprofessional. You'll also risk delivering an incomplete or unclear message, depending on the recipient. (**Examine Exercise #9, page 207.**)

Use Positive Form

Readers will read more efficiently if you tell them what *is* rather than what is *not*.

Don't write this	Write this
She <u>did not understand</u> very much.	She <u>understood</u> little.
I <u>do not want to be thought of</u> as inaccessible.	I <u>want to be thought of</u> as accessible.
We <u>have not found</u> any such purpose.	We <u>have found</u> no such purpose.

Statements written in negative form are like socks paired inside out: they become useful only after someone has turned them. Your readers will not want that job. It slows them down.

This is not to say you should avoid negative-form statements altogether. At times you will need negative form for the specific emphasis it gives, as in "I did not violate his trust." What you need to guard against is using negative form where positive form is more direct, more concise, and more immediately understood. Think of positive form as your default construction, and yield to negative form only when circumstances compel you to do so. (**Examine Exercise #10, page 207.**)

Use Parallel Form

Imagine looking at a perfectly symmetrical building. A vertical center line would divide the building into mirror-image halves. Now imagine looking at a building of such odd proportions that a vertical center line would create two shapes that barely resemble each other. Which image would your mind accept more quickly and hold in visualization longer?

Just as symmetrical objects help viewers accept and retain images, so will symmetrical writing help readers accept and retain information. The sentence you just read is an example of parallel form. Look at it again, followed by two nonparallel counterparts.

Parallel Form

Just as symmetrical objects help viewers accept and retain images, so will symmetrical writing help readers accept and retain information.

Nonparallel Form

Just as symmetrical objects help viewers accept and retain images, so will readers understand and remember what you write longer if you construct it symmetrically.

Nonparallel Form

Visual acceptance and the length of time you remember what you see is helped by symmetry in an object, and when you write, readers will also accept the information quicker and hold it in memory longer if you write it in a symmetrical way.

As bloated and convoluted as that last sentence is, it's not uncommon. Many rambling sentences could be tamed and streamlined with the help of parallel form.

Be especially careful to express entries in parallel form when you construct a list. The characteristic of a list that makes it so useful—entries stacked vertically for easy comparison—makes nonparallel form particularly noticeable and disruptive.

A List in Nonparallel Form

Operators of commercial television face four distinct challenges:

1. The over exposure of commercial ploys.

2. Viewers ignore familiar commercial messages.

3. Muting the sound is easy with a remote control.

4. Cable television's lack of commercials.

A List in Parallel Form

Operators of commercial television face four distinct challenges.
Today's viewers

1. ignore familiar commercial messages,

2. dismiss overexposed ploys,

3. mute the sound of commercials, and

4. turn to cable TV for commercial-free viewing.

Notice that each entry in the parallel list immediately above begins with the same part of speech: a verb. Verbs work well, because the feeling of action propels readers through the list. (Other parts of speech work, too, so long as all entries are treated alike.) Notice also that the original, non-parallel list contains a mixture of complete sentences and sentence fragments. That jumble increases the likelihood that entries will begin with nonparallel parts of speech. It also creates a punctuation challenge. That is, placing periods after each entry leaves two sentence fragments masquerading as sentences, removing them leaves two complete sentences without periods, and punctuating each entry according to its structure accentuates inconsistencies.

Within the constraints of parallel form, a well-written list may consist of complete sentences, sentence fragments, or single words. Entries may be self-contained, or they may be part of a sentence that begins with the stem and finishes at the end of the last entry (as in the parallel list above). And entries may be either numbered or marked with bullets, depending on their length, their complexity, and their relationship to one another.

Just as parallel form between the parts of a sentence or a list makes reading easier, so does parallel form between paragraphs and sections of a document. Whenever you see a parallel relationship between clumps of material in a document you are writing—maybe in the description of specific functions or activities—write one of those descriptions in full and revise it thoroughly until you have exactly what you want. Then cut and paste that writing into subsequent sections as a template, and simply change the details within the template to construct the next description. Not only will you give readers a clean, easily digested parallel form to read, but you'll save yourself time by not having to re-create entire sections from a standstill.

Considering how powerful parallel form is as a tool for clarity, it may be the most underused of all writing techniques. I recommend strongly that you keep it in the top tray of your writing toolbox, ready to be snatched up and used frequently. How will you know when the time is ripe? Any time a sentence or paragraph has an awkward feeling—writing's equivalent of wearing shoes on the wrong feet—check to see if parallel form is the tool you need to set things right. (**Examine Exercise #11 on page 207.**)

Say Something

The ultimate blockade of a reader's path to meaning is word after word that says not much of anything. Playwright George Bernard Shaw once wrote of an acquaintance, "The trouble with her is that she lacks the power of conversation but not the power of speech" (Winokur, 1987, p. 71). Whether opening your mouth or opening a document that you're writing, always use words to say something of consequence. Empty words are the subject of the next chapter.

BREVITY

Make "fewer words" a beacon that lights your way through every sentence and paragraph you write. Monitor your sentences not only for brevity, but also for average length and variability.

CHAPTER 5
MAKE WORDS EARN THEIR SPACE

CHAPTER 6
MONITOR SENTENCE LENGTH

MAKE WORDS EARN THEIR SPACE

A well-known statement from *The Elements of Style*, a classic writer's guide by William Strunk, Jr. and E.B. White (2000, 1979, 1972, 1959), is "omit needless words" (2000, p. 23). That may be the most important advice any writer can receive. In this chapter I'll talk about two categories of needless words that need to be omitted: filler and redundancy.

Avoid Filler

I define filler as words that take space without adding meaning. You may have started using filler years ago when a teacher assigned a five-page paper and you worried about how to fill the pages. *If* became *in the event that*, *while* became *in the process of* and *to* became *for the purpose of*. Eventually, writing filler became a habit.

Think how resentful you'd be as a reader if you were told that for each page of information you want to acquire you will be required to read one-and-a-half or two pages of words. If you bloat your writing with filler, your readers will resent you similarly for wasting their time. Particularly in business, wasted time is wasted money. Writing filler is certainly a habit worth breaking.

Don't write this	**Write this**
<u>In the event that</u> he is late, start without him.	<u>If</u> he is late, start without him.
He did it <u>for the purpose of</u> impressing his boss with <u>a total of</u> 12 new contracts.	He did it <u>to</u> impress his boss with 12 new contracts.

Probably the most common single-word fillers are *the* and *that*, and the most common type of two-word filler phrases are *who is*, *that are*, *which is*, and so on. In the last of the examples below, *it was* launches what I call a slow-start sentence.

Don't write this	**Write this**
Such vague style forces <u>the</u> reader to construct, without benefit of <u>the</u> facts, the message <u>that</u> the writer is supposed to have written. I only wish <u>that</u> I could report that this kind of writing is rare.	Such vague style forces readers to construct, without benefit of facts, the message the writer is supposed to have written. I only wish I could report that this kind of writing is rare.
The test <u>that is</u> given on Saturdays is easy.	The test given on Saturdays is easy.
The conference room, <u>which was</u> warmer than usual, caused discomfort.	The conference room, warmer than usual, caused discomfort.
<u>It was</u> about noon before <u>there were</u> signs of life in the camp.	The camp finally came to life about noon.

Note that *the* and *that* are sometimes filler and at other times important to understanding. Be vigilant about which is which.

Also avoid the filler created by excessive prepositional phrases. In some places you can reduce the number of words by using adjectives, and in other places you can omit the preposition altogether.

Don't write this	**Write this**
Test scores <u>of</u> the A group were significantly higher than test scores <u>of</u> the B group, and more extreme <u>in</u> variability than either those <u>of</u> the B group or those obtained <u>in</u> the experiment conducted <u>on</u> November 15.	A-group test scores were significantly higher than B-group test scores, and more variable than either B-group scores or scores obtained November 15.

And finally, avoid filler that amounts to whole sentences of empty language. You might write such a sentence at the beginning of a paragraph as a kind of mental warm-up—akin to clearing your throat or saying "um" before you speak. If you do write such sentences, take them out when you revise.

Don't write this	Write this
<u>There are many types of approaches to marketing perishable products.</u> The five most common of those approaches are…	The five most common approaches to marketing perishable products are…

Still worse is sentence after sentence of empty language, creating a fluffy style that can be described best as immature writing.

Don't write this	Write this
Choosing a program is not an easy job. There are many programs available, and not all of them are of good quality. Caution should be used in the selection process.	The many programs available vary widely in quality: choose carefully.
Montessori held a certain view of will and obedience. She said that it is a commonly held thought that will and obedience are opposing concepts. Most adults believe that we get children to obey by suppressing their wills and having them conform to the teacher's will. Montessori felt that this was a poor idea. She believed that a child will learn to obey only when his will is developed.	Montessori disagreed with the common view that children learn to obey by conforming to a teacher's will. She believed, rather, that they learn to obey by developing their own wills.

Notice in the example immediately above that Montessori is referred to four times in the original—either by name or by the pronoun *she*—and the term *will* appears five times. In the revision, Montessori and the term *will* are each referred to only twice. Immature writing makes reading laborious in a way that grates on the nerves of intelligent readers. Enrich your vocabulary over time by paying attention to useful words that you see and hear but don't use. You may want to build a personal dictionary (see pp. 245–246). Also, in Appendix A, *A Collection of Useful Verbs,* and Appendix B, *A List of Troublesome Words*, you'll find ample opportunities to enrich your vocabulary.

My advice here to build a vocabulary and write maturely may seem contradictory to Chapter 2's advice to use simple words. It's not. Brevity is as important as simplicity, and one key to using few words is to know many.

Acquire an extensive repertoire of words from which to choose. That will enable you to make judicious use of a mature vocabulary and mature sentence construction while building your sentences on a foundation of simple words.

The quantity and variety of filler to which you might fall prey are unlimited. Examples here—including the modest list of common violations shown in Figure 1—can only reveal the essence of the problem and make you more alert to tendencies in your writing. (**Examine Exercise #12, page 208.**)

Candidates for Omission	**Candidates for Revision**		
the	at that point in time	→	then
that	in order to	→	to
that is	for the purpose of	→	to
(are, was, were)	by means of	→	by
which is	concerning the matter of	→	about
(are, was, were)	during the course of	→	during
who is	in the process of	→	while; during
(are, was, were)	for the simple reason that	→	because
a total of	due to the fact that	→	because
in fact	in the event that	→	if
the fact that	in some cases	→	sometimes
at this time	on a weekly basis	→	weekly
at the present time			(monthly; daily; regularly)
presently, currently	is most likely to	→	usually
make it a point to	last but not least	→	finally
	in the final analysis	→	finally; in the end
	it is anticipated that	→	we expect
	regardless of the fact that	→	although; despite
	it is (was); there is (are, was, were)	}	(identify the true subject and rewrite)

Figure 1. A Few Common Filler Words and Phrases

Avoid Redundancy

Redundancy might be thought of as a variety of filler, but I chose to give it its own category here because of its distinct nature. When you write redundantly, your extra words duplicate (1) something you wrote elsewhere, (2) something you implied elsewhere, or (3) common knowledge.

Most obvious are blatantly repeated words that can be eliminated with a little planning.

Don't write this	Write this
Three hypotheses will be examined within this study.	Within this study I will examine hypotheses of relationships between
1. <u>There is some relationship between</u> longevity and productivity.	1. longevity and productivity,
2. <u>There is some relationship between</u> longevity and loyalty.	2. longevity and loyalty, and
3. <u>There is some relationship between</u> productivity and loyalty.	3. productivity and loyalty.

Just as repeated words are redundant, so are words having the same meaning or a similar meaning. Remove one of them.

Don't write this	For this reason
Stewards distributed <u>free</u> complimentary copies during lunch hour.	Complimentary copies are free.
The <u>intervening</u> years between the wars were lean, but happy.	*Intervening* means *between.*

Besides being redundant to something you've written, words can be redundant to something you've implied. Remove the unnecessary word.

Don't write this	For this reason
They represent several <u>big</u> companies from among the giants of corporate America.	*Giants* implies that the companies are big.
The contract has come under <u>close</u> scrutiny in recent months.	*Scrutiny* implies a close examination.
<u>By comparison</u>, the British were more reliable than were the French.	The statement implies *comparison.*

Less conspicuous than redundancies either to what you've said or to what you've implied are redundancies to common knowledge, as in these five statements. The only correction needed is to omit the unnecessary word or words from each original statement.

Don't write this	For this reason
We learn from <u>past</u> history.	Everyone knows that history happened in the past.
I will improve <u>in the future</u>.	Everyone knows that what *will* be done has to be done in the future.
That is my <u>personal</u> opinion. He was a <u>personal</u> friend.	Opinions and friends are naturally personal.
I joined the two <u>together</u>.	Everyone knows that to join two things you must bring them together.
That is his <u>regular</u> routine.	Without regularity, it would not be a routine.

Like quantities of filler, the number of redundancies you might write is virtually infinite. In Figure 2 you'll see a few common redundancies in list form. **(Examine Exercise #13, page 208.)**

Parting Thoughts About Wordiness

As you read examples throughout this book, notice that most revisions are shorter than the originals. That's because most flawed writing produces wordiness as a byproduct. Stated in reverse, **the more you work to reduce the number of words you use, the more likely you are to uncover and solve other writing problems and improve your general writing style**.

No one wants to read seven pages to get information that can be given clearly and completely in four or five. No one wants to be imposed upon with hours or minutes—or even seconds—of unnecessary reading. As you write, think of yourself as the reader of your work. You'll find yourself becoming as stingy with words as Scrooge was with money.

Here are a few slogans aimed at helping you establish a healthy mindset toward economical writing:

- **As you write, make *fewer words* a beacon that lights your way through every sentence and paragraph.**

- **As you revise, work diligently—almost obsessively—to remove every word unimportant to the completeness, clarity, or intended effect of your writing.**

- **Believe sincerely that words are to writers as strokes are to golfers: accomplished players use fewest.**

---

collaborate together	future plans	proceed ahead
complete stop	indecently assaulted	regular routine
end result	join (or link) together	repeat again
first conceived	past experience	successfully passed
forward progress	past history	sum total
free complimentary	personal friend	totally opposite
free gift	personal opinion/belief	true facts

also. . . as well as . . . both . . . as well as …	*As well as* should not duplicate the function of *also* or *both*.
approximately 30 to 50	A given range (30 to 50) is already an approximation.
close proximity	This common expression means literally "close closeness."
different	Use *different* only if readers might think *same*. "We held three *different* meetings" is redundant, because "three meetings" obviously are not the same meeting.
equally as important	Use either *equally important* or *as important*
preplanning	Isn't that planning?

Figure 2. A Few Common Redundancies

CHAPTER 6

MONITOR SENTENCE LENGTH

The message of the preceding chapter was to use fewer words. The message of this chapter is to monitor the number of words you put into a particular sentence. Rudolph Flesch offers the best advice I've read about sentence length. He characterizes the readability of a piece of writing by its average sentence length as follows: 11 words, easy; 17 words, standard; 25 words, difficult (1946, p. 38), and he recommends an average sentence length of fewer than 20 words (1962, p. 90). That doesn't mean you should aim for all sentences to contain about 20 words. Flesch recommends substantial variability in sentence length. Some should be very short. To achieve optimal readability, construct sentences of variable length that average, across several paragraphs, perhaps 16 to 20 words.

Flesch considers variability of sentence length a virtue in itself. Sentence after sentence of similar length and similar construction blunts readers' attention. In contrast, sentences of only a few words mixed with sentences of many words (averaging no more than 20) invigorate writing and keep readers alert. These first two paragraphs—to give you a feeling for the relationship between average sentence length and readability—contain 223 words and 14 sentences. That gives this chapter an average sentence length of about 16 words so far. Variability in sentence length ranges from 5 words to 41.

When you find yourself saddled with a monstrous sentence, you might consider any of four ways to tame it: you can break it into smaller sentences, use markers, use punctuation, or draw a picture.

Make Smaller Sentences

When a sentence becomes cumbersome because of its length, the first thought is to break it into multiple sentences of more manageable lengths. In most cases, that works well.

One sentence of 70 words

> While critics claim that senators fail to attend to the desires of their constituents, several senators have responded that with a scarcity of office time, and with pressure to attend to important committee work, constant partisan assignments, and routine paperwork, and living with expectations that they will research and introduce their own bills periodically, little time is left to develop the close relationship they would like to have with constituents.

Four sentences totaling 72 words, averaging 18, and ranging from 4 to 39

> Critics claim that senators fail to attend to the desires of their constituents. Several senators have responded. They claim that office time is scarce and demands are great: they must attend to important committee work, partisan assignments, and routine paperwork, and they live with constant expectations that they will research and introduce their own bills periodically. Little time is left to develop the close relationship they would like to have with constituents.

Notice that the periods in the revision above feel like oases, and the four-word second sentence feels like a gift from writer to reader.

You may have a legitimate reason to write a very long sentence on occasion. When you do, probably you'll need the help of some sophisticated punctuation, as shown on the next page and page 108. Generally, though, 70-word sentences are not salvageable if your aim is to do right by your readers. **(Examine Exercise #14, page 209.)**

Use Markers

When an overstuffed sentence has discrete parts, you can help readers by simply providing a few markers along the way. Insert numbers (1, 2, 3) or letters (a, b, c) as cues that the corresponding pieces of information are distinct from each other. An alternative is to create separate sentences beginning with *First*, *Second*, and *Third* (or *Finally*). (Avoid *Firstly*, *Secondly*, and so on.)

One sentence of 46 words

> She found that differences in ATS scores between Koreans and
> Americans were not significant, Koreans were similar to Americans
> in the relationship of their ATS scores to their IQ scores, and Koreans
> scored higher on the verbal subtest of the ATS than on the tactile subtest.

The same 46-word sentence made easier to read with markers

> She found that (1) differences in ATS scores between Koreans and
> Americans were not significant, (2) Koreans were similar to Americans
> in the relationship of their ATS scores to their IQ scores, and (3) Koreans
> scored higher on the verbal subtest of the ATS than on the tactile subtest.

The numbers give readers comfort and security by showing where to shift gears—when to depart one point and engage another. Besides, a reader who has finished the sentence and wants to re-examine a particular point can return to that point easily with help from the markers. A variation is to stack the marked segments below the stem, and thus create a list.

(Examine Exercise #15, page 209.)

Use Punctuation

Punctuation is another tool that can tame overstuffed sentences. When you study Chapters 12 and 13 you'll see the specific principles behind the revision below. For now, just observe and enjoy what can be accomplished by a pair of dashes and a few pairs of parentheses.

One sentence of 56 words

> His indecision was whether to buy the exorbitantly expensive but very durable
> model, which was made of steel, the moderately priced but less durable model,
> which was made of aluminum, or the inexpensive model that he would likely
> have to replace soon because it was made of plastic, but which he actually
> preferred for its appearance.

The same sentence shortened and organized with the help of punctuation

> He was unable to decide whether to buy the exorbitantly expensive but very
> durable model (steel), the moderately priced but less durable model (aluminum),
> or—preferable for its appearance—the inexpensive model that he likely would
> have to replace soon (plastic).

(Examine Exercise #16, page 209. Suggestion: use the example above as a model.)

Draw a Picture

You might find yourself writing an overstuffed sentence against your better judgment simply because you're drowning in details. Maybe your message involves too much numerical information for readers to absorb in sentence format. Rather than stretch the ability of the sentence to do the job, siphon the details from the sentence and present them in a table.

Don't write this	**Write this**
In 1994, overwhelmingly more deaths occurred by gunfire in the United States than in developed Asian countries, with 1 gunfire death per 2 million citizens in Japan, 2 deaths per 2 million in South Korea, 3 per 2 million in Hong Kong, 4 per 2 million in Singapore, and 7 per 2 million in Taiwan, as compared to 285 deaths for every 2 million citizens of the United States.	In 1994, overwhelmingly more deaths occurred by gunfire in the United States than in developed Asian countries. Comparisons are shown in Table 1.

TABLE 1. Deaths by gunfire per 2 million citizens in 1994 for the US and five Asian countries.

Country	Deaths per 2 million
Japan	1
South Korea	2
Hong Kong	3
Singapore	4
Taiwan	7
United States	285

You needn't limit tables to numerical data. You can also present overabundant verbal detail in a table.

Don't write this	**Write this**
Researchers used color codes to designate the grade and sex of each group, with first-grade girls wearing pink and first-grade boys wearing red; second-grade girls wearing yellow and second-grade boys wearing orange; third-grade girls wearing tan and third-grade boys wearing brown; fourth-grade girls wearing sky blue and fourth-grade boys wearing navy blue; and finally, fifth-grade girls wearing lime green and fifth-grade boys wearing forest green.	Researchers used color codes to designate the grade and sex of each group, as shown in Table 1.

TABLE 1. Color codes by grade and sex

Grade	Female	Male
1	pink	red
2	yellow	orange
3	tan	brown
4	sky blue	navy
5	lime green	forest green

When you do use a table or a figure, you can help readers in three ways. First, introduce the table or figure with some reference to it in the preceding narrative. Second, number the table or figure so you can refer readers to it easily from other places in the document. And finally, give the table or figure a concise but descriptive title that makes it somewhat comprehensible even to readers who are breezing through your document casually. (**Examine Exercise #17, page 210.**)

Parting Thoughts About Sentence Length

If you were to combine the problems of complex words (Chapter 3) and filler words (Chapter 5) with a violation of reasonable sentence length (this chapter), you might create a sentence that feels similar to the monstrosity shown below (a real-life example). Imagine reading paragraph after paragraph of this style of writing! The revision shows the extent to which such bloat can be tamed by a diligent use of sensible writing principles.

Don't write this	**Write this**
It is hoped that this study will aid us in evaluating our present and future requirements and will assist us in determining the solutions we will need in the future to maximize productivity and hold deleterious costs in check.	I hope this study will help us achieve maximum productivity at minimum cost.

This kind of bloat may be most common among writers who think of themselves as writing for someone above them in a particular hierarchy—students wanting to impress teachers or professors, and employees wanting to impress superiors or clients. You will do well to just be yourself when you write. Ignore echoes of "the official style" ringing in your ears. Have confidence that your knowledge of good writing principles and your ability to think are sufficient. After all, readers of every stripe are impressed with the same qualities in a piece of non-fiction writing: clarity and efficiency.

PRECISION

Choose the right word over the almost-right word, and construct sentences and paragraphs to say precisely—not approximately—what you intend to say.

CHAPTER 7
CHOOSE YOUR WORDS PRECISELY

Of all the eye-openers during more than 20 years of analyzing and teaching writing, one of the more dramatic to me has been the number of ways a writer can botch the choice of a word. Words are the raw material of language. Nothing is more basic than choosing them well. Choose specific terms over general, respect shades of meaning, and be wary of word popularity.

Choose Specific Terms Over General

Why drop readers into the general neighborhood of your meaning when you can send them to the specific house you have in mind—even sit them down in the very chair that is at the core of your thoughts? "The committee needs your input." What does the committee really need? *Input* is a general term coined to refer to any information or data entered into a computer. How sensible is it to stick the general term *input* routinely into any sentence that refers to a transfer of information from one person to another?

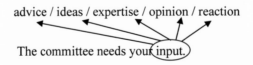

advice / ideas / expertise / opinion / reaction

The committee needs your input.

Use terms that give readers as much specific meaning as possible. Words like *input* become buzzwords—words that come to mind more for their familiar sound than for the value of their meaning. They damage both reading and writing by devitalizing the specific terms they displace. That leaves everyone with a shrunken vocabulary.

Buzzwords sometimes leave readers at a fork in the road. What does *area* mean in this sentence from a newspaper article?

> Scheduled to be released today by the Pennsylvania KIDS COUNT Partnership, the report cites improvements in some areas and points to continued decline in others.

Does the report compare improvement in the Philadelphia *area* to improvement in the Pittsburgh *area*, or is *area* referring to something other than a physical parameter?

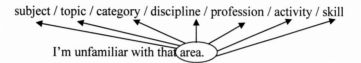

subject / topic / category / discipline / profession / activity / skill

I'm unfamiliar with that area.

The use of *area* as a buzzword is widespread. Dictionaries, generally in about their fourth level of definitions, allow for a figurative use of *area*. Still, if you resolve to use *area* only to describe physical parameters, you will improve both your thinking and your writing.

Two buzzwords that have become popular recently are *look to* and *look at*. They remind me of Voltaire's observation that "we use words to hide our thoughts." If you write "we are looking to win the title next year," you lead readers to imagine that you expect to win, or at least have plans that give you a good chance of winning. In reality, you may just be trying to sound confident in the face of dim hope.

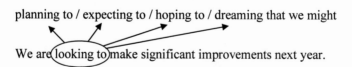

planning to / expecting to / hoping to / dreaming that we might

We are looking to make significant improvements next year.

Look at is used in the same way, giving an impression of effort while avoiding commitment.

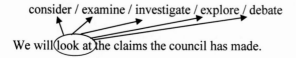

consider / examine / investigate / explore / debate

We will look at the claims the council has made.

Other common buzzwords, shown below, appear also in Appendix B, *A List of Troublesome Words*, and in Appendix C, *Four Business Buzzwords Elaborated Upon*. There you'll find further thoughts about misuse, along with sample sentences and revisions.

address	*Address* used as a verb is a common tool of evasion. Promising to *address* a problem avoids the commitment that comes with promising to *solve* it, or at least *investigate* it thoroughly.
deal with	*Deal with* could mean *resolve, fight, ignore, tolerate, eliminate*, or any one of several other actions.
implement	*Implement* used as a verb displaces many descriptive terms: *start, apply, test, install, initiate*.
leverage	*Leverage* used as a verb displaces *use, apply, take advantage of, exploit*, and other verbs having specific meaning.
ongoing	*Ongoing* commonly displaces such descriptive adjectives as *continual, continuous, constant, long-term, far-reaching*, and *open-ended*.
metrics	As a general term referring to any type of data, *metrics* can leave readers wondering what specifically is involved: *revenue, profits, expenses, scores, measurements, criteria*.
upcoming	This worthless word can always be replaced with specific information (day, date, time), or it can be omitted altogether.
update	Too often *update* displaces such verbs as *revise, report*, and *tell*, and such nouns as *revision, report, summary*, and *overview*.

Apparently some writers find recently coined word-mutants (input, update, ongoing, upcoming) irresistible for their sound, like a familiar song that the mind replays continually. Otherwise, why would those words sometimes appear where they have no function at all?

For years he has valued his ongoing exercise routine.

Don't miss the upcoming concert next Saturday at 8 p.m.

All readers know that a routine practiced for years is "ongoing," and that an event scheduled for next Saturday has to be "upcoming."

The key to choosing words well, and particularly to rejecting buzzwords in favor of terms that carry rich meaning, is simply to THINK. You'll convince readers that you're sincere and believable only if you're willing to think extensively about what you want to say and about the many shades of meaning in the words you use. A writer who expresses multiple actions with one all-purpose word is like a golfer who drives, chips, and putts with one all-purpose club: it's possible, but it's careless and inefficient, and the results are likely to be undesirable.

Think of your use of buzzwords as a self-imposed weakness. As a writer, you begin your work in a strong position. You are in charge. You are the one imparting information, ideas, and opinions to readers. Then, as you use vague words, you empower readers to fill in specific meaning with whatever their biases dictate. You relinquish the power to say as much as you can. Still worse, you lose readers who sense a lack of substance in your writing.

One last thought about buzzwords is that using them extensively inflicts a serious loss beyond the loss of effective writing. **To discard concrete words is to discard concrete thought, and to discard concrete thought is to set into motion an unraveling of the intellectual base our predecessors built. That amounts to human devolution.** (Examine Exercise #18, page 210.)

Respect Shades of Meaning

William Zinsser (1994) says, "You'll never make your mark as a writer unless you develop a respect for words and a curiosity about their shades of meaning that is almost obsessive" (p. 34). That's a powerful thought! No doubt you've written a word, sensed that its meaning wasn't exactly what you intended, and then begun to search for the just-right word. If the just-right word escapes you after you've scratched your head and peered at the ceiling for a while, enter your almost-right word into thesaurus.com and scroll through the possibilities. The just-right word may jump out at you. If it doesn't, refine your search with more thesaurus entries or the help of a good dictionary. Finding that just-right word is worth the search.

Look at the damage done by these almost-right words. If they were left in place, readers would have to conclude that the writer either didn't know the difference or didn't care enough to search for the just-right word. Neither impression is one you'll want to make.

Replace words as shown	For this reason
describe Next I will ~~discuss~~ the setting in which the observations were made.	To *discuss* is to engage multiple views.
corroborate Parents' observations ~~support~~ what the students saw.	*Support* is not strong enough. *Verify* would be another good option.
believe Board members ~~feel~~ that the statistics, as presented, are accurate.	To *feel* is to respond to emotion. To *believe* is to respond to information.
most important One of the ~~biggest~~ contributions of science to cancer research has been…	The issue is not so much size as it is effect.
challenge My new position will ~~allow~~ me to improve my speaking skills.	Lack of the position did not impede speaking-skill improvement. The new position simply provides incentive.
eluding They were tired of ~~avoiding~~ the police after being chased for five days.	To *avoid* is simply to stay away. If police were chasing them, they would have to actively run and hide (elude or evade).

The six sentences above give new meaning to the phrase "scratching the surface." There's virtually no limit to the number of examples of imprecise word choice that might be presented here. Note also that your readers will not be the only persons to benefit from your diligence in choosing words. The very act of searching for that just-right word will help you clarify to yourself exactly what you want to say—and build your vocabulary for future writing.

In addition to committing yourself to using the simplest words needed (Chapter 2) and the fewest words needed (Chapter 5), commit yourself now to knowing the precise meaning of every word you use. If you have any question about the precise meaning of a word you are considering, investigate its meaning thoroughly. Then use that word only if you are convinced that it is more precise than any other word you and your readers know.

Your devotion to shades of meaning needs to extend beyond nouns, verbs, adjectives, and adverbs. You need to give equal attention to the "small stuff." You'll use many small words—conjunctions (and, but, or, nor) and prepositions (in, on, of, for, to, from)—when you write. Those small words do an important job: they join words or groups of words (clauses and phrases) in a way that identifies the relationship between the words they join. If you choose your conjunction or preposition imprecisely, you'll either inconvenience readers or lead them to believe that the relationship is something other than what it is.

Be particularly vigilant about the common but misleading use of *and* when a relationship is causal or oppositional rather than additive.

The traffic was heavy, ~~and~~ *so* he missed his appointment

She forgot to turn the heat on, ~~and~~ *but* the plants survived

Here are a few other examples of imprecise conjunctions and prepositions. Notice the power of these small words to mislead or confuse readers, and take heed as you write.

We used scores ~~for~~ *from* the writing exams to award scholarships.

She wrote 40 pages ~~on~~ *about* Aztec life.

He made statistical comparisons ~~on~~ *between* the two tests.

They compared spatial perception scores ~~and~~ *to* aptitude scores.

The body can move forward, backward, upward, downward, ~~and~~ *or* side to side. (Test the claim of this sentence in its original form at your own risk.)

(Examine Exercise #19, page 211.)

Be Wary of Word Popularity

New words pop up and old words take on new meanings. Be cautious about adopting any of the new arrivals. Ask yourself if the new word or new usage offers a distinct meaning. If it does—if it accomplishes something that no standard term can—use it. If it doesn't, probably the new word is no more than a passing fad. There's no substitute for Standard English if you want to communicate effectively with a cross-section of readers.

Young people are the source of many new words and word uses: *cool*, *hot*, *awesome*, and *radical*—to name a few—have applications that would have been unrecognizable a couple generations ago. No one could have convinced my grandfather that the day would come when a person could be cool and hot at the same time—and gain status for both. Nor would he have had any idea what was meant by being dissed.

Not all faddish words spring from youth. In the business community, the noun *implement* has become a wildly popular all-purpose verb, and the verb *revisit* is used in ways never imagined a generation ago. Conventional use would have us *revisit* the art museum to see a wing we missed, or *revisit* Grandmother when she's feeling better. Recent use has spawned such statements as "When we reconvene next month, we will *revisit* the issue of truancy." Any one of a host of conventional terms would yield more specific meaning: *resume discussion of, debate more thoroughly, reconsider, pursue in earnest*. Failing to pass the test of distinct meaning, the faddish use of *revisit* is likely to disappear as quickly as a bad joke.

The moral of these observations is this: while new words and new word uses might lubricate spoken exchanges in some social circumstance, resist their quick adoption in your writing. Think about meaning and effect. While a new word or new usage appears to be marching toward possible adoption, keep your writing strongest by letting others lead the way. In contrast to scientists, who ply their craft best by riding the front edge of change, nonfiction writers ply their craft best by working skillfully with well-established, standard terms.

CHAPTER 8

PLACE WORDS PRECISELY

When you place material poorly within a sentence or paragraph you give your readers a jigsaw puzzle to assemble. If they assemble it incorrectly, they'll miss what you intended to say. Even if they assemble it correctly, you'll have inconvenienced them—and you'll have put your name on a piece of weak writing. Some readers, feeling burdened with what they see as unacceptable difficulties, will give up on your work altogether. In short, misplacing material is one of the principal ways that you, as a writer, risk a poor relationship with your readers. In this chapter you'll read advice for the placement of four types of material: modifiers, subjects, material that orients readers, and material needing emphasis.

Keep the Modifier and the Modified Together

A modifier is a "word or word group . . . used to limit, qualify, or otherwise describe the meaning of another word or word group" (Kramer, et al., p. 673). Placing modifiers next to the words they modify strengthens and clarifies your message. Notice throughout this section that few of the misplaced modifiers arrive too late. Modifiers are misplaced chiefly out of impatience—failure to think ahead, find the word or words to be modified, and hold onto the modifier until reaching that point.

The word *only* seems to be misplaced more frequently than any other modifier. You may have acclimated to the early *only* as a flaw so common that it seems acceptable: many very good writers are consistent in its use. Still, I believe the weaknesses and the occasional confusion it imposes are sufficiently damaging to justify my making a point of it. These three sentences are weaker than if *only* were re-positioned as the arrow indicates.

We can only do that after the new equipment is installed.

We have only seen the water go down an inch in the last hour.

Telstar's signal was only available across the United States for a short period of time.

The changes create three strong statements: *only after the new equipment is installed*, *only an inch*, and *only a short period of time.*

A still stronger argument for placing modifiers where they belong is that misplacement sometimes obscures meaning altogether. In none of the three following sentences do the circled modifiers modify the words they precede (*wants*; *likes*; *find*), but you'll have to guess at which of the possible locations gives the intended meaning.

He only wants Republicans in his cabinet because they agree with him.

He just likes men in that job because he knows no other way.

Some marketers even find follow-up calls difficult after six months on the job.

I don't want to leave you with the impression that misplaced modifiers are confined to a small number of words, with *only* at the core, so I'll leave you with a few sentences showing a variety of modifiers that the writer might be well-advised to reposition.

Teachers *even* face a great challenge if they like children.

She will *either* have to bring extensive experience or phenomenal instincts.

Some managers may *neither* agree with the policies as written nor the director's modifications of them.

The new drug bears *similar* characteristics to one made by our chief competitor.

An ergonomist from the University of Michigan *specifically* designed the floating-chair workstation for employees in your division.

Do *not* invest your money in our firm on the strength of what I have to say, but on the strength of the track record shown in this performance summary.

Can readers extract intended meaning from these sentences by applying mental gymnastics? Probably. Abundant misplaced modifiers in our reading have made us good at that. But why take chances with your own writing? Why miss opportunities to make strong, clear statements that help readers pass through your sentences with efficiency and immediate comprehension?

By diligently putting together words that belong together, you can steer a reader's thinking to precisely the place you want it to go. In the last sample sentence above, for example, correcting the placement of the modifier causes the sentence to begin with "Invest your money in our firm" rather than "Do not invest your money in our firm." Which first impression would you want to make? How many poorly crafted sentences do you think one can get away with before unknowingly suffering losses?

While you're likely to misplace single-word modifiers early in a sentence through impatience, you're likely to misplace groups of modifying words (phrases) late in a sentence as an afterthought. The misplaced phrase in the following sentence apparently came to the writer's mind too late to be coordinated with the rest of the sentence.

Senator Hunt promised to fight criminal activity in his committee meeting.

Did the criminal activity actually take place in the senator's committee meeting, or did he simply make his promise during the meeting? That's an important distinction—one that could affect the senator's electability. Be careful. Don't let misplaced modifiers have you saying something that you don't want to say. (**Examine Exercise #20, page 211.**)

Follow an Action Phrase with the Action's Subject

The great number of examples you will see in this section is my response to the ubiquitous and damaging nature of this particular writing flaw. I carry in my mind an image from a school book of long ago, probably one I used in high school. In a silly drawing, a large building was riding a bicycle. The caption was "Turning the corner on my bicycle, a large building came into view." The illustration was of a dangling participle, so named because the opening participial phrase—an action in need of its subject—was left dangling when a false subject appeared instead. The caption should have read, "Turning a corner on my bicycle, I saw a large building come into view."

I think this problem of word placement is understood more easily if it's called a *misplaced subject* rather than a *dangling participle*. The guideline is simple: be sure that the first noun or pronoun following an action phrase is the rightful subject of the action. In the sample from my old textbook, the action phrase was followed by a noun (building) that was not the rightful subject of the action (riding my bicycle). As clear cut as the guideline is, compliance seems to be difficult. Misplaced subjects hide in sentences like snakes in long grass.

There are two ways to correct the problem of a misplaced subject. One is to move the correct subject into place following the action.

Don't write this	**Write this**
After gathering and singing the National Anthem, <u>police</u> arrested the demonstrators.	After gathering and singing the National Anthem, <u>the demonstrators</u> were arrested by police.

I changed the sentence from the stronger active voice to the less strong passive voice, but readers are spared the extra work of having to infer that the demonstrators, not the police, gathered and sang the national anthem.

Another way to correct the problem of the misplaced subject is to alter the content of the introductory phrase.

Don't write this	Write this
When driving, <u>these sunglasses</u> may save your life.	When <u>you</u> are driving, these sunglasses may save your life.

The inability of sunglasses to drive allows the meaning to be inferred easily in this case, but still, there is no excuse for putting a bump in the reader's road—even the smallest of bumps.

Sometimes instead of putting a bump in the road, a misplaced subject digs a hole for readers to fall into. Readers will have every right to take the original sentence below literally, in which case they will believe that the prosecutors arrived in Washington. The writer's actual meaning, that the senator arrived in Washington, is captured by the two revisions, which between them show the two ways to solve the problem.

Don't write this	Write this
Shortly after arriving in Washington, <u>prosecutors</u> began to examine the senator's campaign financing.	Shortly after arriving in Washington, <u>the senator</u> had prosecutors examining his campaign financing.
	Shortly after <u>the senator's arrival</u> in Washington, prosecutors began to examine his campaign financing.

Because misplaced subjects are deceptively easy to write, you might see and hear them in unexpected places. Representatives of a major company tried to promote their services by printing in a pamphlet, "In assisting you as a prospective applicant, you can expect us to…." The construction of the sentence has applicants inexplicably assisting themselves. A United States Post Office substation also had patrons serving themselves with a sign reading, "To provide you better service, have forms filled out before you reach the window." The subject in this case is known as the "understood you," an unwritten but nonetheless present subject following the action phrase. Finally, police in a major city some years ago placed copies of this notice by the thousands—in upper-case red letters more than an inch high—on windshields of parked cars.

> IF LEFT UNLOCKED, A THIEF WOULD NOW
> HAVE YOUR VEHICLE

When I agreed with the sentiment, suggesting to a pair of police officers that they not leave the thief unlocked, I found their sense of humor no better than their sense of subject placement. (**Examine Exercise #21, page 211.**)

Orient Readers with Word Placement

When you write information linked to a date, a source, or some other kind of orienting material, most times you should place that material up front. Such a logical placement of orienting material gives readers the perspective they need to read with understanding, and therefore avoid rereading.

Don't write this	Write this
The profits of this division out stripped those of all other divisions combined <u>in 2020</u>.	<u>In 2020</u>, the profits of this division outstripped those of all other divisions combined.
Weights are outside allowable parameters, tolerances are unacceptable, and waste is nearly double the level expected, <u>according to the inspector who was here on the first of the month</u>.	<u>According to the inspector who was here on the first of the month</u>, weights are outside allowable parameters, tolerances are unacceptable, and waste is nearly double the level expected.

The active voice principle presented in Chapter 3 also contributes to reader orientation, because in active voice, too, the actor is identified early and unmistakably. Look at the difference in readability between this passive-voice construction and the revised active voice construction. The latter has its orienting material moved to the front. (Note also the breaking down of a 37-word sentence into two sentences of 10 words and 27 words, respectively.)

Don't write this	Write this
The orientation of new employees to the company and its facilities, to their specific work stations, and to the policies by which everyone is expected to abide, scheduled for next Monday, <u>has been rescheduled</u> for Wednesday.	<u>We have rescheduled</u> next Monday's new employee orientation for Wednesday. New employees will be oriented to the company and its facilities, to their specific work stations, and to the policies by which everyone is expected to abide.

Give information to readers at whatever point they can make best use of it. To do less is to inconvenience the very people you are trying to serve. (**Examine Exercise #22, page 211.**)

Emphasize Material with Word Placement

In conversation you can emphasize points with voice inflection, facial contortions, body language, or finger pointing. In writing, you have none of those aids. The primary tools of emphasis on paper are punctuation and word placement. Techniques for the former will be presented in Chapters 12 and 13. Techniques for the latter are presented here.

Placement for orientation and placement for emphasis often work hand-in-glove. That's because the orienting material misplaced at the end of a sentence is likely to be as weak in that position as it is strong at the beginning. The end of a sentence (or paragraph or document) is the point that draws the most reader attention, and therefore is the point at which material needing emphasis should be placed. Look at the same two examples shown at the beginning of the section on orientation (p. 54), but with emphatic material underlined. Notice that the earlier shifting of orienting material to the beginning of each sentence leaves emphatic material in its ideal location: at the end.

Don't write this	**Write this**
The profits of this division outstripped those of <u>all other divisions combined</u> in 1982.	In 1982, the profits of this division outstripped those of <u>all other divisions combined</u>.
Weights are outside allowable parameters, tolerances are unaccept-able, and <u>waste is nearly double the level expected</u>, according to the inspector who was here on the first of the month.	According to the inspector who was here on the first of the month, weights are outside allowable parameters, tolerances are unaccept-able, and <u>waste is nearly double the level expected</u>.

Of course you can't rely on always hitting two birds with one stone. Sometimes emphasis functions apart from orientation. In those cases you have to simply identify material that you want emphasized and find a way to place it at the end of the sentence.

Don't write this	**Write this**
Most important, <u>strong math skills</u> will be required for the job he has been offered.	Most important, the job he has been offered will require <u>strong math skills</u>.

At other times you can focus the reader's attention on material you want emphasized by relegating other material to the background. Notice in the original version of the sentence below that the conjunction *and* gives a sense of balanced importance to the two halves of the sentence. You want to emphasize the point that traditional surgery is less effective. You can accomplish that by placing the statement about its being old-fashioned between commas in the middle of the sentence. That sends it to the background by making it parenthetical.

Don't write this	**Write this**
Using traditional surgery to make that kind of joint repair is old-fashioned, and it is much less effective than arthroscopic surgery.	Traditional surgery, old-fashioned for that kind of joint repair, is much less effective than arthroscopic surgery.

The revision makes the primary message stand out: "Traditional surgery… is much less effective…."

As you revise your work, you may need to relocate quite a bit of material for emphasis. I do. Material doesn't necessarily come to mind in optimal order during first-draft writing. Sometimes you'll think of key points first, and then add other material. That can leave you with a jumble to untangle to get the spotlight shining on the stars of the show.

One tip I often give about emphasis is this: read your writing aloud. Hearing the words you have written slowed to the rate of normal speech will help you identify points you have emphasized and points you have de-emphasized. That will prepare you to revise in a way that makes key points prominent for readers. **(Examine Exercise #23, page 212.)**

GRAMMAR

Use correct grammar to communicate clearly
and precisely with your audience and to produce
writing that reflects well on you.

CHAPTER 9
LEARN BASIC GRAMMAR

CHAPTER 10
SPEAK WELL TO WRITE WELL

CHAPTER 11
ACCOMMODATE GENDER ELEGANTLY

LEARN BASIC GRAMMAR

Probably you don't like having to follow rules. Most of us would rather do things our own way. It makes us feel free—unencumbered.

That feeling of freedom is an illusion if you're writing. Throwing rules to the wind may feel euphoric now, but over the long term it will imprison you in a cell of incoherence. Conversely, learning and observing the rules, though it feels confining now, over the long term will free you to communicate clearly and easily with others.

This chapter doesn't substitute for a grammar book. You should have one on hand as a source of rules for every occasion. I recommend Diana Hacker and Nancy Sommers' *A Writer's Reference* (2017). As the title makes clear, it's a book to be kept handy for repeated reference.

This might be a good place to insert the caveat that you can overplay devotion to rules. The old adage that "rules are made to be broken" is simply an overstated way of saying that intelligent thought about sensible exceptions should always be entertained. Bureaucracies offer sufficient evidence that a slavish following of rules and policies without applying intelligent judgment produces dreary results. The more you write, the more likely you'll be to encounter a circumstance not considered by the rule makers—a circumstance that calls for creative problem-solving. What you'll need to do is strike a mid-point between two extremes, so that you neither (1) let slavish devotion to a head full of rules wring every bit of creativity and spontaneity from you, nor (2) break fundamental rules that impair readability and make you appear ignorant. It is the latter danger that I've written about here.

The remainder of this chapter is divided into eleven short sections. The first three are simply a review of grammar terms that you may have learned and partially forgotten. The others describe and exemplify the eight grammar rules violated most frequently in the many thousands of pages of writing I've read while advising students working on masters theses and doctoral dissertations, and while working more recently with business writing.

I need to emphasize that to keep this book lean I've ignored grammar violations that are less prevalent. You'll find many more rules of grammar and examples of their violation in books devoted to grammar. Following is an account of the eleven sections of this chapter.

- Parts of Speech
- Parts of a Sentence
- Types of Clauses and Phrases
- Incorrect Word Choice
- Subject/Verb Disagreement
- Wrong Verb Tense
- Dangling Participle
- Split Infinitive
- Careless Use of Prepositions
- Wrong Pronoun Case
- Antecedent/Pronoun Disagreement

Parts of Speech

The parts of speech are eight word-functions labeled to make discussion about language possible. Seven are useful to your thinking about nonfiction writing in an organized way. I've omitted interjections (Wow! Whew. Oh, no.) because they're primarily tools of fiction. Review the seven parts of speech shown in Figure 1 until you recall what they are and how they're used.

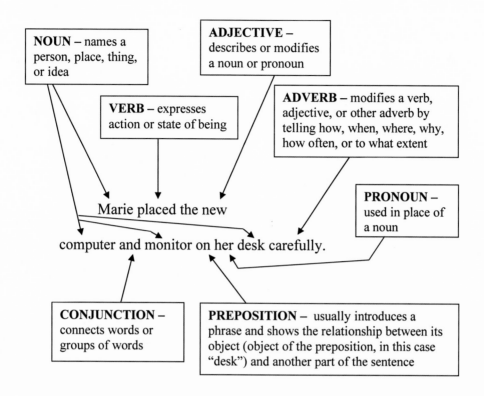

Figure 1. Seven Parts of Speech Defined and Exemplified

Notice that I left *the* unlabeled in Figure 1. *The*, *a*, and *an*—used to modify nouns—are a specific kind of adjective called an *article*. In the Figure 1 sample sentence, *the* (along with *new*) modifies *computer*. Not shown in that sample sentence are uses of the other articles, *a* and *an*. *A* and *an* are indefinite articles (an animal; a dog). *The* is a definite article (the animal; the dog).

Parts of a Sentence

A sentence is a group of words that delivers a complete thought and contains a subject and a predicate (something said about the subject). The basic parts of a typical sentence are shown in Figure 2.

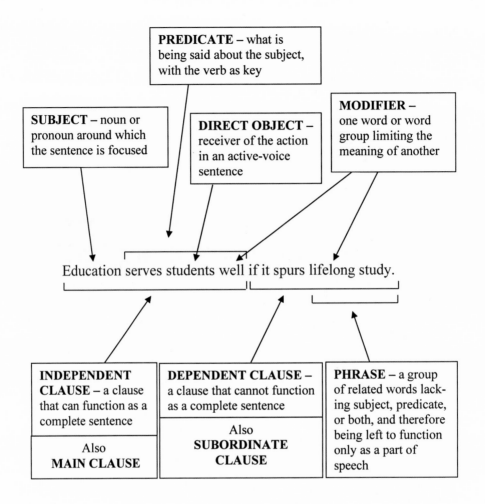

Figure 2. The Basic Parts of a Sentence

Some elements shown in Figure 2 will be absent from other sentences, and some will be used in greater number. A simple sentence is no more than an independent clause. By contrast, some complex sentences have multiple independent and dependent clauses. The number of modifiers in Figure 2 (*well* modifies *serves* by telling how; *lifelong* modifies *study* by telling to what extent) is modest. In a more complex sentence, any number of modifiers might modify any number of words in any number of ways.

In Figure 3 you'll see three additional terms used to describe elements of a sentence.

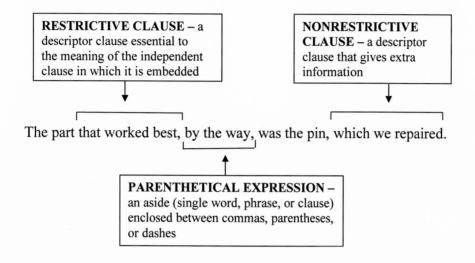

Figure 3. Additional Elements of a Sentence

Phrases and dependent clauses, because they can't stand alone as complete sentences, function as parts of speech, as shown in Figure 4. Parts of speech are fundamental to your understanding how language works. If you're not clear about them, restudy Figure 1.

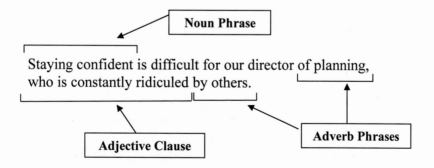

Figure 4. Phrases and Clauses Functioning as Parts of Speech

Incorrect Word Choice

Among the 140 troublesome words, word pairs, and phrases treated in detail in Appendix B, I see eight as common grammar violations. As explained in the appendix, the not-equal sign (≠) between words indicates that one word is commonly misused in place of the other. You'll find details in Appendix B (p. 154), where these words are entered alphabetically. Read about them now.

- amount ≠ number
- latter ≠ last
- lay ≠ lie
- less ≠ fewer

- like ≠ as
- myself ≠ me, I
- where ≠ in which, for which, to which, etc.
- would have ≠ had

Subject/Verb Disagreement

A singular subject needs a singular verb; a plural subject needs a plural verb. Probably you won't write "we was" or "he were," but you might let material that lies between the subject and the verb sway you to the wrong verb tense. This sentence has a singular subject: *column*.

The column of trucks, jeeps, and tanks ~~were~~ was moving slowly.

You might also choose the wrong verb tense when the verb precedes the subject, and then you add a second subject without realizing that you left a singular verb behind where you now need a plural verb.

Of paramount importance ~~is~~ are an interviewer's preparation of questions and ability to elicit honest answers.

Wrong Verb Tense

Past, present, and future are only the surface of verb tense. Don't let all the terms in Figure 5 scare you, but do read the sentences to see how a rich assortment of verb tenses can help you keep readers aware of temporal relationships in your writing.

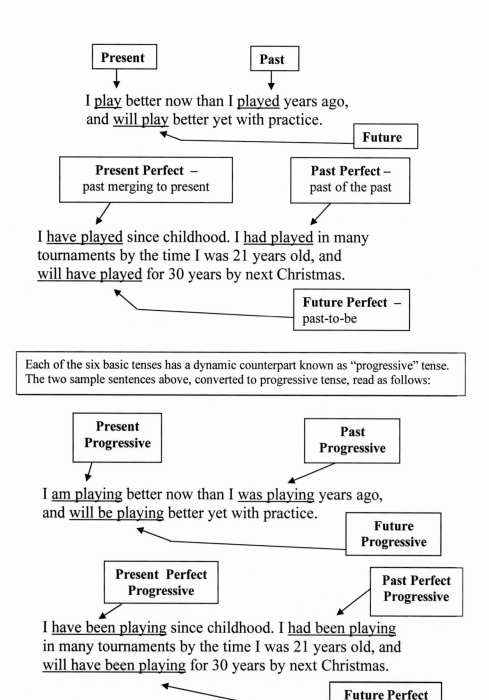

Present → I <u>play</u> better now than I <u>played</u> years ago, **Past**
and <u>will play</u> better yet with practice. **Future**

Present Perfect – past merging to present

Past Perfect – past of the past

I <u>have played</u> since childhood. I <u>had played</u> in many tournaments by the time I was 21 years old, and <u>will have played</u> for 30 years by next Christmas.

Future Perfect – past-to-be

Each of the six basic tenses has a dynamic counterpart known as "progressive" tense. The two sample sentences above, converted to progressive tense, read as follows:

Present Progressive

Past Progressive

I <u>am playing</u> better now than I <u>was playing</u> years ago, and <u>will be playing</u> better yet with practice.

Future Progressive

Present Perfect Progressive

Past Perfect Progressive

I <u>have been playing</u> since childhood. I <u>had been playing</u> in many tournaments by the time I was 21 years old, and <u>will have been playing</u> for 30 years by next Christmas.

Future Perfect Progressive

Think clearly about time frames when you write. You'll need more than past, present, and future tense to make temporal relationships clear.

> had
> When the accounts were pulled last month, those that yielded
> less than a five percent return the previous year were scrutinized.

The past perfect (past of the past) *had yielded* is preferable, because it avoids placing the pulling of the accounts and the previous year's yield in the same temporal plane.

> have doubled
> By this time next year we will double our profits.

The projected doubling of profits by a designated future time calls for the future perfect (past-to-be) *will have doubled.*

> In cultures past and present, primitive and advanced,
> architecture is important.
> has been

The most difficult perfect tense to grasp is present perfect (past moving into present). You can see its usefulness here. The present tense *is important* is not appropriate for cultures past, while the present perfect tense *has been important* accommodates both past and present.

Dangling Participle

A *dangling participle* is the same flaw that I labeled *misplaced subject* in Chapter 8. A participle is a verb form ending in "ing" or "ed" and functioning as the main verb of a clause, either with a helping verb (He was *trying*) or as an adjective (His interest *ebbed*). When a sentence opens with a participial phrase (like *Moving quickly*, . . .), the subject of that phrase should appear as the first noun or pronoun following it. If another noun or pronoun appears first, readers are left "dangling" for lack of the rightful subject. Sometimes the rightful subject appears later:

Don't write this	**Write this**
Moving quickly, <u>no one</u> suspected Allen until after he had left.	Moving quickly, <u>Allen</u> avoided all suspicion until after he had left.

At other times, the rightful subject is absent. In the sentence below, only with the help of the revision do we know who did the packing of the boxes. Further, the sentence's literal message is that everything from his desk was forced to resign!

Don't write this	**Write this**
Forced to resign, <u>everything</u> from his desk was packed into boxes.	Forced to resign, <u>he</u> packed everything from his desk into boxes.

You can see several additional examples of this problem, with solutions, in the section titled "Follow an Action Phrase with the Action's Subject," on pages 52–54.

Split Infinitive

An infinitive is a verb form introduced by "to" and functioning as a noun, adjective, or adverb. To split an infinitive is to insert an adverb after the introductory *to*. Opinion about the incorrectness of the split infinitive is itself split, and it has been for decades. Common sense tells us to avoid splitting the infinitive whenever a reasonably graceful alternative is available. The advantage of keeping the infinitive intact is strength of expression. By relocating the word that splits infinitives in these two sentences, we preserve the strong statements "to resolve" and "to face":

He was determined to forever resolve the differences that had encumbered the partnership for so many years.

The firm would have no choice but to eventually face its financial problems squarely.

Occasionally you'll find that you must split an infinitive to avoid an awkward construction.

We must find a way to adequately equip him to do the job.

To place *adequately* after *him* would be to lose the strong, intact statement "equip him to do the job." Therefore, I'd leave the split infinitive in place as the lesser evil. This illustrates the need I mentioned earlier to let intelligent judgment trump a rule on occasion. That doesn't mean you should throw the rule to the wind. Knowing rules is important. Only then can you conform to the rule as your first choice, and retreat to a violation only after the wisdom of doing so becomes clear. **(Examine Exercise #24, page 212.)**

Careless Use of Prepositions

If you write two prepositions where only one is needed, you'll encumber readers with both a grammatical tangle and an unnecessary word.

You should take his name off ~~of~~ the contract.

We plan to have everyone present except ~~for~~ Daniels and Masterman.

We were surprised by what we found inside ~~of~~ the cash box.

~~Up~~ until Jean spoke, the meeting was going nowhere.

The best-known rule about prepositions is "never end a sentence with a preposition." Over time that rule has been amended to read "almost never end a sentence with a preposition." Some sentence-ending prepositions can be avoided only at the expense of graceful expression.

Awkward: *That point is one <u>over</u> which there is no value in arguing.*

Options: *That point is not worth arguing <u>over</u>.* (end with preposition)
That point is not worth an argument. (restructure)

Avoidance of a preposition at the end of a sentence is standard. Try earnestly to conform to that standard, and then yield to a sentence-ending preposition only when you are forced there by unavoidable awkwardness. Notice that the second option in the example above avoids the preposition altogether, but the first may be preferable as a way to preserve the flavor.

One preposition commonly thrown onto the end of an already-complete sentence is *at*. "Where is the file?" is a complete question. "Where is the file at?" is a common vulgarity. You might want to omit those *ats* from your speech, and you will definitely want to omit them from your writing.

Wrong Pronoun Case

Figure 6 will help you survey pronoun case. "Person" signifies the person on whom the writing is centered. A writer writes about himself or herself in first person, about the reader in second person, and about a third party in third person. A writer uses subjective case (sometimes called *nominative case*) when the pronoun is a subject, objective case when the pronoun is an object, and possessive case when the pronoun possesses.

	Subjective Case	Objective Case	Possessive Case
1st Person			
singular	I	me	me, mine
plural	we	us	our, ours
2nd person			
singular	you	you	your, yours
plural	you	you	your, yours
3rd person			
singular	he, she, it	him, her, it	his, her(s), its
plural*	they	them	their, theirs

* You will read new thoughts about this classification on Page 71 and in Chapter 11.

Figure 6. Personal Pronouns Shown by Person, Case, and Number

Personal pronouns are by far the most common type of pronoun. The relative pronoun (That is the woman *whose* purse was stolen.) does not apply here. For insight into relative pronouns, see p. 97 and *that, which* on p. 191.

I see the most common pronoun case errors in the confusion of subjective case with objective case. Using objective case where subjective belongs (Me and Bill went) sounds more wrong to us than using subjective case where objective case belongs (He gave it to Bill and I). Both are wrong. You'll read more about that in the next chapter, "Speak Well to Write Well."

Another common error in pronoun case is the use of objective case where possessive case belongs.

my
The vice president said he did not mind me shadowing him for a day.

their
Excessive concern about the prices led to them increasing.

his
I appreciated him delivering the documents to me promptly.

What was it that the vice president did not mind? Was it me? No. It was the shadowing. Whose shadowing? My shadowing. Therefore, the possessive case pronoun is needed. The same logic tells us that the prices led to *their increasing,* not to *them,* and that I appreciated *his delivering,* not *him* (although I might have appreciated him, too).

Antecedent/Pronoun Disagreement

An antecedent is simply the noun to which a pronoun refers. As shown in Figure 7, the antecedent may either precede or follow the pronoun.

Our <u>researchers</u> lost all the data. <u>They</u> are distraught.

<u>He</u> was broke, as seemed to be the norm for <u>Joe Bell</u>.

Figure 7. Examples of Pronouns and Their Antecedents

Just as you need a singular verb to refer to a singular subject, you need a singular pronoun to refer to a singular antecedent (noun).

Employees   are
~~An employee~~ who ~~is~~ chronically late will not like their quarterly evaluations.

he
If an NBA player stays fit and healthy, ~~they~~ can play for 20 years or more.

A generation ago, the average elementary school child would have spotted this grammar error immediately. Recently, however, a move away from the sexist language of the past has produced some acceptance of a plural pronoun in reference to a singular antecedent. One consequence seems to be that a measure of tone-deafness has set in relative to that particular grammar violation. As we strive to avoid offensive language, we will want to also avoid becoming desensitized to the basic grammar principal of agreement between pronouns and their antecedents. Otherwise, we may begin to write such absurdities as the sentence above about NBA players, all of whom are male.

Writers have wrestled with many options in the quest to write non-sexist language. Most of those options damage elegance of expression and clarity in one way or another. I've treated the subject of accommodating gender elegantly in a chapter of its own—Chapter 11.

CHAPTER 10
SPEAK WELL TO WRITE WELL

People find their first clues about your intelligence in the words you speak. That's not entirely fair. You could be a genius at engine repair or a first-rate trainer of horses. You could be a brilliant baseball tactician or tracker of animals. You could be highly knowledgeable in any one of a host of ways despite fracturing the language every time you open your mouth. Still, your language makes a powerful first impression.

Bertrand Russell explained the power of language by saying "No matter how eloquently a dog may bark, he cannot tell you that his parents were poor but honest" (Lederer, 1991, p. 235). Language is a uniquely human ability. Birds fly, fish swim, and people use language. Each species has an innate gift. Using the gift well—bird, fish, or person—creates an image of a proficient member of the species.

This is a short chapter. The basic message is this: if you speak clearly, correctly, and efficiently you'll improve your chances of writing clearly, correctly, and efficiently. Your mind has a single language reservoir, and you draw from it whether you're putting words into the air or onto a piece of paper. Only by cleaning up that language reservoir and stocking it with good material will you have the resources you need to use language well in any venue. Because you speak much more frequently than you write, you'll do well to monitor your speech. Think of it as an outward sign of the quality of your language reservoir.

You may have had a slow start in building your language reservoir. You may have grown up hearing, "We was outside when we seen him last, and we don't know where he's at now," rather than "We were outside when we saw him last, and we don't know where he is now." Teachers may have perpetuated the bad habits you picked up by failing to point out flaws in your use of language—spoken and written. A teacher's acceptance of poor speech is tacit permission to continue speaking that way. A paper with a good grade at the top and no suggestions for improvement says, "your writing is just fine as it is." Be thankful for those teachers who corrected your errors—who knew that you'd be better off irritated as a child and competent as an adult than patted on the head as a child and struggling as an adult.

Whatever your language background—rich, impoverished, or somewhere in between—all you can do now is recognize your past for what it is and move on. The most important influence on your language reservoir from this point forward will be your own determination to pay attention to language, to discriminate between effective and ineffective uses, and to teach yourself. Pay attention to the basic points of grammar shown in Chapter 9. For example, don't use objective case pronouns where subjective case is needed.

> He
> H̶i̶m̶ and I will be leaving tomorrow.

And once you've corrected that, don't reverse the problem by using subjective case where objective case is needed.

> me
> She gave the directions to Darla and I̶.

Don't let the second party distract you. You'd never say "Him will be leaving" or "She gave the directions to I." When in doubt, separate the parties referred to and see how each sounds.

Study the points made in Chapter 9 to get the spoken dimension of your language-improvement journey moving, but know that grammar is only a starting point. Above all, try to put together complete, coherent sentences that contain specific information. If the message is this:

> I would never have said anything to him had I
> known it was a secret. Jane was devastated.

Don't deliver it like this:

> He was like "what?" and I was like "Oh, No," and
> she was like "Ahhh!"

Particularly if you want to be a respected professional, you need to discard childish habits in favor of a rich, mature vocabulary.

- Respect the power of words. As William Zinsser recommends, "develop a curiosity about their shades of meaning that is almost obsessive" (1994, p. 34).

- Study Appendix B (pp. 154–195), and as you notice other words that you misuse, or words that are unfamiliar to you but seem useful, build your personal dictionary in the blank pages (pp. 245–246) that follow Appendix D.

- Use the markings recommended at the beginning of Appendix B, and make periodic inventories of your progress.

- Apply what you've read in all the chapters of this book to your daily speech.

In sum, **value proficient language as the powerful tool that it is—spoken and written. Untold numbers of people work beneath their abilities simply for lack of the language proficiency needed to open doors to higher-level responsibilities**.

Language use seems to be at a low point right now. Think of that general failing as an opportunity for you to rise quickly above the crowd by elevating your use of language. As I pointed out in the front of this book, institutions and individuals—businesses in particular—pay dearly for all the misunderstandings, errors, senseless inquiries, and wrong turns generated by individual failures to communicate clearly. If you commit yourself to valuing and respecting language, you can be a part of the solution rather than a part of the problem. Pay attention to how you speak and write. Your efforts to do so will pay big dividends over time.

I should clarify one thing. I don't mean to imply that your speech should be as pristine as your writing. That's not realistic. For one thing, you don't have time to revise when you speak. Nonetheless, your speech will be a stepping-stone to the polished language that you put on paper. Care begets care.

I leave you with a satirical essay that I wrote a few years ago about a common speech habit you'll recognize—a habit that annoys listeners and impoverishes the language reservoirs of both speaker and listener.

Is "Like" Dying an Untimely Death?

I overheard less than one sentence of a conversation between two university students yesterday when I walked past them in a hallway. During the few seconds that I was within earshot, the person speaking used the word "like" five times. All five were examples of using the word "in the nothing way," to quote my youngest daughter.

> I told him that I like wanted to go, like I've really been like planning on it, but like I'm like not sure about ...

We may be suffering the most pervasive and irritating bludgeoning of the English language since the invasion of "you know." Put them together and you have the best three-word combination in the world for someone who wants to speak without taking a chance on saying something—like, you know?

The indiscriminate use of "like" may have started as a hedge against making a commitment. To say that X is beautiful or Y is repugnant is to take a position, and to take a position is to risk criticism. To say that X is like beautiful or Y is like repugnant is to leave an opening at the flank, just large enough to escape with a quick back-peddle.

Since the early days of the "like" phenomenon, use of the word has degenerated to an even lower state. While it continues to function as a hedge, "like" also has become a catch-word for those who have nothing to say, and need to avoid the embarrassment of silence when their turn comes to speak. "She like looked at me like, you know, and like I was like, Ohhh!"

And most recently, the ultimate in degeneration has descended upon us. Frequent, inappropriate uses of "like" have become a subliminal social act—

---

a linguistically meaningless sound that intermittently beeps out the message that "I'm a friendly, not-too-stuffy, nonassertive member of the good guys club," similar to the way an electronic buoy beeps out the message that "friendly waters and a safe harbor are to my left."

If all the "likers" are happy with each other, it might be asked, is there any harm done? Yes, because there is no effective way to segregate the likers from the non-likers. After all, dozens of laws, ordinances, and rules have not kept smokers from contaminating the air of nonsmokers. What hope is there that likers could ever be kept from bombarding the thought processes of non-likers with meaningless, bothersome, misplaced words? Of course confirmed likers will think me prudish, but only because they have long since lost all sensitivity to the difficulties of engaging in straight talk and circuitous listening at the same time.

Suppose that likers and non-likers could be kept out of each other's territory—that likers could freely escalate their practice to glorious heights (depths), unimpeded by the disdain of non-likers. Would that be acceptable? No. We could not in good conscience sanction the horrible intellectual carnage that would take place. "Like," beeping about unchecked with ever-increasing frequency, would turn tens of thousands of potential thinkers into inane talking machines. Just the thought of it is enough to make *Nightmare on Elm Street* seem palatable by comparison.

A final argument for reform of the likers is that the word "like" itself is taking an awful beating. What if "like" should be rendered as impotent as some of the other perfectly good words that have been disemboweled by mindlessness—words like "awesome," "radical," and "totally." Let's face it: we simply cannot afford to lose "like." How would we note similarities, as in "the rising sea was like a demon, swallowing everything in its path"? How would we express our affinity for something, as in "I like ice cream with apple pie"? In the interest of likers and non-likers alike, and in the interest of the language that most of us like to use effectively, I would like to recommend that all thinking people begin to purge the improper use of "like" from their vocabularies.

A liker who reads this might say of me, "he just doesn't like, like like like likers like like, like, you know?" Of course there is no truth to that. If I didn't like like, I wouldn't be waging a campaign to save the poor thing from the most senseless slaughter since the Sioux Nation rode down on Custer.

CHAPTER 11

ACCOMODATE GENDER ELEGANTLY

Background

Contemporary thought has overturned convention. For centuries, feminine pronouns were always gender-specific (Mary attended, but <u>she</u> left early.), and masculine pronouns were either gender-specific (Tom attended, but <u>he</u> left early.) or generic (If a student finished the test, <u>he</u> was allowed to leave early.). Today, *he* is thought of exclusively as a gender-specific pronoun. *He* in reference to a person of indefinite gender (generic masculine pronoun) sounds either archaic or insensitive. Unfortunately, most recent approaches to gender-neutral language inflict their own damage—to clarity and style. As writers, we need a system that avoids replacing injustice to individual readers with injustice to readers in general.

Problem

In the previous paragraph, "If a student finished the test, *he* was allowed to leave early" does not mean that female students were required to stay. Good sense dictates that. Still, the wording fails to project males and females as equal in status. Nor can readers be relied upon consistently to surmise the meaning of a pronoun through context. In short, generic masculine pronouns obscure meaning and perpetuate stereotypes.

If you go to a doctor, I believe <u>he</u> will confirm my suspicions.

A responsible pilot checks <u>his</u> plane thoroughly before takeoff.

He and *his* in the sentences above were once justified as generic uses of the masculine pronoun. Functionally, however, the masculine pronouns in those sentences are likely to reinforce some readers' conceptions of doctors and pilots as male. You as the writer control only half of any communication you offer. Readers are free to interpret your generic pronouns as gender-specific, leaving you open to the charge of perpetuating gender bias.

Wanting to replace generic masculine pronouns to avoid the problems they cause, writers have tried for decades to find an alternative. Look at these examples.

Generic Masculine: the need for a replacement

> If <u>an employer</u> treats <u>his</u> employees with respect, <u>he</u> will increase <u>his</u> chance of being respected in return.

Avoidance of Generic Masculine: candidates to become replacements

1. *either-or approach*:

> If <u>an employer</u> treats <u>his or her</u> employees with respect, <u>he or she</u> will increase <u>his or her</u> chance of being respected in return.

2. *slash approach*:

> If <u>an employer</u> treats <u>his/her</u> employees with respect, <u>s/he</u> will increase <u>his/her</u> chance of being respected in return.

3. generic feminine approach

> If <u>an employer</u> treats <u>her </u>employees with respect, <u>she</u> will increase her chance of being respected in return.

4. *antecedent/pronoun disagreement approach*:

> If <u>an employer</u> treats <u>their</u> employees with respect, <u>they</u> will increase <u>their</u> chances of being respected in return.

These approaches to avoiding generic masculine pronouns all cause problems. The last, antecedent/pronoun disagreement, is gaining acceptance for reasons cited on subsequent pages. First, though, a few words spent on the shortcomings of each approach will be worthwhile.

Either-Or Approach. The either-or approach disrupts sentence flow and breaks the reader's concentration by crowding two pronouns into a space normally occupied by one. It increases reading time not so much by the few words added as by the bumps it puts in the road. A reader can negotiate occasional uses of *his or her* with little or no trouble, but frequent occurrences, as in the sentence above, become an irritating, arrhythmic distraction.

Slash Approach. The slash approach disrupts our natural inclination to convert symbols to latent sounds as we read. How bothersome it is—and how difficult to put full attention on content—when we find ourselves periodically stumbling over *s/he*, *she/he*, and such. In praise of a fellow writer, E. B. White once described Fitzgerald's style in terms of "the sound his words make on paper" (Strunk and White, 2000, p. 67). Readers cannot convert slash symbols into any sensible sound, much less a sound that bodes well for style.

Generic Feminine Approach. Some pursue gender equity by giving equal play to a generic feminine pronoun (If a person works hard, *she* will advance). That creates its own problems. A generic feminine pronoun violates the premise at the root of the generic masculine problem—that a single-gender pronoun can represent all gender circumstances adequately. In short, the two-can-play-that-game approach makes a gesture toward gender equity at a cost of confusion and inconsistency. It throws to the wind the writer's most precious gift to readers: clarity. Pity the poor reader who has to alternate between generic masculine and generic feminine pronouns from one chapter to another, or worse, from one paragraph to another—as some writers have done in a nod to anti-sexism. The one-for-you and one-for-me gender equity game becomes a running subplot that distracts readers from content and impairs their concentration.

Antecedent/Pronoun Disagreement Approach. Disagreement in number between a pronoun and its antecedent, long seen as a grammar violation that grates on literate readers' ears, has recently gained acceptance in response to two conditions. The first applies to the general population and the second to a small subset:

1. Wrong-headed assumptions (doctors and pilots are male) perpetrated by the use of generic masculine pronouns.

2. Persons not wanting to be identified as either male or female.

The first is a reaction to the misleading and offensive nature of generic masculine pronouns, and to the awkwardness of alternate approaches. The second is a reaction to the danger of mis-characterizing individual persons. The use of antecedent/pronoun disagreement as an antidote to gender bias has in fact been endorsed recently in multiple writing manuals. Going forward, I will refer to the practice as *singular they/their* rather than *antecedent/pronoun disagreement*. S*ingular they/their* brings the specific issue to mind quicker than does *antecedent/pronoun disagreement*, and it presents less of a mouthful.

The use of *singular they/their* requires considerable caution. In the fourth sample sentence on Page 79, for example, the first *their* is clearly meant to be a singular reference to the employer. However, readers are likely to initially link *they* to the more-proximate *employees*—with a need to amend that understanding only after having arrived at the final *their*.

> If <u>an employer</u> treats <u>their</u> employees with respect, <u>they</u> will
> increase <u>their</u> chances of being respected in return.

The reader is likely to read the sentence a second time to verify meaning. Any sentence that stops forward motion through your writing is a disservice to readers. It's a snag that distracts them from content and slows comprehension. The best way to avoid inconveniencing readers in that way would be to rework the sentence so as to avoid the pronoun altogether.

> Employers who treat employees with respect will increase the chance of
> employees respecting them in return.

In short, because *they* and *there* are still alive and well as plural pronouns, and because *singular they/their* has a vivid history as a grammar violation, you as a writer will need to work consciously to avoid confusing and exasperating readers with the *singular they/their*. You will not want to yield to inserting *singular they/their* as a substitute for applying intense thought to specific circumstances. This sentence, for example, requires a second reading because of the extent to which—on its surface—it defies logic.

> A mother of three knows <u>they</u> will not have the free time <u>they</u>
> once had.

Readers will almost certainly associate the first *they*, closely preceded as it is by the word *three*, with the children—only to realize the misinterpretation upon completing the sentence. That will prompt a second reading, or at least a second thinking. Readers should not be subjected to such stumbling blocks.

Any time we engage a new act, in this case using *singular they/their*, we find ourselves working through an awkward period of adjustment that requires caution. Always look for opportunities to create the kind of strong imagery that specificity offers. Using *she* as the pronoun in the sample sentence above makes the sentence immediately understandable.

> A mother of three knows she will not have the free time she once had.

The saving grace of the sentence about mothers is that context clues enable readers to understand the meaning of the sentence, albeit as an unfortunate retrospective. The problem becomes ever more serious in the absence of context clues. For example, readers would be unable to decipher the meaning of this sentence at all:

> A member of that club will do anything possible to protect what they have.

Use of *singular they/their* in this case leaves readers with no way to know which of these interpretations applies.

> A member of that club will do anything possible to protect what the club has.

> Members of that club will do anything possible to protect their personal possessions.

This sentence leaves readers at just as great a loss:

> When employees are selfish and unproductive, a manager has to do their job.

How are readers to know which of these meanings applies?

> When employees are selfish and unproductive, a manager has to do the employees' jobs.

> When employees are selfish and unproductive, a manager
> has to manage more effectively.

Careless uses of *singular they/their* are grenades thrown into a piece of writing with the effect of dismantling clarity. In our efforts to marry consideration for individual readers' circumstances with the clear style that readers in general deserve, we will do well to adopt this principle: **Avoid problems altogether rather than create a problem to which you then need to apply a solution.** Specific advice follows.

Avoiding the Problem

The need for gender equity in language can be satisfied without dumping readability. How necessary are generic pronouns, i.e., pronouns whose antecedent nouns (teacher, doctor, pilot, artist) are of indefinite gender? Can sentences be rewritten to exclude generic pronouns without sacrificing clarity or gracefulness? I would answer that question with a qualified "yes." These examples show alternate solutions to sentences shown earlier.

> ~~If an~~ An employer who treats ~~his~~ employees with respect, ~~he~~ will
> increase ~~his~~ the chance of being respected in return.

> ~~If you go to a doctor,~~ a doctor would I believe ~~he will~~ confirm my suspicions.

Reconstructing a sentence to avoid generic pronouns may actually strengthen it. The sentence about the doctor is a case in point: the revision exceeds the original in brevity, directness, vigor, and clarity, and at the same time avoids use of the generic pronoun. What a payoff!

To what extent can you avoid generic pronouns and maintain a strong, clear, graceful writing style? I believe if you commit yourself to doing so, you can avoid them at nearly every turn. When you discover that you cannot eliminate a generic pronoun gracefully (perhaps once every 10 pages or so), you'll have to decide which option to use. I think *he or she* is least cumbersome. Used infrequently, *he or she* will neither annoy readers nor slow them down. I used that compromise two or three times in this book.

Four specific techniques will help you become skillful at avoiding generic pronouns and awkward substitutes in your writing.

Omit the generic pronoun from a sentence that remains essentially unchanged without it.

How can a sensitive, committed teacher teach disruptive students without abandoning either ~~his~~ sensitivity or ~~his~~ productivity?

The CEO may resent having a vice president miss ~~their~~ executive council meetings.

Monitor introductory clauses that contain a singular noun of indefinite gender. Most are conditional clauses that begin with *if* or *when*.

A   who
~~If a~~ director begins to allow late arrivals, ~~he~~ will fight tardiness indefinitely.

After an absence,
~~When~~ a student ~~has been absent, s/he~~ must call me directly.

Convert singular nouns and pronouns to plural as a way to circumvent gender-specific pronouns.

s
~~A~~ sensitive social worker tend~~s~~ to become involved personally with clients, but if ~~she does~~ so excessively ~~her~~ effectiveness will be impaired.   they do   their

workers of the latter type as slackers,
I would diagnose ~~the latter as a slacker,~~ based solely on their meager productivity.

You may need to **reconstruct sentences creatively** to retain good form while eliminating a generic pronoun. In some cases that is as simple as changing one word.

the
The nurse was instructed to inoculate each recruit in ~~their~~ buttocks.

In other cases you'll find that you need to rework an entire structure.

Don't write this	Write this
Does a good manager set an example of company loyalty for <u>his</u> employees? Is it <u>his/her</u> obligation to be a model?	Is a good manager obligated to model company loyalty for employees?

Indecision about how to handle gender in writing can be disorienting, as apparently it was for the writer who used both *his* and *his/her* in the example above. You'll see similar confusion in this last example. The writer seems to rebuff the use of generic masculine pronouns by saying "Two can play that game." Then, as if conscious that the generic feminine pronoun is likely to be disorienting, the writer switches to *he/she* in the last sentence before lapsing back to *her*.

Don't write this	Write this
The ability of <u>a child</u> to organize the content of what <u>she</u> is learning into a sequence that makes learning efficient is critical to <u>her</u> academic success. Not only must <u>she</u> be able to organize content; <u>she</u> must be able to organize content at various rates, depending on the complexity of the learning task. What if <u>a child</u> is unable to organize information at more than one rate? What if <u>he/she</u> becomes easily distracted when <u>he/she</u> tries to diverge from <u>her</u> most comfortable learning rate?	A child's ability to organize content into an efficient learning sequence is critical to academic success. Beyond simply organizing content while learning, children must organize it at various rates, depending on the complexity of the learning task. What if a child is unable to organize information at more than one rate? What if divergence from the child's most comfortable learning rate creates distractions that impede learning?

You'll encounter some awkward circumstances as you try to eliminate generic pronouns. Occasionally you may find yourself calling upon *his or her*—or perhaps the *singular they/their*—as a compromise. More often than not, though, even when you find yourself in a situation as cumbersome as befell the writer of that last example, you're likely to find that diligence rewards you with a work-around that accommodates not only gender-equity, but also clarity and elegance. (**Examine Exercise #26, page 213.**)

PUNCTUATION

Use punctuation wisely to give readers smooth passage through your writing, and to convey tone and emphasis akin to spoken language.

CHAPTER 12
USE THE COMMON
PUNCTUATION MARKS WELL

CHAPTER 13
EXPAND YOUR PUNCTUATION WORLD

CHAPTER 12
USE THE COMMON PUNCTUATION MARKS WELL

Is any tool of writing more overlooked and less understood than punctuation? More useful and less valued? Rudolph Flesch (1946) dubbed punctuation "the most important single device for making things easier to read" (p. 92). Like the gestures of a good speaker, punctuation marks—if you use them intelligently and richly—will accentuate, clarify, and enhance your message. They'll help you organize your writing and at the same time give it life. They stand in not only for gestures, but also for pauses, emphasis, and changes in tone and volume.

Despite punctuation's usefulness, many writers use only periods and question marks confidently, guess where to place commas and apostrophes, and ignore everything else for fear of misuse. You'll want to do better than that. This chapter and the next will help you make good use of all 14 punctuation marks used in the English language.

Chapter 12	Chapter 13
period	parentheses
question mark	dash
exclamation point	semicolon
apostrophe	colon
quotation marks	slash
hyphen	brackets
comma	ellipsis

Note: marks stated in plural form are used only as pairs.

I've categorized six of this chapter's seven marks by function, with the apostrophe appearing in two categories. The comma, a multi-function mark that causes more than its share of trouble and indecision, has a section of its own.

Sentence Enders
period
question mark
exclamation point

Joiners
apostrophe
hyphen

Signs of Ownership and Emphasis
apostrophe
quotation marks

The Comma Coma

If you find yourself in a comma coma, it may be because the comma has a great number of uses—some prescriptive and some subjective. I hope the guidelines contained here will help free you from some of your comma indecision.

Sentence Enders

Chances are good that you know how to end sentences, using a **period** to signal the end of a statement and a **question mark** to signal the end of a question. Use the third sentence ender, the **exclamation point**, very rarely, and only to mark a truly exclamatory statement:

One more season as dismal as this will put us out of business!

An overuse of exclamation marks will irritate readers and condition them to ignore the marks altogether.

An obvious rule for a sentence ender is that it should appear only at the end of a complete sentence (except where a period signals an abbreviation), and a complete sentence contains a subject and a verb. As much as that rule is stressed in grammar school, there are some exceptions. For one, the subject might be "understood." The subject of this sentence is an understood "you."

Go tell Robert that I need to talk to him now.

Furthermore, on rare occasions you might use a sentence-ender at the end of a sentence fragment, helping it to masquerade as a complete sentence. The second "sentence" of this chapter ("More useful, less valued?") is an example. You'll need to meet two conditions to justify violating the complete-sentence rule. Write a fragment only if (1) preceding material gives it the context of a complete thought, and (2) you see no better way to handle the circumstance. Sentence fragments should be extremely rare.

Signs of Ownership and Emphasis

One of the two uses of an **apostrophe** is to show possession. To show possession on the part of a plural noun ending in *s* (*students*, *employees*), add only an apostrophe.

> The employees' benefits have improved little.

To show possession on the part of any other noun, or an indefinite pronoun, add an apostrophe followed by *s* ('s):

- plural noun not ending in *s*:   women's tee; children's clothes
- singular noun not ending in *s:*   receipt's date; Mary's office
- singular noun ending in *s:*   Carlos's desk; bass's tail
- indefinite pronoun: somebody's fault; one's rights

A common perception is that singular nouns ending in *s* should be made plural with an apostrophe alone (Carlos'). There is room for interpretation here. I recommend using *'s* with two exceptions. (1) Some historic names whose plurals traditionally carry only the apostrophe: Moses', Jesus'. (2) Plural nouns made so awkward by the addition of *'s* that they become almost unpronounceable: the Smiths' house; paralysis' devastation. As a writer, you'll make judgments case by case about the need for exceptions to the *'s* rule for singular possessive nouns that end in *s*.

Be sure to say what you intend to say with your apostrophes. For example, the manager's meeting is a meeting called by the manager (singular), but a managers' meeting is a meeting of managers (plural). Be particularly careful with multiple nouns:

- joint ownership: They are Bill and Elsa's clients.
- separate ownership: They are Bill's and Elsa's clients.

Possessive forms of third person pronouns have no apostrophes: his, hers, theirs, yours, ours, and its. Avoid the common misconception that *its* as a possessive pronoun needs an apostrophe. If you add an apostrophe (*it's*), you'll have written a contraction for *it is*.

Treat numbers and acronyms as words when you need to make them either plural or possessive:

Plural	Possessive
Line up in <u>2</u>s.	The <u>2's</u> color is brighter than the <u>3's</u>.
It was made in the <u>1960s</u>.	What was <u>1960's</u> most dramatic event?
He lived in the <u>1800s</u>.	It was the <u>1800s'</u> most tragic war. (Note: *1800s's* is unacceptably awkward)
She bought six <u>CDs</u>.	One <u>CD's</u> case was broken.

There is one glaring exception. In the odd circumstance of needing to indicate that a single letter is plural, you'll use *'s*, as if it were possessive. That's because to write about multiple occurrences of the letters *a*, *b*, and *c*, for example, you'd confuse readers with *as*, *bs*, and *cs*. Convention is to write *a's*, *b's*, and *c's* as if they were possessives, and leave the interpretation of their status as plurals to the reader. My preference is to avoid resorting to that anomaly if I can find an alternative. For example, rather than write "The *s's* look like *f's*," you might write "Every *s* looks like an *f*."

Quotation marks show ownership of something written, said, or thought.

> "Absolutely not," was the only reply he offered. Meanwhile, I was thinking, "what a liar." I knew he had been involved in the scheme.

Use **single quotation marks** to set off quoted material within a quotation:

> He said "she screamed 'no,' but no one listened."

American convention is to place commas and periods inside quotation marks, semicolons and colons outside:

↓

He said, "come quickly," but I knew it was too late when he added, "never mind."

↑   ↓   ↓

He said, "Do it now"; she added, "Yes, now": she always concurred with him.

Place question marks, exclamation points, and dashes inside quotation marks only if they belong to the quotation:

↓

"Are you hired?" she asked. I had a good reason to respond with my evasive "Time will tell"!   [Check out the last two sentences on page 76.]

Quotation marks are used also to mark titles of articles or book chapters.

You should read "Taxes Made Easy" in the newsletter.

Quotation marks should not be used to mark book titles. Book titles should be either underlined or italicized. In pre-computer days, underlining signaled publishers to italicize. Computers now enable you to italicize directly.

Chapter One, "Begin Right," is the perfect way for Jameson (2019) to open How to Set Up an Efficient Home Office.

Chapter One, "Begin Right," is the perfect way for Jameson (2019) to open *How to Set Up an Efficient Home Office.*

Finally, quotation marks can be used to highlight words having special significance or deserving emphasis, but that is only one option:

If he refers to it as "unique," you can trust that it is.

Computers also offer alternatives to the use of quotation marks for emphasis: *italics*, **bold**, ***bold italics***. You may emphasize material by use of any of these tools, and in fact may choose specific tools of emphasis for specific types of material. Just remain consistent. Use marks for emphasis sparingly. Like exclamation points, they can become tiresome for readers. If you are writing for a specific publication, observe their guidelines, as for example the manual for the American Psychological Association (APA).

Joiners

The apostrophe and the hyphen, two very different marks, join two words into one, each in their own way. You can contract (shorten) a pair of words if you combine them and then replace missing letters with an **apostrophe**. Here are just a few examples of contractions:

do not	don't	I would	I'd
I am	I'm	he would	he'd
she will	she'll	will not	won't
they have	they've	it is	it's

The principal function of contractions is to make writing sound conversational. Contractions generally are used in informal writing and avoided in formal writing. The judgment of what writing should be formal or informal (conversational) is up to you, unless you're submitting for publication. Then it's up to your publisher.

Contractions generally are not used in reports, proposals, and other kinds of formal documents, but they are acceptable in letters, e-mail messages, memos, newsletters—any place that you want to give your readers conversation on paper. I wrestled with the decision of whether to use contractions in this book. I've rejected their use in other textbook material I've written, but I decided to make this writing companion feel as friendly and conversational as possible.

A **hyphen** is the other punctuation mark used to join words. You can use it as a tool for brevity by joining separate words into a single compound word.

> He had to contend with a field that had been soaked by rain.
>
> He had to contend with a rain-soaked field.

Most hyphenated compound words are adjectives, but hyphens also can be used to make compound nouns (The fire-tender fell asleep.) and compound verbs (Let's arm-wrestle.). Sometimes more than two words are joined (hit-and-run driver; seat-of-the-pants decision). Because the hyphen is a tool of creativity, there is no limit to the variety of hyphenated words you might form.

Anything that is easily understood and reasonably graceful will serve you and your readers well as long as you don't overuse the hyphen. Any unusual technique used in excess draws attention to itself, and therefore away from content.

The hyphen is used also to divide a single word in deference to space at the end of a typed line. That's a mechanical function unrelated to the use of a hyphen as a creative tool. **(Examine Exercise #27, page 213.)**

The Comma Coma

I see two reasons you might suffer over comma decisions more than over any other punctuation problem. First, you may be unsure of the many rules that govern the use of commas. Second, ironclad rules don't always apply. Commas are required in some places, but they are a matter of choice in others. That is likely to leave you wondering whether a given circumstance is governed by a rule or a judgment.

The most sensible approach here is for me to lay out rules and guidelines for using commas, with examples, and to point out along the way where subjectivity lies.

Use a Comma to Separate Independent Clauses Joined by a Conjunction

A conjunction not preceded by a comma joins information on each side of it into a single thought:

> You will have to complete the job by Monday↓or Tuesday.
>
> The supervisor identified two glaring problems immediately↓and
> confidently.

But when that conjunction separates two independent clauses, you'll need to precede it with a comma to alert readers to the imminent change in your train of thought:

> You will have to complete the job by Monday,↓or Tuesday I will
> assign it to someone else.

93

The supervisor identified two glaring problems immediately,↓ and confidently set about solving them.

In the sentence immediately above, "the supervisor" is understood to carry over as the subject of the second clause, making that clause functionally independent. Without that comma, readers are likely to read "immediately and confidently" as a pair. That bump in the road is likely to prompt a backtrack. The comma, then, is a matter of reader preparation. The better you prepare readers for what lies ahead—similar to the way road signs prepare drivers—the less likely they are to have an accident or lose their way.

Subjectivity. If the clauses are short, and if the meaning is immediately clear without the comma, you might omit the comma prior to a conjunction that joins two independent clauses:

↓

He put his work away and she followed suit.

Omitting the comma between short independent clauses works best with *and* as the conjunction. Even with short sentences, you're likely to need a comma when such conjunctions as *or*, *but*, or *nor* change the direction of thought:

↓

He taught them well, or thought he did.

↓

She knew, but she preferred to keep quiet.

↓

He knew nothing, nor did he care to know.

When you believe that the use of a comma between short independent clauses is subjective, test the need for a comma by saying the sentence aloud. If you pause, give that pause to readers: insert a comma.

Use a Comma to Set Off an Introductory Word, Phrase, or Clause

Sometimes you'll precede the meat of a sentence with introductory information. Help the reader see where the meat of the sentence begins by partitioning off the introductory material with a comma:

> ↓
> Working diligently, the new teaching intern made the professor
> look like a genius.

> ↓
> To avoid error, we counted each ballot twice.

Lack of attention to a comma following introductory material can change the meaning of a sentence. Without a comma in the sentence below, *further* modifies *subject attrition*, meaning "attrition in addition to earlier attrition."

> ↓
> Further subject attrition reduced the researcher's numbers to
> fewer than 20 per cell.

If *further* is meant to indicate that subject attrition is a problem in addition to non-attrition problems cited earlier, then *further* must not be seen to modify *subject attrition*: a comma is needed.

> ↓
> Further, subject attrition reduced the researcher's numbers to
> fewer than 20 per cell.

Don't risk saying something other than what you mean to say. Attend to subtle differences in punctuation.

    Subjectivity. Sometimes bits of introductory material are so short that you know readers will understand the sentence easily without a comma. In such a case you may omit the comma to help reading flow.

> ↓
> After the argument he returned to his office.

Use Commas to Set Off Words That Interrupt the Flow of a Sentence

    Sentences sometimes have parenthetical material interrupting two halves of an intact statement. That parenthetical material must be partitioned off to make the basic sentence apparent. The most common way to set off parenthetical material is to enclose it between commas.

> ↓   ↓
> Communication, spoken and written, is essential to doing business.

Another type of interruptive material, known as an appositive, is to be treated in the same way. An appositive is descriptive information that modifies the noun immediately preceding it.

The manager, the person responsible for operations, must be knowledgeable and firm.

Mrs. Thompson, the new dean, is knowledgeable and firm.

When setting off interruptive material, take particular care to place a comma on each side of that material. Do **not** write these sentences:

Communication spoken and written, is essential to doing business.

Mrs. Thompson, the manager is knowledgeable and firm.

The measure of whether you need a pair of commas enclosing the material is this: read the sentence with the material omitted. If what you read makes sense without the intervening material (Mrs. Thompson is knowledgeable and firm.), enclose the material between commas.

Subjectivity. Sometimes a sentence having parenthetical material is so short that you know readers will understand it easily without commas. In that case you may omit the commas to help reading flow.

He ran without hesitation to her aid.

Use a Comma to Set Off a Nonrestrictive Clause

Without question, the comma errors I see most frequently stem from writers having failed to identify a clause as either restrictive or nonrestrictive. In Chapter 9 (p. 63) you saw a restrictive clause and a nonrestrictive clause exemplified with a sentence similar to this.

Restrictive Clause – a descriptor clause essential to the meaning of the independent clause in which it is embedded	**Nonrestrictive Clause** – a descriptor clause that gives extra information

The part that worked best was the pin, which we repaired.

You must not insert a comma where it would partition a restrictive clause (*that worked best*) off from the rest of an independent clause that depends on it for meaning. Conversely, if a clause amounts only to added information (*which we repaired*), you must partition it off with a comma to guard against having readers attach it to the larger meaning—in this case, see it as a reference to the repaired pin as compared to another pin that had not been repaired.

The following sentences are identical except for the comma. Notice how radically that comma changes meaning.

Nonrestrictive   Please send the documents, which you no longer need.

Restrictive   Please send the documents which you no longer need.

The nonrestrictive clause asks someone to send all the documents, and adds a comment that "you no longer need them." The restrictive clause asks someone to sort documents into two types (needed and not needed), and to send those not needed.

A good practice is to reserve the use of "which" as the relative pronoun introducing nonrestrictive clauses, and to introduce all restrictive clauses either with "that" or with no relative pronoun at all.

Nonrestrictive   Please send the documents, which you no longer need.

Restrictive   Please send the documents that you no longer need.

Restrictive   Please send the documents you no longer need.

Of the two versions of the restrictive clause, the second is superior for having shed an unneeded word. (Read more about this practice in Appendix B under the entry *that, which*, on page 191.)

Use Commas to Mark a Series

In a series of words or phrases, place a comma after each entry in the series—including the entry that precedes the final conjunction. This rule, once ironclad, was relaxed by consensus of many teachers of English about two generations ago. I've heard rumblings to the effect that the final comma, sometimes referred to as the Oxford comma, is "coming back." So far as I'm concerned, the value of that final comma is such that it never should have left.

Omission of the final comma in a series creates problems that range from a slight skewing of perspective to a chaotic impairment of understanding. Notice the slight differences in perspective between these sentences.

The budget is tight for toll booths, bridges and roads.

The budget is tight for toll booths, bridges, and roads.

The comma after *booths* in the first sentence partitions it off from *bridges and roads*. The *and*, in the absence of a comma, functions as a coordinating conjunction that binds *bridges* and *roads* together like bread and butter. Each appears to have a closer relationship to the other than to *toll booths*. Though the skewed perspective is only slight, the three elements in the series strike the eye as more independent in the second sentence than they do in the first. That effect alone is enough for me to favor the final comma, but much greater damage has been wrought by the ill-fated relaxation of that old punctuation rule.

Look at the problems caused for lack of a comma in these three complex sentences.

Buchanan, 67, talked with *Time's* Jeff Chu about American identity, why conservatives will lose the culture wars and the rewards of being a cat lover.

Readers are in danger of reading "the culture wars and the rewards" before having to backtrack to find the real meaning of the sentence.

She offered the Hamilton-Beals Corporation precisely the maturity, experience, wisdom and intelligence and work ethic they were hoping to find in their new vice president.

A reader conditioned to do without the final comma may see the *and* following *wisdom* as the final conjunction in the series rather than as the coordinating conjunction that it is, only to be disturbed by the true final conjunction following *intelligence*. A comma after *intelligence* would give the perspective needed.

Lack of the final comma in technical writing can cause uninitiated readers to misinterpret meaning.

Data will include mean, standard deviation and split-halves and test/retest reliability.

Only by knowing that split-halves and test/retest are two types of reliability will a reader know that the series divides where the arrow is shown rather than two words later. A final comma would have eliminated uncertainty.

Some persons claim that eliminating the final comma makes writing more efficient. When I weigh the tiny space taken by a comma against the confusion its absence can cause, I believe it earns its keep. A compromise position offered by some is to omit the final comma in simple sentences and use it in complex sentences. I reject that approach not only because of the skewed perspective given by the absence of a comma—even in simple sentences (...toll booths, bridges and roads), but also because of inconsistency. If you use the final comma in all series, your readers will grow to expect it. Therefore, they will not be distracted from content by having to stay alert to inconsistencies.

A minimalist view of comma use is that excess commas disrupt reading flow. I agree. But what constitutes excess? To me, a comma is excess only if it has no potential to help readers understand meaning. Commas that alert readers to an impending independent clause, or to some introductory or parenthetical material—or commas that partition off nonrestrictive material or elements of a series—are not excess. Even if you believe that most readers can negotiate a given sentence well without such a comma, use it if you believe it will benefit some readers. So long as it is placed correctly, a comma helpful to some readers will offer no disruption to others. **(Examine Exercise #28, page 214.)**

CHAPTER 13

EXPAND YOUR PUNCTUATION WORLD

In the opening of the previous chapter, I described a common approach to punctuation as using only periods and question marks confidently, guessing where to place commas and apostrophes, and ignoring everything else for fear of misuse. Pessimistic as that sounds, it applies widely. Even if your punctuation skills are more advanced than that, the 14 punctuation marks of the English language offer such a range of possibilities that you probably have room to expand your use of punctuation further. Doing so will be to your advantage, and to the advantage of those who read your writing.

Here is another look at the 14 punctuation marks as I've assigned them to Chapter 12 and to this chapter.

Chapter 12	**Chapter 13**
period	parentheses
question mark	dash
exclamation point	semicolon
apostrophe	colon
quotation marks	slash
hyphen	brackets
comma	ellipsis

Note: marks stated in plural form are used only as pairs.

I've categorized this chapter's seven punctuation marks by function as follows:

Interruptions	Relationships	Specialty Items
parentheses	semicolon	slash
dash	colon	brackets
		ellipsis

Interruptions

One use for commas that I cited in the previous chapter is to set off words that interrupt the flow of a sentence.

Communication, spoken and written, is essential to doing business.

The primary message of that sentence is "Communication is essential to doing business." The phrase "spoken and written" interrupts the primary message. When I presented the comma approach to handling interruptions, I didn't mean to imply that it's the only approach. Two other punctuation tools useful to showing interruptions are parentheses and dashes. Having a choice of three approaches allows you to decide how important each piece of interruptive material is, and then convey that level of importance to your readers.

Consider the use of commas to set off interruptive material as the middle ground. If you wanted to downplay the interruptive material in the sample sentence above, you could enclose it between **parentheses** rather than between commas. That causes the reader to think of the material as an aside, which gives the primary sentence greater prominence.

Communication (spoken and written) is essential to doing business.

If you wanted to highlight the interruptive material, as though you were raising your voice and pointing your finger in the air for emphasis, you could enclose it between **dashes**.

Communication—spoken and written—is essential to doing business.

So you may choose to speak with commas, whisper with parentheses, or shout with dashes. This is one of many ways you can use punctuation techniques to capture characteristics of the spoken word on a two-dimensional piece of paper.

Parentheses encourage readers to see the enclosed material only peripherally, so they work well whenever you want to give readers a bit of information without slowing them down. They're used for citations (Anderson, 2007), for acronyms and abbreviations (CIA), and for numbers or letters used to mark a series, as in (1) or (a).

The dashes in the example above are one of three lengths of horizontal lines used for punctuation. I described the shortest (hyphen) in detail in Chapter 12. The other two are two styles of dash. Because confusion among the three marks is common, and because differences are important to clear communication, I want to elaborate here on the look and function of the three.

- hyphen: joins single words into compound words, for example, rain-soaked

  (also used to break single words across lines of text)

– en dash (or figure dash): primarily separates numbers in a series, for example, 1991–97; pages 4–7. It also connects entities related by distance (May–July) and prefixes connected to multi-word entities (pre–World War II).

— em dash: separates words in text to give an effect of interruption, for example, "He finally agreed—reluctantly but irrevocably—with the majority."

Many writers use a hyphen for en-dash functions. The en dash does give a more elegant appearance (1991–1997), but you'll not cause confusion if you use a hyphen instead (1991-1997). Why? Because those two marks have the same function: they join. (The hyphen actually works well where space is important, as in an index.) **You will cause confusion, however, if you use a hyphen where an em dash is called for**. While their appearance is similar, their functions are opposite: **the function of a hyphen is to join; the function of an em dash is to separate.** When you strike that hyphen key, no matter how firmly you think *separated*, readers will see *joined*.

Don't write this	**Write this**
He gave no indication-at least for now-that he would attend.	He gave no indication—at least for now—that he would attend.

Sometimes you'll see a hyphen or an en dash with a space on each side in place of an em dash. That is not standard. Nothing shows self-interruption more conventionally, emphatically, or convincingly than an em dash. Use the em dash with no space on either side. Its bold length gives readers a clear sense of the intended break without the help of spaces.

Sometimes the material between em dashes contains punctuation of its own.

> Two men from the Properties Department moved everything left in his cubicle—desk, chair, filing cabinet, and shelving— to the storage building.

At other times a single dash sets off an afterthought or amplification at the end of a sentence, in some cases functioning as an informal version of a colon. (You'll read about the colon's function on pages 106–108.)

> When he left the vice president's office, he walked quickly between the desks and out the door as if no one else were in the room—neither word nor glance exchanged with anyone.

In the days of typewriters, a double hyphen stood in for an em dash. You can program your computer to convert a double hyphen to an em dash. Besides that option, you'll find en dashes and em dashes in the *insert* menu on a PC under *symbol*. Shortcut keys let you program symbols into your keyboard, perhaps [Alt + n] for en dash and [Alt + m] for em dash. On a Mac, [Opt + hyphen] produces an en dash, and [Sft/Opt + hyphen] produces an em dash.

Relationships

Semicolons and colons have in common that they show a relationship between the material preceding them and the material following them. The difference in function between the two marks is in the nature of that relationship. Both are elective marks. That is, wherever you might use a semicolon or a colon, you can depend on there being a way to get around it. That doesn't mean that neglecting these marks is a good idea. They enrich and enliven writing in a way that approximates the tone and expression of speech.

A **semicolon** functions as a hard-pause version of a comma. Its most basic use is to link segments of material having commas within them, and therefore alert readers to the location of larger separations. For example, semicolons work well to show a series of citations:

> Several researchers have found supporting evidence (Grunow, 2010; Silvey, 2012; Azzara and Snell, 2016; Culp, 2019).

You can apply the same principle to a complex sentence that contains multiple elements within some or all of its segments:

> A team of ten employees made Information Day an unqualified success. Two researched potential vendors, interviewed them, and issued contracts; one sold advertising to newspapers and electronic media; two created materials, had them printed, and delivered them to the site; three set up tables, chairs, and booths; and two decorated the room, distributed materials, and labeled all the display stations.

So semicolons, oddly enough, allow you to combine and separate simultaneously—combine segments of material within a single sentence to show their relatedness, and at the same time separate them from each other with a mark stronger than the commas separating elements within each segment. Note that the last entry in a series joined by semicolons may be either introduced with a conjunction or left without. That's just a matter of style.

Still one more use of semicolons is worth knowing. When I wrote about commas, I said that independent clauses joined by a comma and a conjunction could be written alternately as separate sentences. A third option is to use a semicolon. Look at these three versions of the same message:

Separate Sentences

> Reinforcement of the levees surrounding New Orleans had been neglected for years. The hurricane dealt a devastating blow.

Comma and Conjunction

Reinforcement of the levees surrounding New Orleans had been neglected for years, and the hurricane dealt a devastating blow.

Semicolon

Reinforcement of the levees surrounding New Orleans had been neglected for years; the hurricane dealt a devastating blow.
↑

When two complete thoughts seem too closely related to be placed in separate sentences, probably you'll combine them into a compound sentence and join them with a comma and a conjunction. A stylistic alternative is to remove the conjunction and replace the comma with a semicolon. The effect is to place the two thoughts next to each other without the interpretive effect of the conjunction. Instead of choosing *and* or *but*, or some other conjunction that hints at the nature of the relationship, you simply present the two thoughts next to each other in one unit (the sentence) for the reader to compare. The semicolon seems to say to the reader, "these thoughts are too closely related for me to place them in separate sentences, but I'll leave the exact nature of that relationship for you to see." (A comma lacks the separating power to accomplish that task. The technical name for a comma placed between two independent clauses without the obligatory conjunction is "comma splice.") So, when you want to display one thought in stark contrast to another, the semicolon is one tool you might consider. This sentence implies animus:

↓

Bill came into the office; I left.

The semicolon is particularly useful where independent clauses are joined by a conjunctive adverb (an adverb acting as a conjunction). No doubt you've used *however, consequently, subsequently, therefore*, or *nevertheless* as a conjunctive adverb. To use a comma in place of a semicolon in such a circumstance is to produce a camouflaged comma splice.

Don't write this	**Write this**
↓	↓
Jacob sent it to every administrator, consequently, long-overdue policies finally were put into place.	Jacob sent it to every administrator; consequently, long-overdue policies finally were put into place.

	↓
OR	Jacob sent it to every administrator. Consequently, long-overdue policies finally were put into place.

Note that the semicolon is only one tool by which to avoid a comma splice prior to a conjunctive adverb. You may write separate sentences, beginning the second sentence with a capitalized conjunctive adverb followed by a comma (alternate example above). And the best option in many cases is to replace the conjunctive adverb with a simple conjunction preceded by a comma. For example, replace *consequently* with *so*, or replace *however* with *but*. For more thoughts about the most commonly abused conjunctive adverb, see *however* on page 174, Appendix B, *A List of Troublesome Words*.

The **colon** has a unique function apart from that of the semicolon. Do not interchange the two. Think of a colon as saying "let me give you detail." That is, the material following a colon should be an illustration, elaboration, or amplification of the material that precedes it.

The colon needs to be preceded by an independent clause, or by a word or phrase that stands in for an independent clause. For example, if you were to write "Warning: do not touch," *warning* stands in for an independent clause that amounts to "This is a warning." Generally the first word following a colon is written in lower case, but upper case is an option if the material following the colon constitutes another independent clause.

A colon is more akin to a period than to a semicolon. It is a stop, not a pause. To test the appropriateness of a colon, try to substitute a period. If a period is out of place, so is a colon.

The nature of the material following a colon is very flexible. A colon can be followed by a series, an independent clause, a phrase, or a single word.

	↓
Series	Howard is home: he has not improved, he feels miserable, and he is grumpy.

106

↓

Ind. Clause   Howard stayed home again: he shows absolutely
                no signs of improvement.

↓

Phrase   Howard stayed home for the same reason as before:
                no sign of improvement.

Word   Howard's lack of improvement has him right where
                you might expect: home.
                ↑

Note that in every case above, the material preceding the colon could function as a complete sentence. In other words, colons function as stops, not pauses. Note also that each colon is saying, in effect, "Let me give you detail."

Colon misuse comes in three primary varieties, each violating the principle that a colon is a stop. In each case, the remedy is simply to remove the colon.

NO   The method we began to use at the first of the month:
        dries quickly, costs less, and requires less effort. ↑

> Awkwardly separating the subject (method) from the verbs (dries, costs, requires)

NO   The method we began to use at the first of the month has
        saved us: time, money, and training headaches.
        ↑

> Awkwardly separating the verb (saved) from the objects (time, money, headaches)

NO   We have begun to use the new method for: efficiency,
        savings, and ease of training. ↑

> Awkwardly separating the preposition (for) from the objects of the preposition (efficiency, savings, ease)

Be particularly vigilant about committing one of these misuses of a colon when you introduce a list. For example, resist the tendency to place a colon after *will* in this modest list:

By insisting that students arrive on time for classes, you will

- maintain concentration on your teaching,
- reduce classroom distractions for the other students, and
- teach an important life skill.

You would use a colon if you were to recast the stem as a full stop:

By insisting that students arrive on time, you will achieve the following:

Each entry would then be independent rather than part of a sentence.

To tie off this section, here is a complex sentence made easier to read by the use of punctuation. I generally recommend against long sentences stuffed with detail, but this one will show how parentheses, dashes, semicolons, and colons—used wisely—can clarify a sentence rife with interruptions and relationships.

> Four important garments (furnished by the company) are worn by workers: a hard hat, to deflect falling debris; rubber gloves, to insulate against electric shock; compartmentalized pants, to hold key tools; and steel-toed boots—available up to size 18—to protect the feet from heavy or sharp objects.

(Examine Exercise #29, page 214.)

Specialty Items

You'll use slashes, brackets, and ellipses (plural for *ellipsis*) infrequently. Still, you should learn their intended use—not only to have them available, but to avoid misusing them or misinterpreting them.

A **slash** is used with space on each side to separate lines of poetry incorporated into text, and with no space on each side to join two words that give readers the task of interpreting meaning. As author, you should decide on meaning, and make that meaning clear rather than pass the task on to readers. Avoid *and/or*, *if/when*, and similar uses. Think your message through and say what you want to say. Also avoid the awkward, disruptive *his/her* and *he/she*, as advised in Chapter 11. Justifiable uses of the slash are extremely limited.

> Put a Y or an N in the yes/no column.
>
> Avoid subject/verb disagreement.

Quotations sometimes need to be adjusted for reader comfort. Use **brackets** to insert information that you believe will be helpful to readers and use an **ellipsis** (three spaced periods) to indicate any point at which you have removed material. Any material removed should be inconsequential to the meaning of the original quotation, or it should be replaced in abbreviated form between brackets to retain the meaning of the original. The motivation for using either brackets or ellipses is likely to be word efficiency.

ORIGINAL   "If Rosemary wants the position, as she says she does,
      she might spend less time with trivial tasks and more time
      talking to the right people—to board members—to show
      them how really bright she is."

ABRIDGED   "If Rosemary wants the [CEO] position . . . she might . . .
      show [board members] how really bright she is."

When you use these devices to alter a quotation, examine the original against your alteration thoroughly to assure an accurate representation of the source's original intent. Ethics dictates that you do so.

One other legitimate use of an ellipsis is to show an incomplete thought. That will be rare unless you are writing dialogue, as in "What in the world are you . . . ." Three dots constitute the ellipsis, and the fourth represents the period that would have been there had the thought been completed. Add a fourth dot to an ellipsis within quoted material when you need to signify that one sentence ended and another began during the course of the removal. That is, you removed, and fused together, information from more than one sentence.

Besides use in quotations, a bracket can be used to insert parenthetical material within other parenthetical material:

He asked permission (from the department's [HHS] head) yesterday.

Another common use for brackets is to insert *sic* into a quotation, meaning "exactly as found." *Sic* flags errors and oddities so readers will know that you have not misquoted a source. Use it almost exclusively to cite outdated word choices and spellings from old documents, and to cite egregious errors—not to point out a typographical error or an embarrassing slip in another author's work. **(Examine Exercise #30, page 214.)**

WRITING AS A PROCESS

The first thirteen chapters of this book have given you a close look at most of the trees in the forest. It's time now to look at the forest itself. I'll finish the body of this book by devoting a chapter to each of the three distinct stages of a major writing project—preparing, writing, and revising:

CHAPTER 14
PREPARE YOURSELF

CHAPTER 15
EMBRACE THE ACT OF WRITING

CHAPTER 16
REVISE AND REFLECT

CHAPTER 14
PREPARE YOURSELF

Regardless of venue or subject, the questions underlying all major writing projects are similar:

- How do I decide where to start?
- What materials do I need?
- How important is an outline?
- What kinds of problems are likely, and how do I solve them?
- How should I handle thoughts and feelings and fears that come over me as I write?
- At what point should I revise?
- How extensively should I revise?

The aim of this chapter and the two that follow is to help you establish an orderly way of sorting out these questions and their related tasks so you can approach a major piece of writing systematically and confidently. The system you establish will be uniquely yours. Still, knowing how I think, how I feel, and what I do when I write may help you create a system that works well for you.

The material in these three chapters is a mixture of firm principles and individual preferences. You'll be inclined toward some more than others, and you may find some irrelevant to your circumstances.

In this chapter, preparation for an extensive writing project will be presented in relation to four distinct steps: (1) identify your audience and your purpose, (2) gather the materials that you expect to need, (3) organize those materials, and (4) establish a timetable for the project.

Identify Your Audience and Your Purpose

Will your document be read by company administrators, board members, stockholders, psychologists, social workers, university faculty, school administrators, school students, parents of young children? The list is endless. Know for whom you are writing. Imagine a representative group of that audience sitting with you, reading your drafts and making comments. An old piece of advice from Rudolph Flesch (1954) is as good today as when he wrote it:

> Imagine how that audience will behave, what they are going to like, what they are going to dislike, whether they will interrupt you with questions, whether they will ask for more of this or less of that, whether they will need an interval releasing their tension or something that will build up their suspense. At every word and every sentence you write you must sense how they are going to take it (p. 136).

If you're writing to a lay audience about technical matters, be particularly diligent about boundaries. Omit information unlikely to be understandable and meaningful. To verify that what you are writing will be understood by your readers, recruit someone of your audience's background to read it and give you an honest assessment.

Above all, know what the purpose is for your writing—what effect you expect it to have on your audience. Writing is a journey of sorts, and a critical first step to any journey is to know precisely where you want to go. Without that kind of direction for a writing project, you'll flail around and frustrate yourself with an incurable lack of cohesiveness. If you find yourself laboring unproductively at the keyboard, get yourself back on track by reviewing your preparation. Ask yourself "who are my readers, and what am I trying to accomplish?"

Gather Materials

When you write, you're called an *author* because of your status as an *authority*. You know more about what you're writing than your readers know. If the reverse were true, they would be writing and you would be reading.

Long before you become the author of a specific writing project, you'll be informally gathering materials that prepare you to be an author. Listen, ask probing questions, read, contemplate ideas, and keep notes. I recommend a computer folder of thoughts, ideas, and potential writing topics that can become a window to your own mind—a reservoir of information that would otherwise dissipate with time. I began such a folder decades ago, and I draw on it frequently.

As particular writing tasks arise, you'll set about gathering project-specific information. Most specific information will be outside your own files, and you may have a company or institutional template within which to work. Information you collect will prepare you to give your document three important qualities: accuracy, sufficiency, and interest.

Accuracy

Accuracy is essential to any good document. You need all your quantitative information absolutely error-free: dates, times, dollar amounts, and all other quantities. You also need to represent events and statements exactly as they happened. That kind of accuracy requires diligent information-gathering and fact-checking. To fail in the accuracy of your content is to lose credibility with readers.

Sufficiency

Sufficiency will depend on your gathering more material than you use. The chief reason for casting a wide net is to be sure you've covered all important aspects of the topic. You want to avoid omitting something that would be conspicuous by its absence. Also, insight that comes to you from knowing more than you say will strengthen the document. That is true because subtle thoughts that occur while you read material beyond that which you use—including thoughts about why you have omitted it—will broaden your perspective on the material you do use, and therefore affect for the better how you write about it.

Interest

Interest tends to be thought about last, if at all, by writers of factual documents—reports, proposals, theses, dissertations, analyses. A common misperception is that entertaining, enjoyable reading is the province of fiction alone. That's not true. You can give factual documents vigor by incorporating nonessential information that adds spice (historical sidelights, record-setting events, pertinent anecdotes) and by referring to people (see pp. 20–21). The closer you come to the flavor of telling a story rather than simply relating facts, the more interesting your document will be to read. Keep brevity in sight as a virtue, but at the same time stay alert for places in which a few words will add substantial interest.

Organize Materials

Before beginning to write a large project, you'll want to organize your materials into manageable compartments of related information and ideas. How you do that is up to you. Some writers make detailed outlines. I find them constricting. I write best by working through a series of trials and errors, discoveries, and changes of mind. That is not to recommend simply pulling information from a pile of material while writing. That would be chaotic, frustrating, and nerve-wracking. You'll need some initial organization.

I open a blank computer file and give it the name of the intended document. Then I identify computer files related to the project, including my own early-stage writing, and I paste those files into the document in a sequence that corresponds to my overall sense of organization. Next, I arrange books, articles, and other hard-copy items into piles that correspond to that organization. I enter, in appropriate places in the document, citations for passages from the hard-copy items to facilitate integrating them with my computer files. At this point I'll probably insert some tentative section headings.

Now I'm likely to begin sketching a tentative outline, using paper and pencil so I can alter it quickly and easily as I go. Letting that outline evolve loosely allows me to strike a balance between organization and freedom. (When the outline becomes messy, I make and print a typed version to be used for further adjustments by pencil.)

I find myself moving through several phases as I prepare to write— developing ideas, writing occasional sentences or passages that come to me in a form too good to lose, incorporating references, and searching for new material needed to fill a hole. These phases unfold in a less-than-predictable sequence, driven by what I discover and think about while exploring materials and organizing them.

Usually I open a separate file for long-shot information so I can find it easily if I needed it. By also depositing periodic half-baked thoughts into that file, I create a kind of electronic junk pile that may be worth picking through later—or that may bring to mind something worth inserting. Finally, I type an easy-to-read version of the outline to serve as a guide, realizing that I'll alter it in unpredictable ways as I go. A complete and polished outline is not a goal. A complete and polished document is.

Now I am ready to begin the actual narrative writing of the document.

Establish a Timetable

Doom hovers over many writing projects days or weeks before the writer begins work—that is, at the point the writer *should* have begun work. You can make no stronger statement about your commitment to quality in a writing project than to allot enough time to read, think, collect material, write, and revise. A document needing five or six weeks of work and given one will be as palatable as a cake needing 25 to 30 minutes of baking time and given five. Plan to complete your document in time to reread it with fresh eyes, recruit others to read it critically, and fine-tune it to a high standard.

CHAPTER 15
EMBRACE THE ACT OF WRITING

Emphasis in this chapter is on your state of mind as a writer—how you think and feel while writing and how you respond to writing's demands. Intermingled also is advice about organization. As valuable as advice from preceding chapters is—simplicity, brevity, precision, grammar, and punctuation—I'll allude to none of it here. I'll assume you've assimilated it. The broadest view of this rather large chapter is that it describes relationships between you and the writing process, and between you and your audience.

The sections of this chapter describe key aspects of writing: an inviting opening, well-ordered paragraphs and sections, recognition of the stages and rigors involved in writing, deliberative thought, sincerity, and an impressionable exit. The order in which I present that material is not necessarily sequential relative to the act of writing, except for the first and last sections (the opening and the exit). Expect to enmesh yourself in other issues in an unpredictable order—at times, simultaneously.

Write an Inviting Opening

You'll want time to sit and think before you write, but be careful not to rationalize your way into too much of it. Be honest about the difference between contemplating your opening and getting stuck in the mud.

To get the juices flowing, you may prefer to begin writing at a point of inspiration. Still, you should tackle the opening as soon as you can. You need to face it quite early to ground yourself—to give yourself a strong sense of where you're going. Also, sequential writing enables you to see whether A leads logically to B, B to C, and so forth.

Your opening may consist of one paragraph or several, depending to some extent on the size of the document. One characteristic that nearly all openings have in common is that they are the most difficult part of the document to write. You can make the writing of your opening less difficult and more likely to pull readers in by incorporating these three aims: (1) Let readers know the purpose of the document. (2) Give readers information about the document's structure. (3) Use language that heightens interest and piques curiosity. Below is a weak opening to a hypothetical document, followed by a preferred revision.

Weak Original Opening

As has been discussed recently, many of us have begun to become aware of long-standing inefficiencies at our Eastwood office that we have been ignoring for some time. My observations of the inner-workings of the office last week have led me to hypothesize that there are specific problems there that we might address. For several years we have been asking the employees at Eastwood to work on assignments that are very much like each other, and that can become mundane because of the repetition involved. That, along with the fact that we have given minimal feedback to the Eastwood employees about what has been accomplished in that office, may be responsible for a lowering of morale. Probably we should also look at the employees there and at two of our other offices to see if we could facilitate an improved working environment through some employee reassignments. I have reason to believe that if we were to implement some initiatives relative to such actions as these, it might result in greater efficiency and morale. Such results would outweigh the cost of our making these changes.

Preferred Revised Opening

We are heading in the right direction. We no longer look at the Eastwood office through the rose-colored glasses we wore last year. Now we need to identify the problems there and find solutions.

Last week I spent about one quarter of my time studying the office dynamics at Eastwood. The fundamental problem seems to be a rut not entirely of the staff's own making. I propose three actions for re-invigorating the office:

1. Introduce more variety in assignments.
2. Give more frequent reports about the office accomplishments.
3. Shift a few personnel between that office and two others.

In the first three sections of this document, you will read detailed plans for each of those three proposed actions. The fourth section is an account of expected results. The last two sections are a cost analysis and a summary.

A good opening serves you, the writer, as well as it serves the reader. By orienting readers, you reduce your need for explanations and transitions along the way. And by outlining the journey, you give yourself a blueprint to follow. That blueprint reduces the chances of your wandering off course or having to puzzle about where to place a specific piece of material.

Expect the writing of your document's opening to be troublesome and time-consuming. If I begin with only a loose design in mind, I may spend considerable time writing an opening that is either unusable or in need of heavy revision later. Sometimes I essentially give up on the opening—leave it in disarray—until I've learned enough about my own piece to come back later and do a better job. Still, I take a good run at the opening right away for two reasons: (1) Thinking through the opening forces me to predict where I'm going, and to set a tone and a plan for getting there. It helps me firm up, and sometimes alter or amend, my perspective on the whole. (2) My first attempt at the opening exposes holes in my thinking. I become aware of the need to plug those holes, first within the document itself, and later—once the details of the document become clear—in my revision of the opening.

Depending on your experience with large writing tasks, you may think, "I know what he means about writing an opening," or you may think, "he can't be serious; that sounds unrealistically rigorous." Either way, you must acknowledge that the opening of a document is critically important. **If the opening of your document fails to encourage readers to read it, the effect of your work will be no greater than if you had written nothing at all.**

Give Order to Paragraphs and Sections

Just as you organize a desk by assigning one type of item to one drawer and other types to other drawers, you'll do well to organize a document by assigning one type of information or line of thought to one paragraph and other types to other paragraphs. On a larger scale, you'll exercise the same type of compartmentalization within and between the sections of an extensive document. Because the paragraph is the basic unit of organization, I'll speak here in terms of paragraphs and leave you to generalize the principles to sections and sub-sections.

A typical paragraph contains three or more sentences, but a two-sentence paragraph is acceptable. Technically, a single sentence is not a paragraph, but on rare occasions you may write a freestanding sentence as a transition between paragraphs. Important characteristics of a paragraph are its unity (commonality of material), sequence (order of material), and cohesiveness (flow of material).

Unity

A good paragraph is unified by the presence of material that belongs together. In the early stages of writing, you may have only vague feelings about combinations of material that will unify your paragraphs. Then as you revise toward a final product, you'll adjust each paragraph until it's built around some main idea. The most common way to organize a paragraph around a main idea is to incorporate a topic sentence—a sentence that states the essence of the paragraph. (Similarly, you'll introduce a section with a topic paragraph.) The most common position for a topic sentence (bolded here) is at the beginning of the paragraph:

> **Federal mandates cost businesses enormous amounts of money.**
> Regulations need to be read and understood. Compliance plans need
> to be designed. Costly modifications and extra personnel need to be
> paid for. And finally, company lawyers need to scrutinize the entire
> process to be sure no stones have been left unturned.

This is a deductively designed paragraph. It opens with the main idea as a topic sentence, and then proceeds through elaborations on that main idea.

Even if a transitional sentence of some kind moves the topic sentence from the absolute front of the paragraph, the paragraph will be deductively designed if elaborations follow the topic sentence:

> Production costs account for only a portion of a company's overhead. **Federal mandates**, for example, **cost businesses enormous amounts of money**. Regulations need to be read and understood. Compliance plans need to be designed. Costly modifications and extra personnel need to be paid for. And finally, company lawyers need to scrutinize the entire process to be sure no stones have been left unturned.

Another option is to design a paragraph inductively. That is, you might first present the smaller pieces of information as clues to the main idea of the paragraph, and then end with a topic sentence that in essence says to the reader, "this is the point to which I have been leading you."

> Production costs account for only a portion of a company's overhead. For example, federal regulations need to be read and understood, and compliance plans designed. Then costly modifications and extra personnel need to be paid for. Finally, company lawyers need to scrutinize the entire process to be sure no stones have been left unturned. In the end, **federal mandates cost businesses enormous amounts money**.

Occasionally a paragraph will lack an explicit topic sentence. Such a paragraph must contain material so unified that the reader can see the main idea clearly in its parts. That is, the topic sentence is there in spirit. It's implicit.

> Someone needs to read and understand the federal regulations. Someone then needs to design plans for compliance. Adding to that cost will be the expense of making modifications and hiring additional personnel. Then we still must pay lawyers to scrutinize the entire process to be sure no stones have been left unturned.

Implicit in the paragraph above is that federal mandates will cost the company enormous amounts of money. The implicit-topic technique is legitimate, and you may find it effective in some circumstances. Still, there is no substitute for a good topic sentence as a way of placing the reader's feet on firm ground; be cautious about dispensing with a topic sentence. And if you do craft a paragraph without a topic sentence, be absolutely sure all the material the paragraph contains belongs to a single, identifiable train of thought.

Having said all that, I need to admit to seldom being conscious of the topic sentence of a paragraph as I write. (Note: I would, however, be conscious of and intentional about writing a topic paragraph to introduce a section.) Nor am I necessarily conscious of whether I'm approaching a paragraph deductively or inductively. Writing intuition takes over, leaving my mind free to think about content. Generally, I see in retrospect that I've instinctively built paragraphs around identifiable topic sentences. The extent to which instinct fails me while I'm wrought up in content is the extent to which I have to reconstruct a paragraph when I revise my work.

Although the chief function of a series of paragraphs is to gather related material into clumps around given topics, a secondary function is to give readers visual breaks. For that reason, your choice of where to begin a new paragraph is seldom absolutely objective. You might make a case for combining several closely related topics into a single paragraph, with one general topic sentence encompassing them all, or you might decide to break a single large paragraph into multpiple smaller paragraphs for ease of reading. I favor smaller paragraphs wherever frequent paragraph changes don't disrupt reading flow. They help readers compartmentalize the information and take it in more easily. Generally, the size of the paragraphs in a document should be somewhat proportional to the size of the document. A long paragraph in a small document looks particularly bloated.

Sequence

In addition to deciding what material belongs within a paragraph, you need to decide the order in which the reader needs to receive that material to understand it most efficiently. In the overstuffed paragraph below, material is scattered illogically.

> Hobbies are important diversions for people of all ages. I was about 12 when I became a numismatist. As I recall, the important-sounding name itself had some appeal. Still, what hooked me for good was the excitement of the hunt. "Numismatic" means "of or pertaining

to currency," and "numismatics" has become the official name for the hobby of collecting coins. I remember striking up a friendship with an older man who introduced me to his hobby when I was young. A young person who has not yet reached the frenetic activity of the teen years needs a hobby around which to begin organizing life; a retired person who has just left the frenetic activity of a profession needs a hobby around which to continue organizing life. Looking for just that right coin becomes a joyful obsession. A numismatist becomes facile at sorting through a handful of change, looking for that 1950D Jefferson nickel or that 1955S Lincoln penny. The letters after the dates are mint marks: lack of any mark signifies Philadelphia, D signifies Denver, and S signifies San Francisco. (The San Francisco mint closed in 1955.) Some old coins have an O mint mark for New Orleans, where there was a mint until early in the twentieth century. Location of the mint mark varies from coin to coin, marks on the face being referred to as "obverse" and marks on the back as "reverse." In time, Mr. Nielson and I came to have much in common.

Pieces of information that should be together appear in various places throughout the paragraph. By contrast, the material in the multiple-paragraph revision below follows a sequence from general to specific, with paragraphs serving as the organizing agents for material that belongs together.

Hobbies are important diversions for people of all ages. A young person who has not yet reached the frenetic activity of the teen years needs a hobby around which to begin organizing life; a retired person who has just left the frenetic activity of a profession needs a hobby around which to continue organizing life. I remember striking up a friendship with an older man who introduced me to his hobby when I was young. In time, Mr. Nielson and I came to have much in common.

I was about 12 when I became a numismatist. "Numismatic" means "of or pertaining to currency," and "numismatics" has become the official name for the hobby of collecting coins. As I recall, the important-sounding name itself had some appeal. Still, what hooked me for good was the excitement of the hunt. Looking for just that right coin becomes a joyful obsession.

A numismatist becomes facile at sorting through a handful of change, looking for that 1950D Jefferson nickel or that 1955S Lincoln penny.

The letters after the dates are mint marks: lack of any mint mark signifies that the coin was minted in Philadelphia, a D signifies Denver, and an S signifies San Francisco (The San Francisco mint closed in 1955.) Some old coins have an O mintmark for New Orleans, where there was a mint until early in the twentieth century. Location of the mint mark varies from coin to coin, marks on the face being referred to as "obverse" and marks on the back as "reverse."

Whenever you reread a paragraph or a series of paragraphs for revision, look for ways to improve the sequence of material. I was faced one time with a paragraph that felt disjointed despite having been built of well-written sentences related to a main idea. After several readings, I reversed the order of the sentences and made a few adjustments for cohesiveness. The new, re-ordered paragraph was perfect. Experience has taught me that calling material to mind in optimal order while writing is difficult. As I revise, I now look routinely for sequence of material as a likely flaw in my first-draft paragraphs.

Cohesiveness

You might think that a paragraph containing a unified and well-sequenced collection of information would read smoothly. That's not necessarily so. The paragraph below encompasses a specific topic and unfolds in a logical sequence, but it still lacks a feeling of flow. Probably most readers can make the inferences necessary to tie the thoughts together, but the revision relieves readers of that inference-making responsibility.

Original

A puzzle some companies need to solve is how to get the most out of their work force, and at the same time take full advantage of technological advances. Veteran employees are rich in information and insight. Technological developments offer new, highly efficient tools that replace each other in rapid succession. Veteran employees are challenged to discard old, comfortable processes and learn new, uncomfortable processes. Probably companies need to spend vast sums on technical support. They risk losing a great amount of valuable intellectual capital to early retirement.

Revision

A puzzle some companies need to solve is how to get the most out of their work force, and at the same time take full advantage of technological advances. Veteran employees rich in information and insight may struggle to adapt to new, highly efficient tools that replace each other in rapid succession. They are likely to feel imposed upon by having to discard old, comfortable processes in favor of new, uncomfortable processes. A company's solution may be to spend vast sums on technical support for veteran employees. To do less may be to risk losing valuable intellectual capital to early retirement.

When you read through a paragraph during revision, be sure the sentences flow well from one to another. In the preceding revision, the second sentence ties veteran employees to struggles with technology, the third sentence maintains veteran employees as the subject by use of the pronoun *they,* and the fourth sentence identifies the aim of the paragraph's advice: *a company's solution may be....*

You'll achieve paragraph cohesiveness by using specific tools to clear the reader's path of unnecessary bumps. If one sentence does not progress clearly to the next sentence, you may incorporate a particular word that ties the two. I did that in the revision above by having the pronoun *they* in the third sentence refer to *veteran employees* (second sentence) as its antecedent. When readers need still more help, you may use a transition word or phrase: *similarly, subsequently, consequently, therefore, nevertheless, in contrast, in a similar way, from a different perspective.* Be sure the word or phrase you use describes precisely the relationship between the information that precedes it and the information that follows. (In Appendix B, see *consequently, subsequently, therefore* on Page 166.) Using a transition word or phrase imprecisely does more harm than good. It misleads readers. They are forced into a second reading—or more—to ascertain meaning.

Note that the same three principles of tying sentences together within a paragraph (unity, sequence, cohesiveness) apply to tying paragraphs together within a document. Paragraph two may follow paragraph one logically by content, but if not, you'll need to make an explicit connection. You'll need to incorporate words that reflect back on the preceding paragraph, or use some kind of connective word or phrase. You may even begin the new paragraph with a full sentence of transition that connects it to the preceding paragraph.

Finally, keep in mind that the principle of placing emphatic material at the end applies to paragraphs as it does to sentences. When you need a paragraph to make a particular point emphatically, design it to end with a strong concluding sentence (perhaps the topic sentence). That will help pull its elements together into a strong, cohesive whole.

Acquire a Feel for Writing

If you play baseball, you know how it feels to stand at the plate, watch the ball leave the pitchers hand, and make solid contact with your bat. If you play violin, you know how it feels to tuck the instrument securely under your chin, tighten the bow hairs to exactly the right tension, tune the strings, and coordinate movement between fingers and bow arm. Writing is like other skills: the more you write the more you acquire a feel for it—a feel that lets you predict what lies ahead, judge the formidability of various segments of the process, and react to difficulties without overreacting to them. Following is an account of how I feel at various stages of a given session of writing, followed by thoughts about the relative contributions of inspiration and hard work.

Recognize the Stages of Writing

Something that Rudolph Flesch refers to as **the call** impels me to sit at my computer and begin to write. He warns us against getting in our own way—or in the current vernacular, "psyching ourselves out." He says "Don't overestimate either the difficulty of the task or the grandness of the product-to-be. That tends to shut you down—to keep the call from ever coming" (1960, p. 131). Clear your mind of self-imposed distractions so you can get to work.

Even with a healthy perspective on a given writing project, I find the strength of the call varies with the depth of suffering I expect. I expect the greatest early-stage suffering when I say to myself, "I'd better work on that now; time is flying by, and I need to make some progress." I expect the least early-stage suffering when new ideas are firing like rockets in my head, and I say—with enthusiasm and passion—"I have to write. If I don't, I'll lose something important."

During **the early stage** of a writing session, I feel awkward and uncertain. I write some bad sentences that make me shake my head at myself later when I revise them. During this stage (unless I'm responding to those rockets firing in my head) I'm distracted easily. Without strong self-discipline, I might abandon my writing at the drop of a hat to watch television, eat, read, play with the dog, or talk to my wife. I have to muscle my way through with the faith that eventually I'll penetrate a vein of productivity. I've written enough to know that most gateways to productivity require me to pass through this painful period of discombobulation.

During **the middle stage** of a writing session my view clears. I begin to see what I need and want. Sentences written in the early stage look deficient, but my exhilaration over revising them into something good is stronger than my embarrassment at having written them in the first place. (No one else sees them!) I enter a mental state similar to sleep, with my work developing like a smoothly moving dream while I remain completely unconscious of everything else in the world. Nothing else exists. Normal daily benchmarks like mealtime or bedtime become irrelevant. If someone were to ask me a simple question suddenly—what day is it; what time of day is it; when are your daughters' birthdays—I'd have to "come to" to answer, much as I have to "come to" when someone interrupts my sleep and poses a quick question. It's during this stage that writing becomes a form of intense pleasure and gratification. Productivity and quality soar. Recollections of time spent in this stage create the hunger to return to writing later.

If, during this very active stage, my thoughts shoot ahead to sections that should follow, I tab down a few spaces and type in what I have in mind. I might even develop a few fragments of content if I have in mind something of value that I fear losing. Then I return and resume my writing. I've accomplished two things: I've improved concentration on my current writing by dumping distracting thoughts onto paper where I know I'll find them later, and I've given myself a sketchy roadmap that will make subsequent writing easier and more complete.

As I enter **the late stage** of a writing session, I've been productive—but at a cost. I'm weary. Realization of my weariness sometimes descends suddenly and without warning. I can force myself onward to a stopping point that will make my return easier, but only if it's a short way away. When the saturation point strikes, I have a strong urge to flee. I must get away and refresh myself mentally and physically. I may almost run from my writing area, feeling that I can't escape soon enough. When I do collapse with a cold drink, food, a walk outdoors, or whatever indulgence I choose as reentry to the world outside writing, I feel what's commonly called a "good tired." I feel satisfaction coupled with relief and rest. Sometimes I need 15 minutes away from the project, sometimes hours, and sometimes a day. I'll recognize the call back when it comes. If I'm writing without a deadline, I can afford to wait until the call back is motivated by desire. If a deadline looms, the call back is more likely to be a matter of finding the shortest respite that will allow me to recharge my battery and regain a reasonable level of effectiveness.

Two ploys during the late stage help me energize my next call back to writing. One is to time my writing break to coincide with an interesting embryonic thought about material to come—something to mull while resting. The other is to tab down a few spaces and type a fragment, maybe a few isolated phrases or bullets, about where I believe my writing will go next. Then while I'm away from the writing I tend to keep thinking through my next move. The conscious and the subliminal meld. When I return to my writing, I am—to use a cliché—ready to hit the ground running.

Acknowledge Perspiration and Inspiration

All that you just read about the stages of writing rests on an important underlying fact: the act of writing is fed by both perspiration and inspiration. Writing is work because sustained thinking is work. Fatigue always descends at some point. On one occasion you'll need to hold your feet to the fire; on another you'll need to give yourself a break. Only you can judge. How long you can sustain productive writing without a break and how many total hours per day you can write will depend on your temperament and on the intensity of the task.

Balancing this oppressive picture is knowledge that your writing at times will spring free and flow faster than your fingers can record. Euphoria erupts! You need to seize those times. Jump from section X to section Y if you suddenly have a strong feeling about how to write something that belongs in section Y. Unless a deadline looms, I'll even jump to a different project momentarily to capture a first-rate thought. While away from my writing, if I'm struck by an outstanding thought or by a superb idea for constructing a sentence or a paragraph, I will—if at all possible—leave whatever I'm doing and write. I carry blank note cards and a pencil with me almost everywhere I go. I hate to let a sudden flash of inspiration dissipate if there's a way to capture it.

I should add one last thought about inspiration. You may be struck by an idea bursting with potential, but when you begin to write you're unhappy with your expression of it. That's no time to nag yourself about constructing pristine sentences. Write what comes to you. As a temporary technique, stream-of-consciousness writing can be valuable. You may write poorly at that moment, but you're preserving the general thought to be packaged in better form later.

Think on Your Seat

The ability to think well while speaking to an audience has come to be known as "thinking on your feet." I guess that makes the ability to think well while writing to an audience a matter of "thinking on your seat." An advantage that writing has over speaking is that you can rework your language until you have something ready for the audience's eyes. That's called *revision*, the subject of the next chapter.

Writing is indeed a process. If you feel a need for instant gratification, you should turn to something other than writing. Inspired writing will account for only a small part of your time at the keyboard; deliberative, mind-wrenching writing will be more common. You'll need to think deeply and clearly about your purpose, about what to say, and about how to say it. You'll need to accept the fact that writing is thought made visible, meaning that you cannot expect to write more clearly than you think. As difficult as thoughtful writing is to produce, embrace it. Enjoy it. Take satisfaction from accomplishing it. It will pay big dividends in the end.

George Orwell, in his 1946 essay "Politics and the English Language," decried a growing trend to dodge the responsibility of writing thoughtfully. "Prose consists less and less of *words* chosen for the sake of their meaning, and more and more of *phrases* tacked together like the section of a prefabricated henhouse" (1954, p. 165). What a colorful description of careless, impatient writing!

Impetuousness may masquerade as inspiration, but you need to recognize it for the imposter that it is. If you're an impetuous writer, one who begins striking keys before assembling thoughts, try this exercise in restraint. It's artificial in that you could never do a great amount of writing in this fashion, but as an exercise it will build writing muscles much as ankle weights build running muscles.

1. Construct a sentence mentally. Speak it to yourself to hear what works. Fix inconsistencies, redundancies, vague expressions, and so forth in your mind.

2. When you've recited a good sentence, type it. Construct a whole paragraph this way, sentence-by-sentence. Print the paragraph, then put it aside for a while.

3. When you come back, read the paragraph aloud. Listen for places that sound awkward or unclear. Diagnose problems by using your ear for language, along with the advice you recall from having read this book. Repair problems with a pencil, and then type a clean copy.

4. The next day, read the clean version and look at the penciled version to see your train of thought. Make a new revision based on whatever comes to mind with the fresh look. You may be pleasantly surprised at how time and thought improve your writing. If you like what you see, remember how you achieved it.

A final admonition about careless writing is to avoid leaning on outside information as a substitute for thinking. Never insert a citation into your writing as if it has the strength to mean something in isolation from your message and your structure. When you do that, you pass responsibility to the other author. That means you've lost control over your own work. The legitimate function of a citation is to support and augment what you have to say. The message is yours, and it must remain so—with you steering all the way. If a powerful, stimulating citation tempts you to alter your piece fundamentally, inspect all your other material relative to the changes you contemplate. Ask yourself if the new inspiration has the strength and validity to override all that you've planned. Then if you decide to restructure the piece, do it thoroughly, from the roots up. You'll need to retrench back to the preparation stage to be sure everything fits together well.

Be Sincere

Straining for effect is a common writing fault. When you're in a muddle you may strain to decorate a paragraph that you know to be substandard. When you're on a euphoric binge you may strain from headiness and delusions of grandeur. Either way, strained writing gives an air of artificiality. Genuineness versus artificiality has a way of shining through writing as it does through personal relationships. If you feel yourself levitating a bit, pull yourself back to Earth and take an honest look at what you've written.

Another important dimension of sincerity is honesty with yourself. You may spend a great amount of time writing a paragraph (or something larger) that is best left unused. A day or two later you may need to talk frankly to yourself: "How could you have spent an hour writing something as bad as that? Trash it." Or the issue may be appropriateness rather than quality. You may need to say something like this to yourself: "I know you've worked hard on the material about X, and it reads well, but it doesn't belong in this piece. Take it out." Neither the number of hours spent writing nor the quality of the work justify using material in a piece. **To a sincere writer, the only justification for using anything, from a single word to multiple pages, is that the piece will be poorer without it.**

If you've written something good, but inappropriate for the current piece, park it in one of the files of your ideas folder. It may become useful as part of another piece. It may even inspire another piece!

Think of this issue of sincerity as a matter of being a friend to your readers. Among people you know well and like, you don't display the kind of artificiality that sometimes shows up in your writing. I encourage you to court a similar feeling of good will and helpfulness toward your readers. You'll naturally lose some readers who are uninterested in your content or opposed to your views, or who lack the background to understand what you've written. That's to be expected. But **you should not lose readers for having burdened them with unwarranted tasks**. I'm only saying explicitly what I've said implicitly multiple times in earlier chapters. Adhering to sound writing principles, as expressed in this book or elsewhere, is not just a matter of being correct or incorrect. It's a matter of being respectful and courteous toward your readers—showing regard for the time and effort they invest in your writing.

Being a friend to your readers, in a nutshell, is a matter of pulling out every tool you can find to make your writing easily understood. This book's keys to good writing constitute the bedrock of readability, but a few additional techniques and reminders are worth thinking about:

- Relate whatever you are writing about to something your readers know; compare and contrast the familiar with the unfamiliar.

- Use humor. An occasional smile or chuckle does wonders for a reader's progress through a document.

- Insert direct quotations where you can, depending on the type of writing. That makes readers feel that someone is talking to them. How much more friendly can you get?

- Use a question-and-answer format where it works. Readers will be drawn in by feeling that they are asking the questions and getting answers.

- Tell anecdotes about people. Rather than simply describe a process, use people and their actions to demonstrate it.

- Do all you can to tell a story rather than simply present information.

Rudolph Flesch is insistent on those last two points—on the importance of writing about people and telling stories: "If there are no people on the scene, it's your business to put them there. If there's no story to tell, you'll have to invent one" (1974, p. 73). When people read stories about other people doing things, they picture themselves in action. They become engaged. Rather than begin an instruction with "One will be able to make use of the machine only after having first done A, B, and C," try something like this: "Harold turned on the new machine left by the company representative only to find it dead, as if the power were off. What he hadn't realized was that . . . ."

Can you make every aspect of every piece of writing interesting? Probably not. The dryness of some subjects may thwart your efforts. Can you write so well as to spare readers unwarranted tasks? That's probably no more likely than an amateur golfer shooting par on every hole. All any of us can do is work on technique, approach each writing job with commitment and concentration, have reader comfort always in mind, and keep bad strokes to a minimum.

Make an Impressionable Exit

The end of your document will be most effective if you unify your main points in some kind of summary. To encourage readers to retain what you've said, incorporate into that summary a few memorable highlights of the document. An excellent technique is to tie your summary back to the opening statement of purpose. By tying the whole document together in this way, you'll leave readers with a strong impression of your planning and organization. You'll also promote long-term recall of your most salient points.

CHAPTER 16
REVISE AND REFLECT

All writers revise—some lightly, some extensively. Some favor revising as they write and others after they've finished a first draft. I think both are important. I've devoted a full section to each approach, followed by short sections on sharing your writing with others and on self-reflection. But first we should think about what revision is.

Have a Perspective on Revision

When you revise, you're silently asking questions of yourself, answering them, and responding with changes. That's true whether you work on a paragraph, a sentence, or a word or two. Here are some of the latent questions about sentences and paragraphs that you might ask yourself as you try to deliver a clear, concise message that others will read efficiently. There are others, but this list offers a good start.

- Is it meaningful?
- Is it completely true and accurate?
- Is it stated precisely?
- Is it stated clearly?
- Is it active? Alive?
- Is it free of unneeded words?
- Is it free of unnecessarily long and complicated words?
- Does it hold together logically?
- Does it let the reader read through smoothly?

Notice that these questions are more reader-oriented than writing-principle oriented. That's because readers, rather than seeing technical errors, simply judge the extent to which your writing is comfortable or uncomfortable to read. There's no better perspective by which to judge your own writing. Read it as if you expect everything to be as it should, and then as you come across places where it is not, decide on the revisions needed to make rough spots smooth.

Revise as You Write

To keep my writing cohesive, I reread frequently as I write—as long as doing so doesn't distract me from where I'm heading. Some common revisions I make while writing are changes in word choice, changes in the order of sentences or clauses, improvements in flow between sentences and paragraphs, and adjustments in tone. Most common—both as a direct aim and as a by-product of other repairs—is a reduction in the number of words.

To not make changes as I go would add to the job of post-writing revision. Besides, a sentence that feels suspicious usually can be revised best and most efficiently while it's still warm. Also, I know that what I write now may lead to what I write a few minutes from now. I'll do better taking clues from good writing than from mediocre writing. All the while, it's important to keep in mind that there are many good ways to construct a given sentence or paragraph. Poor writing stems not so much from failure to find *the* good way as from a lack of diligence in pursuing and arriving at *a* good way.

When I resume writing after a period of time away (maybe an hour; maybe a day), I reread the last few paragraphs I wrote—sometimes more—to orient myself to what I'm about to do. More often than not I revise lightly during that time. Sometimes I see need for a major change, and may spend that session revising rather than writing new material. Also, when I've finished a section of writing—say a few pages of a 20-page piece—I reread that section to be sure it holds together well and flows logically. Usually I change a word here and there, and I may reconstruct a sentence or paragraph that strikes me as awkward. Typically, I make changes to the beginnings or ends of paragraphs in the form of transitions that ease the reader through. I feel more prepared to write the next section buoyantly and confidently if I know that the section I just finished is closer to final form than to first-draft form. I make an exception to that practice if ideas for the next section are bursting at the seams: to suppress those ideas is to risk losing them.

While revising along the way, I may find that I lack conviction about a change. To avoid the risk of replacing it with a lesser version, I copy the questionable passage immediately below the original, or at the end of the document, or in a new, temporary document. Then I revise the original freely, knowing that a copy is easily recoverable. Seldom do I need it, but knowing that it's there lets me revise freely. If I'm unhappy with both versions after I've made the revision, I'll write a third—maybe some blend of the two.

Be careful not to revise too heavily as you write. A compulsion to leave no trash strewn through a piece can keep you from unleashing your thoughts fluently. It can also cause you to destroy some good writing. A corollary to the infamous Murphy's Law states "If you play around with a thing long enough, eventually it will break." Writers revising compulsively tend not to stop revising when the sentence or paragraph is good. When you sense that you can no longer distinguish between a change that improves and a change that simply changes, you need to move on and let the passage cool for a time.

An unfortunate effect of over-revising is a condition I call *reader's block*, a loss of all ability to judge the quality of your own writing. It comes from having reread and re-thought a piece or a section too extensively. You're susceptible to reader's block either while you're writing or when you immerse yourself too deeply in post-writing revision. All you can do then is let the material sit—the longer the better—and return to it later with a fresh perspective.

Revise After You Write

I do my first post-writing revision at the computer screen. I always find a few unquestionable changes to be made as I scroll through: typographical errors, imprecise word choices, awkward sentences. Had I printed those defects they'd have been annoyances.

Next, I print the document (always double-spaced). With printed copy in hand, I'm ready to work the piece over at a deeper level. I read intensely and critically, pencil-marking as I go. I cross out words, write in words, circle sections, draw arrows showing relocation, cross out full sections, and sometimes handwrite extensive additions. Why not do all that revising at the computer? First, the document looks different in hard copy from the way it does on a computer screen, and the hard copy version is what most readers will see. Second, the pencil leaves a trail that shows where I've been and what I've changed. It gives me a sense of the whole—of how one change interacts with another. Sometimes I make a change that prompts me to undo an earlier change. I'd have lost that perspective had I revised on screen.

After marking the first draft, I open the computer file and transfer changes from the pencil-marked copy. That's primarily a mechanical process. I put faith in the thinking I did while making the pencil marks. Occasionally I see something I missed, and I change it on the screen. Then I print a new copy.

The next copy isn't likely to be the final. I read it later (maybe the next day) and pencil in more changes. Some pieces need six or seven revisions—or more; others need only two or three. With each subsequent revision I read more quickly, consciously trying to get a sense of how the pieces fit into a whole. At the last stage of revision I may repair a slightly awkward spot or two—maybe rhythmic clumsiness or alliteration—that I've let stand several times previously out of uncertainty.

If you're revising a large work—major proposal, book, thesis—lay out the Table of Contents, including lists of figures, tables, etc. Then check every page of the document against those pages to be certain that (1) page numbers correspond to the page numbers in the Table of Contents, and (2) titles of chapters, sections, subsections, tables, and figures all coincide with the Table of Contents in terms of wording, capitalization, italics, underlining, and every other detail. I usually find errors. You might even want to copy and paste chapter titles, section headings, etc. from the document itself into a single, compact page or two that makes the document's skeleton easy to see. That will help you see inconsistencies, and it will give you a greater sense of the whole to carry with you as you revise in detail.

Solicit a Fresh Perspective

Your writing can look wholly different to you after time passes. I remember writing a paragraph some time ago that was exactly what I wanted. The next day I read it—not to revise but to enjoy my masterpiece—and I was shocked that I could have written something so mediocre and thought it was good. Looking at it with fresh eyes allowed me to see what I hadn't seen earlier.

Of course the freshest eyes belong to someone else. Make the lonely craft of writing a little less lonely: find a writing partner. As much as you try to see the holes in your own writing, your intimate knowledge of content puts a low ceiling over the amount of "ignorance" you can impose on yourself. Another person will see problems that have become invisible to you, especially words and expressions that you tend to overuse. Whether you work in business, government, education, or some other professional pursuit, **join forces with a colleague. Make a pact that you'll read each other's work and make frank comments**. I no longer consider anything a final version until at least one other person has offered suggestions for revision.

You might read each other's writing periodically even when a major project isn't at stake. Reading and commenting on short pieces (memos, e-mail messages) is an exercise well worth the time. Each of you will catch tendencies in the other's writing, and the small adjustments you make will amount to major improvement over time. The outside-reader approach isn't a matter of a better writer helping a lesser writer; it's simply a matter of fresh eyes. Anyone can learn from almost anyone if communication is honest and minds are open.

Reflect on Your Work and Its Meaning to You

Let's end with a brief foray into the philosophical. What I will say here about your relationship to the reader is reinforcement of advice I've already given. That should indicate how important I believe it to be. Following that, I'll finish with thoughts about three important personal R-words: Reputation, Responsibility, and Rewards.

Protect Reader Comfort

My aim here, as I bring the body of this book to a close, is to emphasize the danger—especially among technicians and academicians—of assaulting readers with unnecessarily complex writing.

Wisdom has many faces. One is the good sense to recognize that everything we're capable of doing isn't necessarily something we should do. My car will go 120 miles per hour. I decline. My credit card will allow me to spend $30,000. I decline. My vocabulary will let me use five-syllable words in place of perfectly serviceable two-syllable synonyms. I decline.

If you have a large vocabulary, you need to judge how much of that vocabulary is usable for particular pieces of writing. To me, the upper end of my vocabulary is most useful for reading difficult literature, thinking expansive thoughts, and locating that occasional just-right word. It is not serviceable for wholesale communication. Large-vocabulary writers commonly intimidate readers with painfully long, complex sentences and complex words much as thugs intimidate people with weapons. In both cases, those intimidated are bullied into acquiescence. You, too, can bully and alienate readers with your writing: use many-syllabled words, choose noun-forms over verb-forms, write passively, avoid specificity when you see an opportunity to be vague, and craft convoluted sentences that average 30 words. Or instead, you can value readers and communicate with them: embrace one-syllable and two-syllable words and the occasional short sentence; devote yourself to lively verbs and active voice; say—in a forthright way—precisely what you mean to say; and write clear, direct sentences that average fewer than 20 words.

Remain ever conscious that complex language has value over simple language only when it conveys information more precisely, completely, and clearly. Many complex subjects can be described only with complex language (in which case mixing in as much simple language as you can becomes particularly important to readers). So, when you absolutely need complex language, use it. But where simple language offers the precision, completeness, and clarity needed to do the job, complex language is nothing more than a barrier that shuts some readers out, makes others work harder than necessary, and lets you feel bright at the expense of your readers.

Of course, some readers' lack of understanding must be laid to their limitations. All will not have sufficient background to understand what you write. You can do nothing about that. What you can do, though, is choose to write in a way that keeps to a minimum the number of readers you shut out.

Protect Your Reputation and Acknowledge Your Responsibility

When you put a document together for others to read, be aware that what you've written represents you. The quality of the writing represents your ability and care in the use of language. The clarity and brevity represent your respect for the reader's time and comfort. The content—including whether you're careful with facts, forthright in argument, and responsible about citing other persons in context—represents your honesty.

Over time your writing will earn a reputation of one kind or another for its level of readability. Colleagues may become faithful readers, or they may become conditioned to just skim what you write. Worse, they may routinely skip over your writing altogether to save the unwarranted time they know it will consume. That last condition is deadly. Your success and advancement will depend in part on your having cultivated an appreciative and faithful audience of readers for what you put on paper.

As the quality of your writing grows, so does your obligation to be careful, forthright, and responsible on behalf of your readers. That's because skillful writing attracts a larger audience and carries more credibility than mediocre writing. Know the power of the tool you're honing, and use it responsibly.

Reap Your Rewards

As you hone your writing skills to an ever-sharper edge, you'll find fewer and fewer basic flaws in your early drafts. That will free you to make higher-level revisions, which in turn will lead to documents that please both you and your readers more than you'd ever thought possible. That's the ultimate reward for a diligent approach to writing—a reward that I hope you'll reap and enjoy.

Bibliography

Bernstein, Theodore and Jacques Barzun (1976, 1965). *Watch Your Language.* New York, NY: Macmillan Publishing Company.

Flesch, Rudolph, and A. G. Lass (1946). *The Way to Write.* New York, NY: Harper & Brothers, Publishers.

Flesch, Rudolph (1954). *How to Make Sense.* New York, NY: Harper & Brothers, Publishers.

Flesch, Rudolph (1960). *How to Write, Speak, and Think More Effectively.* New York, NY: Harper & Brothers.

Flesch, Rudolph (1962). *How to Be Brief.* New York, NY: Harper & Row, Publishers.

Flesch, Rudolph (1964). *The ABC of Style: A Guide to Plain English.* New York, NY: Harper & Row, Publishers.

Flesch, Rudolph (1974). *The Art of Readable Writing.* New York, NY: Harper & Row, Publishers.

Hacker, Diana and Nancy Sommers (2017). *A Writer's Reference* (9th ed.). Boston, MA: Bedford Books of St. Martin's Press.

Kramer, Melinda G., Glenn Leggett, and C. David Mead (1995). *Prentice Hall Handbook for Writers* (12th ed.). Englewood Cliffs, NJ: Prentice Hall.

Lanham, Richard (2007, 1991). *Revising Prose* (5th ed.). New York, NY: Pearson Education, Inc.

Lederer, Richard (1999, 1991). *The Miracle of Language.* New York, NY: Pocket Books, a division of Simon and Schuster, Inc.

Orwell, George (1954). "Politics and the English Language," in *A Collection of Essays.* New York, NY: Doubleday Anchor Books, Doubleday and Company, Inc.

Strunk, William Jr. and E. B. White (2000, 1979, 1972, 1959). *The Elements of Style* (3rd ed.). New York, NY: Macmillan Publishing Co., Inc.

Winokur, Jon (2011, 1992, 1987). *The Portable Curmudgeon.* New York, NY: Plume, a division of Penguin Books.

Zinsser, William (1994). *On Writing Well* (5th ed.). New York, NY: Harper Perennial, a division of Harper Collins Publishers. (2001, Logan, IA: Perfection Learning)

A COLLECTION OF USEFUL VERBS

This appendix contains two lists of verbs: *Reminders* (commonly used verbs that you probably know well) and *Mind Provokers* (more-challenging verbs that will help you express yourself vividly). Read this introductory material to understand the thought behind the appendix, and then use the lists periodically to refresh your reservoir of verbs.

Mind Provokers is the longer of the two lists because I've included common words having imaginative uses beyond their usual context. A few words you might not expect to find on the more-challenging *Mind Provokers* list, for example, are *buckle*, *stock*, *shield*, *bathe*, and *capture*, but they are there because of their potential for expansive use that enlivens writing:

> I expected all research subjects to *buckle* under the last few
> questions, but one young lady had *stocked* her mind with
> ready answers and *shielded* her pride with willful indifference.

> He *bathed* himself in unrealistic expectations, ignoring the truth
> that to *capture* their hearts he must first *capture* their attention.

To avoid burdening you with too many entries, I excluded three types of verbs from the lists, as described in the following paragraphs.

First, I have excluded verbs that are minimally useful because of their obscurity. Most are useful in the right circumstance, but as a whole they yield little return for time spent. Your likely path to these verbs is through a thesaurus (or www.thesaurus.com) in response to a specific, narrow need. Here is a sample of ***obscure verbs:***

adumbrate	elinguate	manducate	nidificate	perigrinate	reducrucate	urticate
cadge	inculpate	mizzle	oppilate	prate	repugn	vellicate
cohobate	lucubrate	nesslerize	oppugn	ratriocinate	sparge	wintle

Second, I excluded verbs having so singular an application that you're likely to bring them to mind when you need them. Here's a sample of *specifically applied verbs:*

blink	debate	faint	molt	picket	solder	trawl
breed	dismount	gargle	neuter	redistrict	stitch	triage
cremate	elope	italicize	oxidize	refract	sublet	void

Finally, I excluded verbs so common that you can recall them at will. Here's a sample of *extremely common verbs:*

ask	drive	listen	open	ride	smile	teach
bite	give	look	pick	run	stand	think
cry	grin	move	read	see	take	understand
cut	hear	need	rest	sit	talk	write

I also excluded fancy versions of more common verbs (*orientate* = *orient*; *pacificate* = *pacify*; *systematize* = *systemize*), and some verbs that can be constructed easily by adding a prefix to another verb (*de-emphasize*). I must tread lightly in that last category; many such words belong on the list (*degrade*; *disengage*; *retrace*). I've included some words that are more common as nouns than as verbs, but only if they double as active, uniquely useful verbs (*cloak*; *frame*; *label*; *heap*; *mound*).

As subjective and unavoidably flawed as these lists are, they'll help you enlarge your vocabulary of verbs and write more active sentences. You might want to **study the lists in small portions**, giving yourself time to sense the usefulness of words and to form tentative sentences. You might also want to read across rows at times to avoid the distraction of alliteration that comes with reading down alphabetized columns. To introduce yourself to unfamiliar words and find deeper meanings and wider uses for familiar words, you'll need a good dictionary. You may find some unfamiliar words only marginally useful, but others you'll want to study and incorporate into your vocabulary.

Be adventurous. While you generally want to attune your writing vocabulary to your intended audience, there's nothing wrong with stretching readers' vocabularies here and there. Context usually illuminates meaning. Just be sure your purpose is never to impress, but rather to say what you have to say as efficiently and precisely as possible.

Reminders

(Easily Recalled Verbs: An Alphabetical List of About 1,100)

A	audit	bluff	chant	complicate	degrade
abbreviate	authenticate	board	characterize	compliment	delegate
abide	authorize	boil	charge	compromise	delete
abolish	automate	bombard	charm	conceive	delight
absorb	avoid	borrow	chart	condense	depreciate
abstain	await	bother	chase	confide	depress
accelerate	awaken	bounce	chatter	confine	deprive
acclaim	award	bow	cheapen	confirm	descend
accom-	**B**	box	cheat	conquer	desert
modate	babble	brag	cheer	consent	designate
accomplish	backfire	braid	chill	conserve	despise
accumulate	backslide	brainwash	chime	consult	destine
acquaint	backstab	brake	chip	contain	detach
acquire	bail	branch	chirp	contest	detain
acquit	balance	brawl	choke	contract	detect
activate	band	break	chop	contradict	devise
adapt	bank	breathe	chronicle	contrast	devote
adjust	baptize	breed	circulate	convene	dictate
administer	bar	breeze	claim	convert	dignify
admire	bargain	bribe	clamp	coordinate	dilate
adopt	bark	brighten	clang	cope	diminish
adore	barnstorm	bring	clank	corrupt	dimple
advance	bat	broadcast	clap	counsel	direct
affect	battle	broaden	clash	crackle	disassemble
allege	bawl	broil	clasp	cram	disband
alter	bear	bruise	classify	craze	disburse
alternate	beautify	brush	clatter	creak	discard
ambush	beg	bubble	claw	crease	disclose
analyze	behave	bump	clean	creep	discolor
annoy	behold	burst	clear	criticize	discount
anticipate	behoove	bury	clench	croak	discourage
appeal	believe	button	click	crop	disgrace
applaud	belong	buy	clinch	crouch	disguise
appoint	bend	**C**	cling	cuddle	disgust
approximate	benefit	cage	clip	cuff	dishonor
arbitrate	beware	calculate	clock	**D**	disillusion
articulate	bid	calm	clog	dam	disinfect
assemble	bide	cap	clothe	damage	disinherit
assert	blackmail	capitalize	clump	dart	dislocate
assess	blame	capsize	coagulate	dash	dislodge
assign	blast	carve	coast	deactivate	dismiss
assist	blat	catalogue	cock	debrief	disorient
associate	blaze	caucus	coil	decay	display
assume	bleach	caution	collate	decline	dispute
assure	bleed	cease	collide	decompress	disqualify
attach	blend	celebrate	combine	decree	disregard
attack	bless	cement	command	dedicate	disrespect
attempt	blind	censor	commem-	deduct	disrobe
attend	block	center	orate	deepen	disrupt
attract	bloom	certify	commence	deface	dissatisfy
attribute	blow	chain	commend	deform	dissect
auction		challenge	complement	defy	distinguish

Reminders (continued)

distract	evaluate	forerun	guzzle	inform	mate
distress	evaporate	forfeit	**H**	inherit	materialize
distribute	evict	formalize	hack	initiate	mature
distrust	exaggerate	freewheel	halt	inject	maximize
disturb	excavate	freeze	handcuff	insist	measure
diversify	exceed	frighten	handicap	inspect	mechanize
divorce	excel	frost	hanker	instruct	medicate
donate	except	froth	hash	insult	melt
doodle	exchange	frustrate	haul	insure	mention
doom	exclaim	fulfill	heal	intend	miff
double-	exclude	function	heft	interfere	minimize
check	exhume	fuss	hemorrhage	interrupt	miscopy
double-cross	exile	**G**	hesitate	interview	miscount
double-dip	expedite	gag	hibernate	irrigate	miscue
doze	expel	gain	hightail	irritate	misdate
drain	expend	gallop	hijack	itch	misemploy
dramatize	expire	gamble	hike	itemize	misfile
drape	expose	gash	hire	**J**	misfire
drawl	extend	generalize	hiss	jerk	misinterpret
dread	externalize	gesture	hole (up)	jiggle	misjudge
drizzle	extort	gibber	holler	jingle	mislabel
drown	extradite	giggle	honk	jinx	mislay
duck	**F**	glad-hand	hook	jitter	mislead
duplicate	facilitate	glamorize	hoot	join	misplace
E	fade	glance	howl	jot	misplay
eavesdrop	fake	glare	huff	judge	misprint
egg (on)	falsify	glaze	hulk	junk	mispro-
elect	familiarize	glitter	hull	justify	nounce
eliminate	fantasize	gnash	humidify	**K**	misquote
embezzle	fascinate	gobble	hunt	kibitz	misread
emigrate	feast	goof	hydrate	kink	misspell
emphasize	fetch	gore	hypnotize	**L**	mistake
enable	finagle	gorge	**I**	land	mistrust
enact	finesse	govern	identify	launder	misunder-
enclose	fizzle	grab	ignore	lease	stand
endanger	flabbergast	grade	illustrate	lecture	modernize
endeavor	flake	graduate	imagine	legislate	mooch
energize	flank	graft	imitate	license	motivate
enforce	flatten	graph	immigrate	limit	motorize
engage	flavor	grease	immunize	link	munch
engrave	flick	greet	impersonate	litigate	**N**
enlarge	flip	grieve	imply	litter	nationalize
enlighten	float	grind	import	load	navigate
enslave	flock	grip	impress	lob	necessitate
envy	flood	gripe	improve	locate	neglect
equalize	flop	grit	inbreed	lust	negotiate
equate	flow	groan	include	**M**	nip
equip	flush	group	inconven-	maintain	nitpick
erase	foam	grunt	ience	manage	nod
escape	focus	guarantee	increase	manufacture	nominate
escort	fold	guard	indent	march	normalize
estimate	foliate	guide	indicate	mark	notice
evacuate	forecast	gulp	individualize	master	notify
	foreclose	gust	influence	match	

Reminders (continued)

O	overcomp-	participate	pretest	refer	rule
obey	ensate	pat	prevent	refine	**S**
object	overcrowd	pause	preview	reflect	
obligate	overdevelop	paw	proceed	refresh	sag
observe	overdo	peek	process	refund	sail
obtain	overdraw	peel	procrastinate	refuse	sample
occupy	overdress	penalize	profit	regain	satisfy
occur	overestimate	perceive	progress	register	scare
offend	overexcite	perch	promote	regret	schedule
offer	overexert	perfect	pronounce	regulate	score
officiate	overexpose	perform	prop	reject	scrap
offset	overfeed	permit	propel	relate	scratch
omit	overfill	personalize	propose	relax	screw
operate	overflow	persuade	prorate	relay	scribble
oppose	overhang	pertain	prosecute	release	scrub
orient	overhaul	phase	prosper	relieve	seal
originate	overhear	(in/out)	protect	remain	search
outargue	overheat	philosophize	protest	remake	seat
outbid	overlap	phrase	provide	remark	secure
outbluff	overlay	pin	publicize	remove	seek
outdo	overload	pinch	pump	renegotiate	segregate
outdraw	overlook	pity	punish	renew	select
outfit	overmatch	place	pursue	repay	sense
outflank	overorganize	plaster	puzzle	repeat	sentence
outlast	overpay	please	**Q**	replace	separate
outlive	overpopulate	pledge	qualify	reply	settle
outplay	overpower	plop	quarantine	report	shake
outrank	overproduce	plot	question	represent	shape
outrun	overrule	plow	quiet (down)	reproduce	share
outsell	oversell	pluck	quiz	request	shine
outshine	overshoot	plug	quote	require	shock
outshoot	oversleep	poke	**R**	rescue	shrink
outsleep	overspend	police	race	research	simplify
outsmart	overspill	polish	raise	reserve	sip
outstare	overspread	pop	rate	resign	skip
outstay	overstate	popularize	ration	resist	slam
outswear	overstay	populate	rationalize	respect	slap
outtalk	overstep	position	rattle	respond	slice
outthrow	overstock	possess	react	restore	slide
outvote	overstudy	post	realize	restrain	slip
outwait	overstuff	postdate	reason	restrict	slit
outwalk	oversub-	postpone	reassure	resume	slop
outwear	scribe	pound	rebel	reveal	slope
outweigh	oversupply	pour	recalculate	reverse	slosh
outwork	overthrow	practice	recite	review	slug
(out, over,	overuse	praise	reclassify	revise	slurp
under, etc.	overweigh	preach	reconsider	reward	smash
are endless	overwork	prearrange	reconstruct	rinse	sniff
as prefixes)	**P**	predict	recover	rip	snoop
overbid	pack	prefer	recruit	risk	snort
overbuild	package	prepackage	recycle	rub	soak
overbuy	panic	pressure	redevelop	ruin	soar
overcharge	park	pretend	redirect		sob
overcome					socialize

Reminders (continued)

soil	subdivide	transfer	upstage
solve	subscribe	transform	**V**
sort	subsidize	translate	vacate
sound	substitute	transplant	vaccinate
spare	subtitle	transport	value
sparkle	subtract	treat	vandalize
specialize	suck	trespass	vanish
specify	suffer	trim	vary
spill	suffocate	trip	verbalize
spin	suggest	trot	verify
splash	summarize	tuck	veto
split	supervise	tug	vibrate
spoil	support	**U**	victimize
sponsor	suppose	uncover	view
spot	surrender	underbid	violate
sprain	surround	underbuy	visit
spray	survey	undercharge	visualize
spread	survive	undergo	vocalize
spring	suspect	underpay	volunteer
sprinkle	suspend	underprice	voyage
spy	swear	underquote	**W**
squash	sweep	underrate	wad
squeak	swing	undertake	waddle
squeeze	**T**	undervalue	wade
squirt	table	undress	wag
stab	tack	unfasten	wake
stabilize	tackle	unfold	warn
stack	tag	unite	wave
stain	tap	unload	wed
stall	tattle	unplug	welcome
stamp	tear	unroll	whine
stampede	tease	unscrew	whip
standardize	testify	unseal	whisper
stare	theorize	unsnap	whistle
station	threaten	unstick	whiten
steal	tighten	untangle	widen
steer	tip	untie	wiggle
stereotype	title	untune	wine (and
stockpile	toast	untwist	dine)
strain	tolerate	unwind	wink
strangle	toot	unwrap	winterize
strap	top	unwrinkle	wipe
stretch	torture	unzip	**Y**
strip	toss	upgrade	yank
struggle	tow	uphold	yawn
stuff	trade	uplift	yell
stump	train	upset	**Z**
subcontract	transcribe		zip

Mind Provokers

(Less Easily Recalled Verbs: An Alphabetical List of About 2,000)

A	annihilate	befog	brood	cohabit	converge
abandon	annotate	beget	browse	cohere	convey
abate	anoint	begrudge	buckle	coincide	correlate
abet	antagonize	belabor	budge	collaborate	correspond
abhor	appall	belie	bundle	collapse	corroborate
abjure	appease	belittle	bungle	collude	corrode
abort	append	bemoan	buoy	commingle	counter-
abridge	apprehend	bemuse	burden	commiserate	reply
abscond	apprise	benumb	burnish	compel	countermand
absolve	arouse	beseech	bustle	compensate	countervail
abuse	array	beset	butcher	compile	covet
abut	arrest	besmirch	buttress	complement	cower
accede	ascend	bestow	bypass	comply	cradle
accentuate	ascertain	betray	**C**	compound	craft
acclimate	ascribe	bewail	cajole	comprehend	crave
accost	aspire	bewilder	calcify	compress	crest
accrue	assail	bicker	camouflage	conceal	crimp
acquiesce	assault	bilk	canvass	concede	cringe
adhere	assimilate	bind	capitulate	conciliate	cripple
adjoin	assuage	bisect	captivate	concoct	crisscross
admonish	astonish	blanch	capture	concur	crucify
adorn	astound	blaspheme	careen	condescend	crumble
adulterate	atone	blazon	carom	confer	crusade
advocate	atrophy	blemish	carouse	confiscate	crystallize
affiliate	attain	bloat	carp	conform	cull
affirm	attenuate	blot	cast	confound	culminate
affix	attest	bludgeon	castigate	confute	cultivate
afflict	attune	blunder	catapult	congeal	curb
afford	augment	blunt	censure	congest	curry (favor)
affront	avail	blur	chafe	conjoin	curtail
aggrandize	avenge	blurt	champion	conjure	cushion
aggravate	avert	boast	char	connive	cycle
agitate	**B**	bob	cherish	connote	**D**
agonize	backpedal	bode (evil;	chide	consecrate	dab
alert	badger	well)	churn	consign	dabble
alienate	baffle	boggle	circumscribe	console	dampen
alight	balk	bolster	circumvent	consolidate	dangle
align	balloon	bolt	cite	consort	daub
allay	ban	bond	clamber	conspire	daunt
alleviate	banish	boost	clamor	consternate	dawdle
allocate	banter	bore	cleanse	constrain	dazzle
allot	barge	bound	cleave	constrict	debase
allude	barricade	boycott	cloak	construe	debauch
amalgamate	bask	brace	cloister	consume	debilitate
amass	batch	bracket	cloud	consummate	debunk
amble	bathe	brand	clutch	contaminate	decelerate
ambulate	batten	brandish	coalesce	contemplate	decimate
ameliorate	batter	breach	coax	contend	decipher
amend	bedazzle	brew	coddle	contort	decry
amplify	bedevil	bridge	codify	contravene	deduce
anchor	befall	bristle	coerce	controvert	defame
animate	befit	broach	cogitate	convalesce	defect

Mind Provokers (continued)

defer (to)	disable	divert	embody	envelop	fashion
defile	disabuse (of)	divest	embolden	envision	fathom
deflate	disaffect	divine	embrace	epitomize	favor
deflect	disallow	divulge	embroil	equilibrate	fawn
defraud	disarm	dodder	emend	equivocate	faze
defray	disassociate	dodge	emerge	eradicate	feature
degenerate	disavow	doff	emit	erode	feign
degrade	discern	dole (out)	emote	err	fend (off)
deign	discharge	dominate	empathize	erupt	ferry
deject	disclaim	don	empower	escalate	fester
deliberate	discomfit	dote	emulate	eschew	festoon
delineate	disconcert	douse	encapsulate	espouse	fetter
delude	discredit	dredge	encase	estrange	feud
deluge	discriminate	drench	enchant	etch	fidget
delve	disdain	dribble	encircle	evade	filibuster
demean	disembark	drift	encompass	eventuate	filter
demolish	disenchant	drone	encounter	eviscerate	flag
demonize	disencumber	droop	encroach	evoke	flail
demur	disenfranch-	drub	enculturate	evolve	flap
denigrate	ise	drudge	encumber	exacerbate	flare
denote	disengage	dub	endorse	exalt	flash
denounce	disentangle	dun	endow	exasperate	flaunt
denude	disenthrall	dwarf	endure	excise	flee
deprave	disestablish	dwell	enervate	excoriate	fleece
depict	disfigure	dwindle	enfeeble	exculpate	flesh (out)
deplete	disgruntle	**E**	enfold	exemplify	flex
deplore	dishabituate	earmark	engender	exert	flinch
deploy	dishearten	ease	engross	exhaust	fling
depose	dishevel	ebb	engulf	exhibit	flirt (with)
deprecate	disincline	echo	enhance	exhilarate	flit
depredate	disintegrate	edge	enlist	exhort	flog
derange	disinter	edify	enliven	exonerate	flounce
deride	disjoin	efface	enmesh	exorcize	flout
derive	dismantle	effuse	ennoble	expand	flower
derogate	dismay	eject	enrage	expatiate	fluctuate
desecrate	disparage	eke	enrapture	expiate	fluster
desiccate	dispatch	elaborate	ensconce	explicate	flutter
desist	dispel	elapse	enshrine	exploit	foil
despair	dispense	elate	ensue	expound	foist (on;
despoil	disperse	elevate	ensure	expropriate	upon)
despond	dispirit	elicit	entail	expunge	foment
deter	displace	elide	entangle	extinguish	fondle
deteriorate	dispossess	elongate	enthrall	extirpate	forage
detest	disprove	elucidate	enthrone	extol	forbid
detract	disseminate	elude	enthuse	extract	forebode
devastate	dissent	emaciate	entice	extrapolate	foredoom
deviate	disserve	emanate	entitle	extricate	forefeel
devolve	dissipate	emancipate	entrap	extrude	forejudge
devour	dissociate	emasculate	entreat	exuberate	foreknow
differentiate	dissuade	embark	entrench	exude	foreordain
diffuse	distend	embed	entrust	**F**	foresee
digress	distill	embellish	entwine	fabricate	foreshadow
dilapidate	distort	embitter	enumerate	falter	foreshow
dilute	diverge	emblazon	enunciate	fare	forestall

Mind Provokers (continued)

foretaste	glean	herd	implant	institute	jeer
foretell	glide	hew	implicate	insulate	jell
forewarn	glimpse	highlight	implode	integrate	jeopardize
forge	glint	hinder	implore	intensify	jest
forgo	glisten	hinge	impose	intercede	jettison
formulate	gloat	hint	impound	intercept	jibe
forsake	glorify	hitch	impoverish	interchange	jilt
forswear	gloss (over)	hoard	impregnate	interconnect	jockey
fortify	glower	hobble	imprint	interject	jog
foster	glut	hobnob	improvise	interlace	jolt
foul	gnarl	(with)	impugn	interlock	jostle
founder	gnaw	hoist	impute	interlope	journey
fracture	goad	hone	incapacitate	intermingle	jubilate
fragment	gouge	honor	incarcerate	intermit	juggle
frame	gradate	horrify	incense	intermix	jumble
frazzle	grant	hose	inch	interpolate	jut
fret	grapple	hound	incinerate	interpose	**K**
fringe	grasp	house	incise	interrelate	key
fritter	grate (on)	hover	incite	interrogate	kindle
(away)	gratify	huddle	incline	intersect	knead
frolic	gravitate	hug	incorporate	intersperse	knit
front	graze	hum	incriminate	intertwine	knot
fulminate	grimace	humble	incubate	intervene	knuckle
(against)	groom	humiliate	inculcate	interweave	(down;
fumble	grope	hunker	indemnify	intimate	under)
fume	grouse	(down)	indict	intimidate	**L**
funnel	grovel	hurdle	indispose	intone	label
furnish	grumble	hurl	induce	intoxicate	labor
fuse	gurgle	hurtle	induct	intrigue	lace
G	gush	hush	indulge	introspect	lacerate
gall	gyrate	hustle	inebriate	intrude	lack
gallivant	**H**	hypothesize	infect	inundate	lade(n)
galvanize	habituate	**I**	infer	inure (to)	lag
gape	haggle	idealize	infest	invade	lambaste
garble	hail	idle	infiltrate	invalidate	lament
garner	hallucinate	idolize	inflame	inveigh	lance
garnish	hammer	ignite	inflate	(against)	languish
gasp (out;	hamper	ill-treat	inflect	invert	lap
forth)	harangue	illuminate	inflict	invest	lapse
gather	harass	image	infringe	invoke	lash
gauge	harbor	imbibe	infuriate	irk	latch (onto)
gawk	harden	imbrue	infuse	irrupt	laud
gaze	harness	imbue	ingrain	isolate	launch
gear	harp	immerse	ingratiate	issue	lavish
generate	harry	immobilize	inhabit	iterate	layer
genuflect	harvest	immortalize	inhere	**J**	leach
germinate	hasten	impair	inhibit	jab	leak
gerrymander	hatch	impale	innervate	jabber	lean
gestate	haunt	impart	inoculate	jam	leap
gesticulate	heap	impeach	insinuate	jampack	leash
gild	heave	impede	inspire	jangle	leech (onto)
gird	hedge	impel	install	jar	leer
gladden	heed	impend	instigate	jaundice	legitimate
gleam	hem (& haw)	impinge	instill	jaunt	lend

Mind Provokers (continued)

level	mash	mishandle	mystify	outwit	perforate
levitate	mask	mishear	**N**	overarch	perish
levy	masquerade	misinform	nag	overawe	perk (up)
liberate	massacre	misknow	nauseate	overbalance	permeate
lilt	massage	mislocate	needle	overbear	permute
linger	mastermind	mismanage	negate	overburden	perpetrate
lionize	mat	mismatch	neologize	overgrow	perpetuate
liquefy	maul	misname	nestle	overindulge	persecute
liquidate	maunder	misremem-	net	overjoy	persevere
loaf	meander	ber	neutralize	overrate	persist
loath	meddle	misreport	nick	overreach	personify
lobby	mediate	misrepresent	niggle	override	perturb
lodge	meld	missend	nominalize	overrun	peruse
loft	memorialize	misshape	nourish	oversee	pervade
log	menace	misspeak	nudge	overtake	pervert
loiter	mend	misspend	nullify	overtax	pester
loll	merge	misstate	numerate	overtire	petrify
lollygag	merit	misteach	nurse	overturn	piddle
loom	mesh	mistreat	nurture	overwhelm	(away)
loop	mesmerize	misuse	nuzzle	overwrite	piece
loot	mete (out)	misvalue	**O**		(together)
lop	migrate	miswrite	obfuscate	**P**	pierce
lope	militate (for;	mitigate	oblige	pace	pilfer
lounge	against)	moan	obliterate	pacify	pillage
lubricate	mill	mob	obscure	pad	pioneer
lug	(around)	mobilize	obsess	paint	pique
lull	mimic	mock	obstruct	pair	pit (against)
lump	mince	moderate	obtrude	palaver	pitch
lunge	mingle	modify	obvert	pale	pivot
lurch	minify	modulate	obviate	palpitate	placate
lure	mire	moil	occlude	pamper	plague
lurk	misapply	moisten	ooze	pander	plateau
luxuriate	misappre-	mold	opine	pant	plead
lynch	hend	molest	oppress	paraphrase	plod
M	misapprop-	mollify	opt (for)	parlay	plumb
machinate	riate	monitor	orate	parley	plummet
magnify	misbehave	monopolize	ordain	parody	plunder
maim	misbelieve	moon	ornament	part	plunge
malfunction	miscalculate	mortify	oscillate	partition	ply
malign	miscarry	mound	ossify	patch	poise
malinger	miscast	mount	ostracize	patronize	polarize
malleate	mischoose	mourn	oust	patter	poll
manacle	miscolor	mow	outdistance	pattern	pollute
mandate	misconceive	muddle	outgrow	(after)	ponder
maneuver	misconstrue	muffle	outmaneuver	pave	pontificate
mangle	miscounsel	mull (over)	outmatch	peak	pool
manifest	misdeem	multiply	outmode	peal	portend
manipulate	misderive	mumble	outrage	peddle	portray
map	misdescribe	murmur	outreach	peep	pose
mar	misdirect	muse	outsoar	peer	postulate
maraud	misdo	muster	outspan	peeve	posture
marinate	misestimate	mutate	outstretch	pelt	pounce
maroon	misgovern	mutilate	outthink	penetrate	pout
marvel	misguide	muzzle	outweep	perambulate	prance
				percolate	

150

Mind Provokers (continued)

prattle	prolong	ransom	rehash	resound	ruffle
precede	promenade	rant	reign	respire	rumble
precipitate	prompt	rap	reimburse	resurface	ruminate
preclude	promulgate	rarefy	rein (in)	resurge	rummage
preconceive	propagate	rasp	reinforce	resurrect	rumple
precondition	prophesy	ravage	reiterate	resuscitate	rupture
predate	propitiate	raze	rejoice	retain	rush
predestine	propound	reactivate	rejoin	retaliate	rustle
predicate	proscribe	ream	rejuvenate	retard	**S**
predispose	protract	reanimate	relegate	retire	sabotage
predominate	protrude	reap	relent	retort	sack
preempt	provoke	reapportion	relinquish	retrace	sacrifice
preen	prowl	rebound	relish	retract	sadden
preexist	pry	rebuff	remand	retreat	saddle
prefabricate	puff	rebuke	remedy	retrench	salivate
preface	pulsate	rebut	reminisce	retrieve	salute
prefigure	pulverize	recalcitrate	remit	retroact	salvage
preform	pummel	recant	remonstrate	retrogress	salve
preincline	punctuate	recap	remunerate	revamp	sanctify
preindicate	purge	recapitulate	rend	revel	sanction
preinform	purify	recapture	render	reverberate	sanitize
preinstruct	purport	recede	rendezvous	revere	sap
prejudge	purvey	recess	renege	revert	sate
prelimit	putrefy	reciprocate	renounce	revile	satiate
premeditate	**Q**	reclaim	renovate	revive	satirize
preoccupy	quaff	recline	repair	revoke	saturate
preordain	quake	recoil	repatriate	revolt	saunter
prepossess	quarrel	recompose	repel	revolve	savor
prerelease	quaver	reconcile	repent	rhapsodize	scale
prerequire	quell	reconstitute	rephrase	rid	scamper
presage	quench	recount	replenish	ridicule	scan
prescribe	query	recoup	replicate	rigidify	scandalize
preselect	quibble	recreate	repose	rile	scar
preserve	quicken	re-create	repossess	ring	scatter
preside	quip	recriminate	reprehend	riot	scavenge
press	quiver	rectify	repress	ripen	scheme
presume	**R**	recuperate	reprieve	ripple	school
presuppose	rack	recur	reprimand	rise	scintillate
prevail	radiate	redeem	reprise	rival	scoff
prevaricate	rage	redeploy	reproach	roam	scold
prey	raid	redouble	reprove	roar	scoop
prime	rail (at;	redress	repudiate	rob	scorch
primp	against)	reduce	repulse	rock	scorn
prize	rake (over;	reform	repute	roister	scour
probe	through)	refrain	requite	romanticize	scourge
proclaim	rally	refurbish	rescind	romp	scout
procure	ram	refute	resemble	roost	scowl
prod	ramble	regale	resent	root	scramble
profess	ramify	regard	reset	rot	scrape
prognosti-	rampage	regenerate	reshape	rotate	scrawl
cate	ramrod	regiment	reside	rouse	screech
prohibit	range	regress	resolve	rout	screen
project	rank	regurgitate	resonate	routinize	scrimp
proliferate	rankle	rehabilitate	resort	rove	scroll

Mind Provokers (continued)

scrounge	shove	slump	squelch	submerse	tailor
scrunch	shower	slur	squint	submit	taint
scrutinize	shriek	smack	squirm	subordinate	tally
scuff	shroud	small-talk	stage	subside	tamp
scuffle	shrug	smear	stagger	subsist	tangle
sculpt	shuffle	smirk	stagnate	substantiate	tantalize
scurry	shun	smite	stake	subsume	taper (off)
scuttle	shunt	sneer	stalk	subvert	tar
sear	shutter	snicker	stammer	succumb	tarnish
season	shuttle	sniffle	stanch	suffuse	tarry
secede	side (with;	snip	startle	sulk	tatter
seclude	against)	snipe	stash	summon	taunt
secrete	sideline	snivel	stave (off)	super-	teem
secularize	sideswipe	snub	steel	annuate	telescope
sedate	sidle	snuggle	steep	supercharge	temper
seduce	(lay) siege	sock (in;	stem	supererogate	terminate
seep	(to)	away)	stifle	superimpose	terrorize
seesaw	sift	soft-pedal	stigmatize	superintend	thaw
seethe	sigh	sojourn	stimulate	super-	thicken
segment	sight	solemnize	sting	saturate	thin (out)
segue	signal	solicit	stipulate	superscribe	thirst
seize	signify	solidify	stock	supersede	thrash
[self-govern]	silence	souse	stoke	supplant	thread
[self-inflict]	simmer	space	stoop	supplicate	thresh (out;
[self-teach]	simulate	span	storm	suppress	over)
etc., though most compound words beginning with self are not verbs	singe	spar	stow	surge	thrill
	sinuate	spatter	straddle	surmise	thrive
	siphon	spawn	strafe	surmount	throb
	situate	spearhead	straggle	surpass	throng
sensitize	sketch	speculate	strand	sustain	throttle
sentimental-	skew	spew	stratify	swagger	thrust
ize	skewer	spice	stray	swamp	thunder
sequester	skid	spiral	streak	swap	thwart
sermonize	skim	spite	stream	swarm	tilt
sever	skimp	splatter	stress	swash	tinge
shackle	skirt	splay	strew	swat	tingle
shade	skitter	splice	stride	sway	tinker
shadow	skulk	splinter	string	swell	tinkle
shag	slacken	splurge	strive	swelter	titillate
shame	slander	sprawl	stroke	swerve	titter
shatter	slant	sprout	stroll	swill	toddle
shave	slash	spruce (up)	strove	swindle	toe (in)
shear	slate	spur	structure	swirl	toggle
shed	slaughter	spurn	strut	swish	toil
sheer	slay	spurt	stultify	switch	topple
shelter	slight	sputter	stumble	swivel	torment
shelve	sling	squabble	stun	swoon	totter
shield	slink	squall	stupefy	swoop	tousle
shift	slither	squander	stylize	synchronize	tout
shimmer	slobber	square	stymie	syncopate	tower
shirk	slouch	(with)	subdue	synthesize	toy
shiver	slough (off)	squat	subjugate	systemize	trace
shoo	sluice	squawk	sublimate	**T**	track
shoulder	slumber	squeal	submerge	tabulate	traduce

Mind Provokers (continued)

trail	tussle	unglue	usher	waiver	whirl
trample (on;	twinkle	unhand	(in; out)	waken	whisk
upon; over)	twirl	unhinge	usurp	wall	whitewash
tranquilize	twist	unlearn	*utilize	wallop	whittle
transact	twitch	unleash	utter	wallow	whoop
transcend	twitter	unloose	**V**	waltz	wield
transfigure	typify	unmask	vacillate	wander	wile
transfix	tyrannize	unmuzzle	validate	wane	will
transfuse	**U**	unnerve	vanquish	wangle	wilt
transgress	unbend	unpile	vaporize	ward (off)	wince
transmit	unbind	unravel	variegate	warm	wind
transpire	unblock	unreel	varnish	warp	winnow
transpose	unbridle	unruffle	vault	warrant	wither
traumatize	unburden	unsaddle	vaunt	water	witness
traverse	unclog	unscramble	veer	(down)	wobble
tread	undercut	unseam	vegetate	water-soak	worm
treasure	under-	unseat	veil	waver	wrangle
trek	develop	unsettle	venerate	wax	wreak
tremble	under-	unshackle	ventilate	weaken	wrench
trickle	estimate	unsheathe	venture	wean	wrest
trifle (away)	underexpose	unshroud	vest	weasel	wriggle
trifurcate	undergird	unsnarl	vex	weather	writhe
trigger	underlay	unteach	vilify	weave	**Y**
triplicate	underlie	unthink	vindicate	wedge	yammer
trisect	undermine	untuck	vitalize	weep	yaw
triumph	under-	unveil	vitiate	weigh	yearn
trivialize	nourish	upend	vivify	weld	yelp
troop	underpin	upheave	vociferate	well (up)	yield
trounce	underpraise	upraise	vouch	wend	yowl
trudge	underscore	uprear	vow	wheedle	**Z**
trump (up)	understate	uprise	vulgarize	wheel	zag
trumpet	undo	uproot	**W**	whet	zig
truncate	undulate	upsurge	waft	whiffle	zig-zag
trundle	unearth	upturn	wage	while	zing
tumble	unfetter	urge	wail	(away)	zoom
	unfurl		waive	whimper	

* *Utilize* is a word you might want to avoid altogether. Its original meaning, "convert to usefulness," has long-since been driven into obscurity by widespread use of *utilize* as a pretentious substitute for *use* (even modern dictionary writers have finally succumbed). Your readers will appreciate your writing *use* when that is what you mean. You will spare them the extra two syllables, the pretentious sound, and the fuzzy meaning.

A LIST OF TROUBLESOME WORDS

What Is This List and How Can You Use It Well?

This appendix is an alphabetical list of words and short phrases I see misused or poorly used by students and business professionals. Some words shown here have appeared on similar lists throughout the ages, as in Flesch's *How to Be Brief* (1962), Bernstein & Barzun's *Watch Your Language* (1976, 1965), and Strunk & White's *Elements of Style* (2000, 1979, 1972, 1959,). The criterion for entry here is for me to have noticed misuse during my decades as an advisor for graduate research projects and a writing clinician for businesses.

You may want to **study this information-rich material in small batches**. Some entries, even though they appear simple on the surface, call for concentrated thought (see *and* or *however*). I recommend that you keep track of your progress. For example, you might place one of the following symbols in the margin of your book as you read each entry the first time. Those symbols would then keep you aware of where you stand with each term, and as you restudy entries over time you could build from — to ++. Probably you will eliminate a great number of entries with ++ at the outset

++	I use this correctly.
+—	I am inconsistent.
—	I use this incorrectly.
?	I disagree or do not understand.

By using this appendix in such a systematic way, you'll begin to build a personal dictionary. As you come across other words that are troublesome to you, either because of incorrect usage or unfamiliarity, enter those words with their definition and a sample sentence onto the blank pages (pp. 245–246) that follow Appendix D. In time you'll have, in a convenient place between here and the index of this book, a personal account of word-use that you can refer to periodically to enhance your working vocabulary.

Another approach would be to use the alphabetical list on the next page to predict what I have to say about each word before you read the corresponding entry. Such pre-reading experimentation might make learning more vivid and enduring.

Orientation to the List

Some of the 140 entries in this list have been presented earlier in the book, and four are elaborated upon extensively in Appendix C (pp. 196–201). I chose to present all of them again here, along with entries that do not appear elsewhere (the preponderance of the list), to make this a complete independent reference for frequently seen troublesome words.

Words commonly mistaken for each other are entered with a not-equal sign (≠) between them. A bee (🐝) marks "buzzwords," so called because they are typically brought to mind for their familiar sound more than for the value of their meaning.

Weaning yourself from the 22 buzzwords on this list may frustrate you at first. You may feel confined—deprived of some old friends. But in time you'll realize that you suffer greater confinement and deprivation from **using** those buzzwords than you do from avoiding them. Their use confines you and your readers to shallow, general labels, and it deprives you and your readers of the rich, specific, meaningful descriptions that good thinking generates.

Misuses of each word are shown in the left column and **revisions are shown in the corresponding right column**, with key words underlined. To accommodate your search for specific entries, I've cross-referenced pairs of words that are alphabetically distant from each other.

Words and Phrases Contained in the List

above, below, over, under
access (as a verb)
address (as a verb)
affect ≠ effect
aggravate ≠ irritate
allow ≠ enable
all ready ≠ already
all together ≠ altogether
allude ≠ elude
allusion ≠ illusion
alternative ≠ alternate ≠ option
amount ≠ number
and
another
anticipate ≠ expect
anxious ≠ eager
any and all
any way ≠ anyway
appraise ≠ apprise
approximately, about
area
around ≠ about
assist ≠ help
as well as
before
beside ≠ besides
between ≠ among
both ≠ each
center around, focus around (coined titles)
compliment ≠ complement
comprise ≠ constitute

concern
confront
consequently, subsequently, therefore
continual ≠ continuous
correlation
counsel ≠ council
currently ≠ presently
deal with, dealt with
determine
diagnose
different, separate
different than ≠ different from
dilemma ≠ problem
discover
discussed, discussion
disinterested ≠ uninterested
divided
done
eminent ≠ imminent
enormity
equally
essential, necessary
everyday ≠ every day
exists
experience (as a verb)
farther ≠ further
feel ≠ believe
finalize
firstly, secondly, etc.
flaunt ≠ flout
flush out ≠ flesh out

however
i.e. ≠ e.g.
if and when
impact (as a verb)
implement (as a verb)
imply ≠ infer
importantly
in ≠ into
include
individual
initiative
input
insure ≠ ensure
integrate ≠ incorporate
involve
it's ≠ its
latter ≠ last
lay ≠ lie
less ≠ fewer
leverage (as a verb)
like ≠ as
limited
literally ≠ virtually
look at, look to, look for
lots of, a lot of
maximum ≠ optimum
may, might
metrics
mute ≠ moot
myself ≠ me, I
nor
often
one and the same
ongoing
only
onset ≠ outset
pension ≠ penchant
people ≠ persons
pinch hit
plus
possess
potentially

principle ≠ principal
process
proximity
reason, because
reason why
relatively
resiliency
resources
result in
revisit
share in common
significance, significant
since ≠ because
site
some time ≠ sometime
stationery ≠ stationary
statue ≠ statute ≠ stature
taunt ≠ taut
tenant ≠ tenet
that
that, which
the
the ≠ a, an
this, these
torturous ≠ tortuous
unknown
upcoming
update
utilize, utilization
veritable
very
where ≠ in which, for which, to which, by which, through which
whether or not
would
would have ≠ had

about (see **approximately** and **around**)

above, below, over, under

Literally, these words signify location. Used figuratively, they may displace stronger, more precise terms.

NO Profits are <u>above</u> what was expected.	**YES** Profits are <u>greater than</u> expected.
All means were <u>over</u> 24.5.	All means <u>exceeded</u> 24.5.
The rise in temperature was <u>under</u> (or <u>below</u>) five degrees.	The rise in temperature was <u>less than</u> five degrees.

access

As a verb, this term is clumsy and imprecise (though gaining acceptance). Use it exclusively as a noun for best results. ("Do you have direct access from the parking lot?").

NO How do you <u>access</u> your files?	**YES** How do you
	   - <u>open</u> your files?
	   - <u>enter</u> your files?
	   - <u>retrieve</u> your files?

	What access do you have to your files?
He <u>accessed</u> the voting machine with help from the precinct captain.	He <u>opened</u> the voting machine with help from the precinct captain.
Access used effectively as a noun ⟶	Do you have <u>access</u> to those files?

address (see also p. 44)

Except for such specific phrases as "address the envelopes" and "address the crowd," _address_ as a verb creates weak generalizations.

NO We need to <u>address</u> the problem of poor attendance.	**YES** We need to <u>solve</u> the problem of poor attendance.
	We need to <u>investigate</u> the reasons for poor attendance.
	We need to <u>induce</u> members to be more diligent about their attendance.

affect ≠ effect

Generally, _affect_ is a verb and _effect_ is a noun.

NO The rain did not effect our plans.	**YES** The rain did not affect our plans.

For occasional cases when the reverse is true, *affect* as a noun (accent on the first syllable) means *feeling* or *emotion* (Children need art and music for the affect.). *Effect* as a verb means *make happen* (I did effect a change.). Both of these uses are rare compared to *affect* as a verb and *effect* as a noun.

aggravate ≠ irritate

Think of irritation as typically preceding aggravation. To irritate is to annoy (psychologically) or to chafe or inflame (physically). To aggravate is to make the irritation worse or more severe; to intensify.

NO   His late arrival <u>aggravated</u> me.

YES   His late arrival <u>irritated</u> me.

She has been badgered enough. The last thing she needs is the <u>irritation</u> of being asked again.

She has been badgered enough. The last thing she needs is the <u>aggravation</u> of being asked again.

Tight clothing will <u>irritate</u> your sunburn problem.

Tight clothing will <u>aggravate</u> your sunburn problem. (Note: The sun did the irritating; the clothing will do the aggravating.)

Note: An action can begin as an irritation, and grow into aggravation with repetition.

allow ≠ enable

Do not use the more-common term *allow* (give permission) in place of the less-common term *enable* (give power, means, competence, or ability) where *enable* is more precise. To do so is to err by understatement.

NO   The course is demanding, but completing it will <u>allow</u> me to be a valuable assistant to our chief financial officer.

YES   The course is demanding, but completing it will <u>enable</u> me to be a valuable assistant to our chief financial officer.

all ready ≠ already

All ready means *completely prepared.*   *Already* means *previously.*

NO   That department is <u>already</u> to be moved.

YES   That department is <u>all ready</u> to be moved.

We <u>all ready</u> moved that department.

We <u>already</u> moved that department.

all together ≠ altogether

All together means *simultaneously. Altogether* means *wholly* or *completely*," as in "I am not altogether confident that we are doing the right thing."

NO   Now I want you to meet <u>altogether</u>.

YES   Now I want you to meet <u>all together</u>.

He has not handled the personnel problems <u>all together</u> well.

He has not handled the personnel problems <u>altogether</u> well.

allude ≠ elude

To *allude* is to make an indirect reference (an allusion). To *elude* is to escape attention, either physically or intellectually.

NO She was <u>eluding</u> to what I said yesterday.

YES She was <u>alluding</u> to what I said yesterday.

They <u>alluded</u> the police across three states for more than a week.

They <u>eluded</u> the police across three states for more than a week.

I am embarrassed that his embezzlement <u>alluded</u> me for nearly two years.

I am embarrassed that his embezzlement <u>eluded</u> me for nearly two years.

allusion ≠ illusion

An *allusion* is a passing, indirect reference (something alluded to). An *illusion* is an impression that seems real but is not.

NO The <u>illusion</u> he made to Mr. Brooks that I cannot be trusted has devastated me.

YES The <u>allusion</u> he made to Mr. Brooks that I cannot be trusted has devastated me.

The feeling of motion when a car next to you moves is an <u>allusion</u>.

The feeling of motion when a car next to you moves is an <u>illusion</u>.

alternative ≠ alternate ≠ option

An *alternative* is a choice between two possibilities. An *alternate* is a substitute, one available to fill the position of another. An *option* is a choice from among any number of possibilities.

NO We have several <u>alternatives</u>.

YES We have several <u>options</u>.

I see no <u>alternative</u> to what we are doing.

Here is a precise use of *alternative*. ⟶

Maybe you can back up Marian as an <u>alternative</u>.

Maybe you can back up Marian as an <u>alternate</u>.

among (see **between**)

amount ≠ number

Amount refers to volume. *Number* refers to countable quantities. Write about the amount of work, but the number of jobs; the amount of scoring, but the number of points. Also, avoid inserting *amount* into a sentence that is adequate without it, as in the last example.

NO The <u>amount</u> of students registered does not justify hiring a teacher.

I cannot handle the <u>amount</u> of problems I am facing.

Drivers leaving before 5:00 a.m. encounter the least <u>amount of</u> traffic.

YES The <u>number</u> of students registered does not justify hiring a teacher.

I cannot handle the <u>number</u> of problems I am facing.

I cannot handle the <u>amount</u> of trouble I am facing.

Drivers leaving before 5:00 a.m. encounter the least traffic.

and (see also p. 47)

When you use *and*, take into account issues of cause and effect (first example) and subordinate material (second example).

NO He <u>was the best</u> student in his high school class, <u>and earned</u> a full college scholarship.

<u>Betty Bix earned</u> a Ph.D. at Columbia <u>and moved</u> here recently to be with her ailing mother.

YES Being the best student in his high school class, he <u>earned</u> a full college scholarship.

<u>Betty Bix</u>, a Ph.D. graduate of Columbia, <u>moved</u> here recently to be with her ailing mother.

<u>Betty Bix</u>, who moved here recently to be with her ailing mother, <u>is</u> a Ph.D. graduate of Columbia.

In the second example, the lack of relationship between Betty Bix's moving and her having earned a Ph.D. at Columbia requires that the two events not be weighted equally— as the coordinating conjunction *and* implies in the original. The two revisions show that either event might be treated subordinately, depending on the desired emphasis.

another

Join two things with *another* if they are the same in number and kind: X and another X, not X and another Y.

NO Sixteen computers arrived yesterday, and <u>another</u> 10 today.

YES Sixteen computers arrived yesterday, and 10 today.

Sixteen computers arrived yesterday, and <u>another</u> 16 today.

anticipate ≠ expect (see also p. 13)

These words are close in meaning, but *anticipation* implies more forethought and preparation than does *expectation*. I see *anticipate* used commonly where the less-involved *expect* is more precise.

NO I <u>anticipate</u> that the package will arrive tomorrow.

YES I <u>expect</u> the package to arrive tomorrow.

Your reaction is not what I <u>anticipated</u>.

Your reaction is not what I <u>expected</u>.

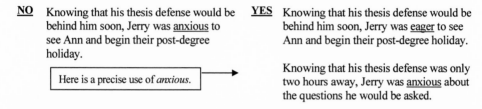

Here is a precise use of *anticipate*.

The other team won because we failed to <u>anticipate</u> their next move.

anxious ≠ eager

Do not use *anxious* where you mean *eager*. Both terms imply anticipation, but anxiety is driven by uneasy apprehension; eagerness by impatient longing.

NO Knowing that his thesis defense would be behind him soon, Jerry was <u>anxious</u> to see Ann and begin their post-degree holiday.

YES Knowing that his thesis defense would be behind him soon, Jerry was <u>eager</u> to see Ann and begin their post-degree holiday.

Here is a precise use of *anxious*.

Knowing that his thesis defense was only two hours away, Jerry was <u>anxious</u> about the questions he would be asked.

any and all
This is a cliché. Choose one term or the other.

any way ≠ anyway

Most circumstances call for *any way*. Use *anyway* only when you mean "in any case" ("The battle is lost anyway").

NO Data collection was difficult <u>anyway</u> we tried.

YES Data collection was difficult <u>any way</u> we tried.

appraise ≠ apprise

To *appraise* is to make a professional estimate of value, as to appraise a home or a diamond ring. Use *apprise* to refer to a notice or a warning.

NO We should <u>appraise</u> him of the changes we made today.

YES We should <u>apprise</u> him of the changes we made today.

approximately, about

Avoid using these terms in a way that makes them redundant to another term (first example, *estimated*) or to a given range (second example, *five to seven years*). In the second case, if the range is too constricting, enlarge it rather than duplicate its function with a redundant term.

NO University enrollment is <u>estimated</u> to be <u>approximately</u> 28,000 next fall.

YES University enrollment is <u>estimated</u> to be 28,000 next fall.

Building it will take <u>about five to seven years</u>.

Building it will take <u>five to seven years</u>.

Building it will take <u>about six years</u>.

Approximately and *about* differ slightly in meaning. *Approximately* means "within reasonable limits of accuracy" (We have approximately a one-inch clearance.). *About* is a more relaxed estimate (Will you be free about 4 o'clock?). Avoid using the five-syllable *approximately* where the two-syllable *about* will do.

🐝 **area** (see also p. 43)

Avoid using *area* to describe anything other than a literal, physical parameter (...the Detroit area; ...the area of the conference room). For greater precision and strength, replace figurative uses with more specific terms.

NO In what <u>area</u> does this belong?	**YES** In what <u>category</u> does this belong?
I need to know more about his <u>area</u> to make a judgment.	I need to know more about his <u>profession</u> to make a judgment.

around ≠ about

These words can be used interchangeably, but the principal meaning of *around* is *encircling*, and the principal meaning of *about* is *near* or *almost*. For greatest precision, avoid using *around* when you mean *about*.

NO By 1:00 o'clock, <u>around</u> 50 persons had gathered in the square.	**YES** By 1:00 o'clock, <u>about</u> 50 persons had gathered in the square.
More than 50 persons had gathered in the square by <u>around</u> 1:00 o'clock.	More than 50 persons had gathered in the square by <u>about</u> 1:00 o'clock.

as (see **like**)

assist ≠ help

The meanings of these words overlap. Still, to *assist* is to lend help or support "especially as a subordinate or supplement," implying that an *assistant* works side by side with one who is the primary source of knowledge or skill. In contrast, to *help* is simply to "provide what is necessary to accomplish a task or satisfy a need." Be precise. Save *assist* for circumstances in which the recipient of the assistance is the primary doer. Use *help*, the broader and simpler term, where someone is just helping to get a job done.

NO I will ask Ed Parker to <u>assist</u> you with the packing and carting in the morning so you can have your office moved by noon.	**YES** I will ask Ed Parker to <u>help</u> you with the packing and carting in the morning so you can have your office moved by noon.
Here is a precise use of *assist*. ⟶	I can assemble the machine in about half a day, but some of the parts are heavy and cumbersome. Can you send someone over to <u>assist</u> me?

as well as ∫see also p. 35)

This cliché sometimes replaces a simple term unnecessarily,

NO	They came with pencils <u>as well as</u> papers in hand.	**YES**	They came with pencils <u>and</u> papers in hand.

It sometimes distorts the truth by implying equality of importance,

NO	Medical quackery threatens the pocketbooks <u>as well as</u> the lives of patients.	**YES**	Medical quackery threatens the pocketbooks, <u>but more important</u>, the lives of patients.

And it sometimes duplicates the function of *both* or *also*.

NO	Higher rates will create a hardship for <u>both</u> the manufacturer of the product <u>as well as</u> the customer.	**YES**	Higher rates will create a hardship For <u>both</u> the manufacturer of the product <u>and</u> the customer.

Rarely do I use *as well as* other than to equate value, as in "He does the job as well as anyone."

because (see **reason, because**; see **since ≠ because**)

before

Either omit the word *before* or follow it with information that answers the question "before what?"

NO	I have never done anything like that <u>before</u>.	**YES**	I have never done anything like that.
			I never did anything like that <u>before</u> I worked with Wilma.

believe (see **feel**; see also p. 46)

below (see **above**)

beside ≠ besides

Though these words look like singular and plural, they carry distinct meanings. Reserve your use of the word *beside* to mean *next to*. If you mean *also* or *except*, the word you need is *besides*.

NO	And he earned a six-figure income <u>beside</u>.	**YES**	And he earned a six-figure income <u>besides</u>.
	<u>Beside</u> that, what complaints do you have?		<u>Besides</u> that, what complaints do you have?

between ≠ among

Between implies a two-party relationship; *among* implies three or more.

NO Debate <u>between</u> the five doctoral committee members ultimately led to passage of the dissertation.

YES Debate <u>among</u> the five doctoral committee members ultimately led to passage of the dissertation.

Here is a precise use of *between*.	➔

The debate <u>between</u> Dr. Schmidt and Dr. Harrington ultimately convinced the committee to pass the dissertation.

both ≠ each

Use *both* to indicate "the two together," and *each* to indicate "the two (or more) separately."

NO He met with <u>both</u> clients for one hour. ⟵ **YES** He met with <u>each</u> client for one hour. (unless he met them jointly)

Do not use *both* where the alternative, one alone, would be impossible.

<u>Both</u> parties resumed talks at midnight.

<u>The</u> two parties resumed talks at midnight.

The talks resumed at midnight.

center around, focus around

Revolve around and *gather around* make sense. *Center around* and *focus around* do not, because *center* and *focus* imply reference to a specific point.

NO Her leadership style was <u>centered around</u> respect for individual skills.

YES Her leadership style was <u>centered on</u> respect for individual skills.

NO Probably he will <u>focus</u> his political campaign <u>around</u> negativism toward his opponent.

YES Probably he will <u>focus</u> his political campaign <u>on</u> negativism toward his opponent.

(coined titles)

Do not turn a descriptive phrase into a proper noun, as if it were part of someone's title.

NO <u>Renowned Jazz Musician</u> Billy Taylor performed at the Main Street Station last night.

YES Billy Taylor, <u>a renowned jazz musician</u>, performed at the Main Street Station last night.

compliment ≠ complement

To *compliment* is to praise or commend, or give as a gratuity. To *complement* is to add to in a way that completes or brings to perfection.

NO He will <u>complement</u> you if you accomplish something outstanding.	**YES** He will <u>compliment</u> you if you accomplish something outstanding.
I mailed your <u>complementary</u> tickets.	I mailed your <u>complimentary</u> tickets.
We hired him as your partner because his strengths <u>compliment</u> yours.	We hired him as your partner because his strengths <u>complement</u> yours.
Please use <u>complimentary</u> colors.	Please use <u>complementary</u> colors.

comprise ≠ constitute

The whole *comprises* (encompasses) the parts; the parts *constitute* (collectively create) the whole. So few readers understand the meaning of the word *comprise* that you might want to use it only where no other term or construction works as well. Good alternate terms are *encompass,* or *embrace*, or *consist of.* Use of *comprise* as shown in the left column has gained some acceptance through prominence, but I would avoid it.

NO Five villages <u>comprise</u> the metropolitan area.	**YES** Five villages <u>constitute</u> the metropolitan area.
	The metropolitan area
	- <u>comprises</u> five villages.
	- <u>encompasses</u> five villages.
	- <u>consists of</u> five villages.

concern

This double-meaning word may confuse readers in any of a number of ways, so use it and its variations with caution. It may leave readers wondering whether it means *involve* or *worry.*

NO Does this <u>concern</u> him?	**YES** Does this <u>involve</u> him?
	Does this <u>worry</u> him?

Sometimes it is used to say not much of anything.

NO Let us reopen discussion of the issues <u>concerning</u> our last meeting.	**YES** Let us reopen discussion of the issues <u>from</u> our last meeting.

Other times it takes on the mysterious quality of an unspecified possession.

NO I regret that some members have <u>concerns</u>.	**YES** I regret the <u>ambivalence</u> of some members.

The word has become so tainted in my mind that I avoid its use except where context is absolutely clear, as in "I am concerned about his poor health."

confront

To use this word in place of *face* or *meet* or *begin* is to make an unintentional over-statement. *Confront* implies assertiveness, aggressiveness, or even combativeness (With truth as his only weapon, he confronted his accuser.).

NO   When the preliminary work I just described is complete, I will <u>confront</u> the data collection stage of my study.

YES   When the preliminary work I just described is complete, I will <u>begin</u> the data collection stage of my study.

consequently, subsequently, therefore

Consequently and *therefore* signal cause-and-effect relationships; *subsequently* does not. *Consequently* means "because of" in the sense of a direct and implicitly unavoidable consequence. *Therefore* means "because of" in the sense of a response. *Subsequently* means simply "afterward."

NO   He annoyed me continually. <u>Consequently</u>, I fired him.

YES   He annoyed me continually. <u>Therefore</u>, I fired him.

He dropped a hot match into the wastebasket before leaving. <u>Therefore</u>, the office burst into flames an hour later.

He dropped a hot match into the wastebasket before leaving. <u>Consequently</u>, the office burst into flames an hour later.

After many struggles and much soul searching, she bought her first home last year. A very interesting young man moved in across the street from her.

After many struggles and much soul searching, she bought her first home last year. <u>Subsequently</u>, a very interesting young man moved in across the street from her.

The firing alluded to in the first example was not an unavoidable consequence, but merely one of several potential responses. In the second example, *therefore* lacks the power to show the direct consequence. The third example simply shows a way to emphasize sequence in the absence of a cause-and-effect relationship.

continual ≠ continuous

Continual means "repeatedly." *Continuous* means "without ceasing." Rabbits run continually; waterfalls run continuously.

NO   His <u>continuous</u> disruption of instruction scuttled the six-month experiment.

YES   His <u>continual</u> disruption of instruction scuttled the six-month experiment.

She has been a member of the New York Philharmonic <u>continually</u> since 1982.

She has been a member of the New York Philharmonic <u>continuously</u> since 1982.

An unfortunate habit of many speakers and writers in recent years is to plug in the buzzword "ongoing." That eliminates any need to know the distinction between continual and continuous. It also shrinks vocabularies and forfeits opportunities to give readers precise, unambiguous descriptions. Read more about *ongoing* on pages 44–45 and 183.

correlation

Correlation has specific meaning in statistical statements. You can avoid confusion in scientific reports by not using it in non-statistical statements.

NO   I suspect a correlation between his leniency and the disrespect his employees show toward him.

YES   I suspect that his leniency contributes to the disrespect his employees show toward him.

Here is an example of statistical use.	→	I found a high correlation (.79) between management leniency ratings and employee disrespect as measured on the Cheryl Hanks Anarchy/ Organization Scale (CHAOS)

counsel ≠ council

To give advice is to *counsel* (verb). The advice given is referred to also as *counsel* (noun). The word *council* (noun) refers only to an assembly of persons.

NO   I am uncertain about how to council him.

YES   I am uncertain about how to counsel him.

We all need wise council at times.

We all need wise counsel at times.

Four men and three women were appointed to the counsel.

Four men and three women were appointed to the council.

currently ≠ presently

Both terms are used to mean *now*, but *presently* is used also to mean *soon* (We expect him to arrive presently.). Tense usually makes meaning clear, but you can avoid all chances of ambiguity by using *presently* only when you mean *soon*.

NO   You should think of me presently as the leader of the group.

YES   You should think of me currently as the leader of the group.

In many cases, this being one, the word could be omitted altogether.

deal with, dealt with (see also p. 44)

If you use this vocabulary eater in place of specific information, it will mean whatever the reader wants it to mean.

<u>NO</u> The social worker was unable to <u>deal with</u> him yesterday.

<u>YES</u> The social worker

  - was too busy to give him any time yesterday.

  - was too stressed to see another client yesterday.

  - handled his case poorly yesterday.

Yesterday, after enduring his wrath quietly for months, the social worker lost composure.

determine

While *determine* can mean either *to decide* (The judge will determine the outcome.) or *to ascertain* (We are trying to determine what happened.), you can improve clarity by using *determine* for the first meaning and another term (ascertain; identify) for the second.

<u>NO</u> Last, we have to <u>determine</u> which instructors have had some experience with this.

<u>YES</u> Last, we have to <u>identify</u> the instructors who have had some experience with this.

diagnose

Conditions are diagnosed; afflicted persons are not.

<u>NO</u> The doctor <u>diagnosed him</u> as suffering from carpal tunnel syndrome.

<u>YES</u> The doctor <u>diagnosed carpal tunnel syndrome</u> as the cause of his suffering.

different, separate

Do not insert *different* or *separate* into sentences unnecessarily. Omitting *separate* from the first example below will not have readers believe the three meetings were held collectively, nor will omitting *different* from the second example have readers believe the three fonts were alike.

<u>NO</u> The board held three <u>separate</u> meetings in an attempt to resolve the problem.

<u>YES</u> The board held three meetings in an attempt to resolve the problem.

On one page he used three <u>different</u> fonts.

On one page he used three fonts.

Also, when you use *different* you must give the reader a clear answer to the question "different from what?" If *different* means "different from each other," use an efficient word to say so.

NO He demonstrated <u>different</u> approaches to the problem.

YES He demonstrated <u>various</u> (<u>a variety of</u>) approaches to the problem.

different than ≠ different from

To move *from* X to Y is to move *from* one thing to another, which is why X is said to be *different from* Y. *Different than* is an imprecise colloquial substitute for *different from*.

NO His style is <u>different than</u> any I have ever seen.

YES His style is <u>different from</u> any I have ever seen.

dilemma ≠ problem

A dilemma leaves nothing but unacceptable options. If your difficulty does not place you between the proverbial "rock and a hard place," you are facing a problem—not a dilemma.

NO She worried constantly about her <u>dilemma</u> with poor college grades.

YES She worried constantly about her <u>problem</u> with poor college grades.

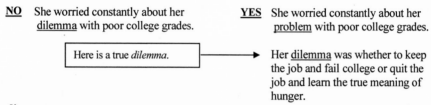

Here is a true *dilemma*. ⟶ Her <u>dilemma</u> was whether to keep the job and fail college or quit the job and learn the true meaning of hunger.

discover

To be discovered, a thing must be in place but unknown. Discovery may be universal (Sims discovered a new species of butterfly in the rainforest.) or personal (He discovered the richness of Shakespeare's sonnets.). An entity brought into being is not a discovery.

NO Montessori <u>discovered</u> a new approach to teaching young children.

YES Montessori <u>developed</u> a new approach to teaching young children.

McCarthy <u>discovered</u> a four-quadrant method by which to categorize that type of information.

McCarthy <u>created</u> a four-quadrant method by which to categorize that type of information.

discussed, discussion (see also p. 46)

A *discussion* is a conversation between at least two persons. While use of the term *discussion* has been stretched to describe written text in which the author presents multiple points of view, as at the end of research articles, you will do well to avoid using these terms where no exchange of information or views is present.

NO The method by which the interviews were conducted will be <u>discussed</u> in the next chapter.

YES The method by which the interviews were conducted will be

- <u>described</u> in the next chapter.

- <u>presented</u> in the next chapter.

disinterested ≠ uninterested

Disinterested has two meanings. Its secondary meaning duplicates *uninterested*. For clarity, use its primary meaning almost exclusively, i.e., to describe someone detached or unbiased. (Before you and I begin negotiating, we should ask the opinion of a disinterested party.)

NO Perhaps too proud of his status as an Olympic athlete, he was <u>disinterested</u> in coaching high school track.

YES Perhaps too proud of his status as an Olympic athlete, he was

 - <u>uninterested</u> in coaching high school track.

 - <u>not interested</u> in coaching high school track.

Disinterested is used to mean *uninterested* primarily where interest has been present and lost: "After struggling for two years, he became *disinterested* in the project.

divided

To *divide* is to break a whole into parts. A group of persons can be divided, but individual persons, despite the fuzzy language of some research studies, are left whole.

NO Subjects were <u>divided</u> into high, moderate, and low IQ.

YES Subjects were <u>categorized</u> by IQ scores as high, moderate, or low.

Subjects were <u>divided</u> into three treatment groups.

Each subject was <u>assigned</u> to one of three treatment groups.

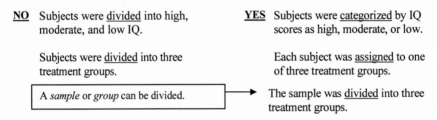

A *sample* or *group* can be divided.

The sample was <u>divided</u> into three treatment groups.

done

Done, as commonly used, is a colloquialism. Pot roasts are done; tasks are finished or completed.

NO Once I was <u>done</u> with data collection and analysis, I began to write in earnest.

YES Once I had <u>finished</u> data collection and analysis, I began to write in earnest.

each (see **both**)

eager (see **anxious**)

effect (see **affect**)

e.g. (see **i.e.**)

elude (see **allude**)

eminent (eminence) ≠ imminent (imminence)

Eminent means "high in station, rank, or repute." *Imminent* means "likely to occur at any moment." The first error below is more common than the second.

NO I fear that a breakout of gang violence is eminent.

YES I fear that a breakout of gang violence is imminent.

His imminence as an author is unquestioned.

His eminence as an author is unquestioned.

enable (see **allow**)

enormity

Enormity does not mean simply "of enormous size." It also means "of a monstrous or heinous nature" (The enormity of the mass murderer's deed could be seen immediately with the opening of the front door.).

NO The enormity of the bulk-mailing task overwhelmed our staff; we had to call part-time helpers.

YES The magnitude of the bulk-mailing task overwhelmed our staff; we had to call part-time helpers.

The enormity of her love gave him courage to persevere. (This is a most unfortunate misuse.)

The depth of her love gave him courage to persevere.

ensure (see **insure**)

equally

Be careful not to make *equally* redundant to the word *as*.

NO The weekend staff is equally as competent as the weekday staff.

YES The weekend staff is as competent as the weekday staff.

The weekday staff does well, but the weekend staff is equally competent.

essential, necessary

You will overstate if you use *essential* or *necessary* to describe something conceivably dispensable.

NO Networking skills are essential to anyone seeking a good professional position.

YES Networking skills are important to anyone seeking a good professional position.

A good teacher's aide is necessary to the operation of a successful preschool classroom.

A good teacher's aide is extremely helpful to the operation of a successful preschool classroom.

171

everyday ≠ every day

Everyday is a single-word adjective; *every day* is a statement of frequency.

NO Just wear your <u>every day</u> work clothes.

YES Just wear your <u>everyday</u> work clothes.

He puts some time in on his writing <u>everyday</u>.

He puts some time in on his writing <u>every day</u>.

🐝 exists

The least you can say about anyone or anything is that it *exists*. Why use words to say so little?

NO The technology <u>exists</u>.

YES The technology <u>is available</u> now.

The technology <u>will be on the market</u> in six months.

Unfortunately, that approach <u>exists</u> within the profession.

Unfortunately, enough of <u>our colleagues practice</u> that approach to taint the profession as a whole.

expect (see **anticipate**; see also p. 13)

🐝 experience

As a verb, *experience* is vague, bland, and impotent. Find the specific descriptions you have in mind and share them with readers.

NO I want to <u>experience</u> the Native American culture.

YES I want to <u>live among</u> Native Americans, <u>learn</u> their history, and <u>share</u> their emotions.

I have not <u>experienced</u> music in any depth.

I <u>listen</u> to music only when driving my car, and I have never learned to <u>play</u> an instrument or <u>sing</u>.

farther ≠ further

Use *farther* for physical references and *further* for non-physical references.

NO We traveled <u>further</u> the second day than we had the first.

YES We traveled <u>farther</u> the second day than we had the first.

We should explore the possibilities <u>farther</u>.

We should explore the possibilities <u>further</u>.

feel ≠ believe (see also p. 46)

Avoid using *feel* for *believe* (I never see the reverse error) by asking yourself whether you are referring to an emotion (based on feeling) or an opinion (based on information).

NO I <u>feel</u> that Piaget has been woefully misunderstood.

YES I <u>believe</u> that Piaget has been woefully misunderstood.

fewer (see **less**)

finalize (see also pp. 13–14)

Finalize amounts to a pretentious version of some useful, descriptive, down-to-earth words.

NO I will <u>finalize</u> my research by the end of the month.

YES I will <u>complete</u> my research by the end of the month.

I expect to <u>finalize</u> the first draft by noon on Friday.

I expect to <u>finish</u> the first draft by noon on Friday.

The committee <u>finalized</u> its day's business with a vote on the Perkins proposal.

The committee <u>concluded</u> its day's business with a vote on the Perkins proposal.

firstly, secondly, etc. (see also pp. 13–14)

To describe events as "in first place, in second place," etc., avoid the affectation and imprecision of these terms. What you mean is that X occurs *first* (adjective), not that the manner in which X occurs is *firstly* (adverb).

NO <u>Firstly</u>, you should check the inventory to be sure we can deliver what we promise, and <u>secondly</u>, you should process the order quickly.

YES <u>First</u>, you should check the order to be sure we can deliver what we promise, and <u>second</u>, you should process the order quickly.

flaunt ≠ flout

To *flaunt* is to display in a way that is conspicuous, defiant, or bold. To *flout* is to show disdain, scorn, or contempt.

NO If you <u>flaunt</u> the rules here, soon you will find yourself on the outside.

YES If you <u>flout</u> the rules here, soon you will find yourself on the outside.

Here is a precise use of *flaunt*.

We respected his awards until he began to <u>flaunt</u> them around the office.

flush out ≠ flesh out

To *flush out* is to break a thing free or expose it. To *flesh out* is to add detail to a thought or design sketched in skeletal form—metaphorically put flesh on the bones. Generally, we *flush out* problems and *flesh out* ideas, though conceivably the reverse might be done.

NO   I need to <u>flush out</u> the proposal before I send it to her.

YES   I need to <u>flesh out</u> the proposal before I send it to her.

focus around (see **center around**)

further (see **farther**)

had (see **would have**)

help (see **assist**)

however (see also p. 106)

You will create a run-on sentence, and probably some confusion, if you join two independent clauses with *however* surrounded by commas when *however* is a conjunctive adverb that introduces the second of the two clauses.

NO   He has misgivings, <u>however,</u> she helps him all she can.

YES   He has misgivings, <u>but</u> she helps him all she can.

She helps him all she can, despite his misgivings.

The simple constructions shown above are preferable to the more ponderous-sounding *however*. If you do want to contrast thoughts with *however*, do it in one of two ways: Begin a new sentence with *However,* or partition *however* off from the first clause with a semicolon (He has misgivings; however, she helps him all she can).

NO   The researcher was ready, the subjects eager, and the equipment in place, <u>however,</u> a power failure ruined the first day of data collection.

YES   The researcher was ready, the subjects eager, and the equipment in place. <u>However,</u> a power failure ruined the first day of data collection.

> A run-on sentence is not created, however, when *however* is a parenthetic expression referring to the clause that precedes it—as in the sentence you are reading now.

The researcher was ready, the subjects eager, and the equipment in place; <u>however,</u> a power failure ruined the first day of data collection.

i.e. ≠ e.g.

Think of the *i* in *i.e.*, to interpret it as *in other words*, or *that is*. Think of the *e* in *e.g.*, to interpret it as *for example*. When these abbreviations appear mid-sentence, place a comma after them. Avoid them altogether in formal writing: write out *that is* or *for example*.

NO Take some weapon, <u>i.e.</u>, an axe or a knife.

YES Take some weapon, <u>e.g.</u>, an axe or a knife.

NO He was finished, <u>e.g.</u>, fired and removed.

YES He was finished, <u>i.e.</u>, fired and removed.

if and when

Do not hedge at your reader's expense. Decide what message you want to send, and then send it by using one word or the other.

NO I will use that approach <u>if and when</u> I am hired.

YES I will use that approach <u>if</u> I am hired.

I will use that approach <u>when</u> I am hired.

illusion (see **allusion**)

impact (see also p. 18, and see Appendix C for extensive details)

Impact works best as a noun ("The impact of this decision will be felt for generations"). As a verb, it leaves too many possibilities open to have meaning beyond a dramatic ring.

NO We are trying to predict the extent to which that law will <u>impact</u> our business.

YES We are trying to predict the extent to which that law will <u>enhance</u> our business.

We are trying to predict the extent to which that law will <u>impede</u> our business.

NO We hope this petition will <u>impact</u> the legislature.

YES We hope this petition will <u>influence</u> the legislature in our favor.

implement (see also p. 44, and see Appendix C for extensive details)

Although you will find *implement* defined secondarily as a verb, its primary function is as a noun, meaning "any article used in some activity; an article of equipment; a means." If you use *implement* as a verb, you are likely to lose specific, meaningful communication power.

NO We want to <u>implement</u> the policy in your department for three months to get a feeling for the wisdom of <u>implementing</u> it across the whole company.

YES We want to <u>test</u> the policy in your department for three months to get a feeling for the wisdom of <u>introducing</u> it across the whole company.

NO The teacher found the techniques shown at the conference impressive, but <u>difficult to implement</u>.

YES The teacher found the techniques shown at the conference impressive, but

- <u>difficult to use</u> without practice.
- <u>cumbersome</u> in large classes.
- <u>impractical</u>.

imply ≠ infer

To *imply* is to send an indirect message—make an implication. To *infer* is to receive an indirect message—make an inference. I never see *imply* used for *infer*, but the reverse is a common mistake.

NO By saying that, are you <u>inferring</u> that I let you down?

YES By saying that, are you <u>implying</u> that I let you down?

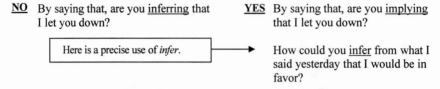

Here is a precise use of *infer*. ➔

How could you <u>infer</u> from what I said yesterday that I would be in favor?

importantly (see also pp. 13–14)

This word is used commonly to tell readers what is of highest priority (*important*), but the *ly* creates an adverb that makes it sound like a matter of how a thing should be done (*importantly*). Used and accepted widely, this word nonetheless sounds imprecise and affected.

NO Most <u>importantly,</u> establish a firm schedule before you begin to collect data.

YES Most <u>important,</u> establish a firm schedule before you begin to collect data.

in ≠ into

"Go jump in the lake." That old colloquialism, taken literally, conjures a picture of someone standing in the lake and jumping up and down. The real message is "go jump into the lake." In other words, transport yourself from out of the lake to in the lake.

NO He went <u>in</u> the office.

YES He went <u>into</u> the office.

Students were asked to sing <u>in</u> the microphone

Students were asked to sing <u>into</u> the microphone.

The second example above could be correct as written only if the student were very small or the microphone very large.

include

When you write *includes, included, or including*, you imply "but not limited to." To keep readers from wondering if your list is partial, i.e., if you have *excluded* something, introduce complete lists with *are, consists of, encompasses*, or a similar all-inclusive term.

NO The services he offers <u>include</u> writing, editing, and ghost-writing.

YES The services he offers <u>are</u> writing, editing, and ghost-writing.

The group <u>included</u> two violins, a viola, and a cello.

The group <u>consisted of</u> two violins, a viola, and a cello.

incorporate (see **integrate**)

individual

Any object or person can be either individual or grouped. *Individual*, an adjective, therefore makes a poor noun by which to cite a person. The appeal of the plural, *individuals*, may stem from discomfort with the use of *persons* (see **people** in this list).

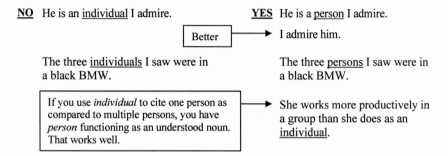

NO   He is an <u>individual</u> I admire.

          | Better |

The three <u>individuals</u> I saw were in a black BMW.

> If you use *individual* to cite one person as compared to multiple persons, you have *person* functioning as an understood noun. That works well.

YES   He is a <u>person</u> I admire.

I admire him.

The three <u>persons</u> I saw were in a black BMW.

She works more productively in a group than she does as an <u>individual</u>.

infer (see **imply**)

initiative

Initiative as a trait is the ability and energy to see what needs to be done, and to do it. The act itself, *an initiative*, means simply "an introductory step," but the term seems to have gained prestige in some business circles as a big-picture descriptor.

NO   The Westwood <u>initiative</u> is nearing completion.

If you take over that division, I expect to see some new <u>initiatives</u>.

YES   The Westwood <u>project</u> is nearing completion.

If you take over that division, I expect to see some new

  - <u>ideas</u>.   - <u>products</u>.
  - <u>approaches</u>.   - <u>thinking</u>.

In a business or institution whose in-house jargon has given *initiative* the meaning of "new, creative piece of work," it might carry specific meaning for persons in the know. Outside readers, however, are likely to have difficulty seeing specificity in the term.

input (see also p. 42)

Give your readers precise meaning. *Input* is one of the most vague of all buzzwords.

NO   Please give us your <u>input</u>.

YES   Please give us your

  - <u>advice</u>.   - <u>viewpoint</u>.
  - <u>opinion</u>.   - <u>insight</u>.
  - <u>reaction</u>.   - <u>assessment</u>.

insure ≠ ensure

To *insure* is to promise to replace whatever is lost, or make compensation for it. One who *insures* might replace a building that burns, or pay health or death benefits. To *ensure* is to take care to make something secure or safe. One who *ensures* is conscientious about fulfilling a promise, but bears no contractual responsibility for replacement or compensation. I see *insure* used for *ensure*, but not the reverse.

NO I need you to <u>insure</u> that these documents will be delivered by noon tomorrow.

YES I need you to <u>ensure</u> that these documents will be delivered by noon tomorrow.

I have ordered extra supplies to <u>insure</u> that everyone will be comfortable for the week.

I have ordered extra supplies to <u>ensure</u> that everyone will be comfortable for the week.

integrate ≠ incorporate

These words are close in meaning. Both describe an intermingling of multiple entities, but *incorporate* works more precisely than *integrate* to describe the drawing of one or more entities into an already-existing body or mass.

NO We decided to <u>integrate</u> the recently acquired distributorship into our parent company.

YES We decided to <u>incorporate</u> the recently acquired distributorship into our parent company.

Here is a precise use of *integrate*. ⟶ We might improve the team if we were to <u>integrate</u> the players socially.

involve

Whenever you can, give specific information rather than lean on the general term *involve*.

NO The researcher will <u>involve</u> assembly line workers in the study.

YES The researcher will <u>use</u> assembly line workers <u>as observers</u> for the study.

Managers were heavily <u>involved</u> in the decision.

Managers <u>cast the deciding vote</u>.

irritate (see **aggravate**)

it's ≠ its (see also pp. 90 and 92)

Use an apostrophe only for the contraction of *it is* ("It's a dreary day"). All other uses are possessive pronouns that call for *its*.

NO The hospital lost <u>it's</u> CEO.

YES The hospital lost <u>its</u> CEO.

<u>It's</u> price is <u>it's</u> principal drawback.

<u>Its</u> price is <u>its</u> principal drawback.

178

latter ≠ last

Latter refers to the second of two; *last* refers to the final entry of three or more.

NO Writers should own a dictionary, a thesaurus, and a handbook of usage. The latter may be the most difficult to select.

> In most circumstances, you might want to avoid using either *latter* or *last*, and instead reuse the specific term to avoid making readers backtrack.

YES Writers should own a dictionary, a thesaurus, and a handbook of usage.

- The last may be the most difficult to select.

- A handbook may be the most difficult to select.

lay ≠ lie

When you place yourself down, you *lie* down; when you place an object down, you *lay* it down. *Lay* is commonly used where *lie* belongs; the reverse is rare. (Note: "Now I lay me down to sleep" is an interesting twist; *me* creates a grammatical shift from *lie* to *lay* by objectifying the speaker.)

NO Lay down for a 20-minute power nap.

He spent all day laying around the house.

YES Lie down for a 20-minute power nap.

He spent all day lying around the house.

The various tenses of these words can be troublesome:

present tense	May I *lie* on the couch?	May I *lay* it here?	Particularly disorienting is *lay* as the past tense of *lie*.
future tense	I will *lie* on the couch tomorrow.	I will *lay* it down soon.	
past tense	I *lay* on the couch for an hour.	I *laid* it down yesterday.	
perfect tenses (present, past, future)	I have *lain* (had *lain*; will have *lain*) on the couch all day.	I have *laid* (had *laid*; will have *laid*) it here daily.	

less ≠ fewer

To describe a reduction in something that can be counted, use *fewer*, not *less*. *Less* is the counterpart to amount (amount of water; less water); *fewer* is the counterpart to number (number of bottles; fewer bottles).

NO We have had less customers today.

YES We have had fewer customers today.

We have had less business today

You cannot rescue an incorrect use of *less* by adding *amount* to it. That only accentuates the absence of *fewer* in your working vocabulary, as seen in a recent newspaper article:

NO Compared to last week's effort, they made less amount of mistakes.

YES Compared to last week's effort, they made fewer mistakes.

Exception: *Less* may apply to a countable entity if the issue is uncountable. For example, "…less than five miles" works, because the issue is distance (uncountable), not miles.

🐝 **leverage** (See Appendix C for extensive details)

Leverage is a noun pressed into service as a verb at the expense of specificity.

NO It takes time to <u>leverage</u> all the resources available to you in this position.

YES It takes time to

- <u>become conversant with</u>
- <u>make full use of</u>
- <u>take advantage of</u>

all the resources available to you in this position.

like ≠ as

Like modifies nouns, noun phrases, and pronouns (She looks like a lady, but she acts like Jim.). *As* modifies other phrases and other parts of speech (He was on time, as he should have been. She was late, as usual.). I see *like* used for *as*, but not the reverse.

NO Data collection was time consuming, <u>like</u> she predicted it would be.

YES Data collection was time consuming, <u>as</u> she predicted it would be.

Like I said, he is blatantly insubordinate.

<u>As</u> I said, he is blatantly insubordinate.

In today's speech, *like* takes a beating that defies explanation (I was like going to go, but he was like "no."). As an adult, jettison that habit along with other vestiges of childhood. For elaboration, read the satirical essay that begins on page 75.

limited

Avoid describing as *limited* anything that is highly unlikely to ever be unlimited.

NO <u>Limited</u> funding forced Carl to abandon his dream of owning a diner.

YES <u>Insufficient</u> funding forced Carl to abandon his dream of owning a diner.

> The use of *limited* works here because it is used in a comparative sense rather than an absolute sense. ➤ Carl's aspirations to own a diner were <u>limited</u> more by money than by ability or ambition.

literally ≠ virtually

Literally means "without exaggeration or inaccuracy." *Virtually* means "practically; almost, but not quite." Avoid the curious practice of using *literally* for *virtually.*

NO When he heard the news he was <u>literally</u> blown away.

YES When he heard the news he was <u>virtually</u> blown away.

Virtually is technically correct in the example below, but it is not needed. Where exaggeration is great, readers will recognize the hyperbole without your help.

The appointment was virtually handed to him on a silver platter.

The appointment was handed to him on a silver platter.

look at, look to, look for (see also p. 43)

To give readers the specific information they want, reserve these terms for literal use, as in "Look at the moon," or "Look to see if he is in the yard," or "Look for my keys."

NO We will <u>look at</u> that issue next time.	**YES** We will <u>discuss</u> that issue next time.

We are <u>looking to</u> win.	We <u>are trying</u> to win.
	   - <u>expecting</u> to win.
	   - <u>planning</u> to win.
	   - <u>hoping</u> to win.

We are <u>looking for</u> a break in the weather.	We are <u>hoping for</u> a break in the weather.

lots of, a lot of

In formal writing, be careful not to overuse these colloquial expressions.

NO <u>Lots of</u> administrative assistants would do well to improve their use of language.	**YES** <u>Many</u> administrative assistants would do well to improve their use of language.
<u>A lot</u> has been written about that topic.	<u>Much</u> has been written about that topic.

maximum ≠ optimum

Remember the old saying that more is not always better. *Maximum* means "the greatest quantity or amount possible," and *optimum* means "the best or most favorable." Before you use *maximum,* ask yourself this question: am I writing about the most, or am I writing about the most effective? *Optimum* is commonly needed, as is its corresponding adjective, optimal: "The *optimal* temperature for this phase is 160 to 180 degrees."

NO We need weather conditions to be at their <u>maximum</u>.	**YES** We need weather conditions to be at their <u>optimum</u>.
Only if we have <u>maximum</u> participation will we get the qualitative data we need.	Only if we have <u>optimal</u> participation will we get the qualitative data we need.

may, might

You risk undercutting what you have to say when you try to tread lightly with the help of these words. If something is certain to vary, use *will* rather than *may.*

NO Effects <u>may</u> vary with temperature and climate.	**YES** Effects <u>will</u> vary with temperature and climate.

If you have some reason beyond pure chance that something will happen, *might* will weaken your message.

<u>**NO**</u> Considering the potential he has shown, he <u>might be</u> promoted soon.

<u>**YES**</u> Considering the potential he has shown, he <u>is likely to be</u> promoted soon.

metrics (see Appendix C for extensive details)

To refer to quantitative data of all stripes as *metrics* is to leave readers hunting for specific information with the help of context clues and inferences.

<u>**NO**</u> We need to know more about the <u>metrics</u> before making a decision.

<u>**YES**</u> We need to know more about the

- <u>revenue</u>
- <u>expenses</u>
- <u>profit and loss statistics</u>
- <u>measurement criteria</u>

before making a decision.

mute ≠ moot

Do not use the common term *mute* (silent) in place of the less common term *moot* (of little practical value; debatable).

<u>**NO**</u> Now that the property has been bought out from under us, its value to our firm is <u>mute</u>.

<u>**YES**</u> Now that the property has been bought out from under us, its value to our firm is <u>moot</u>.

myself ≠ me, I

Myself, and other pronouns that end in *self* or *selves*, have only two potential functions: They can serve as the object of the verb (He asked *himself* why.) or they can be used to intensify a noun or pronoun (I *myself* won first place. She did the same thing *herself*.) Avoid using *myself* where *me* or *I* belongs.

<u>**NO**</u> He heaped embarrassing compliments on my partner and <u>myself</u>.

<u>**YES**</u> He heaped embarrassing compliments on my partner and <u>me</u>.

Frank and <u>myself</u> will attend the meeting.

Frank and <u>I</u> will attend the meeting.

necessary (see **essential**)

nor

Keep in mind that the connotation of *nor* is negative (related to *no*, *not*, and *never*). Do not use it where *or* belongs. Either pair *nor* with *neither* or use it to introduce a clause antithetical to the preceding clause. As a rare tool of emphasis, you can use *nor* as the first word of a new sentence.

NO   The interrogation was not long <u>nor</u> difficult.

YES   The interrogation was

- not long <u>or</u> difficult.

- <u>neither</u> long <u>nor</u> difficult.

- not long, <u>nor</u> was it difficult.

The interrogation was not long. <u>Nor</u> was it difficult.

number (see **amount**)

often

Use *often* only where frequency is the issue, as in "Often we find ourselves short of petty cash."

NO   To improve cash flow, retailers <u>often</u> reduce inventory and rely on daily deliveries.

Here, *often* implies that retailers resort to this practice at frequent intervals. The real issue is not frequency, but prevalence.

YES   To improve cash flow, <u>many</u> retailers reduce inventory and rely on daily deliveries.

A <u>common practice</u> among retailers is to improve cash flow by reducing inventory and relying on daily deliveries.

one and the same

Omit the first two words of this stale, redundant phrase.

NO   The producer and the director are <u>one and the same</u> person.

Better ➝

YES   The producer and director are <u>the same</u> person.

The producer <u>is also</u> the director.

ongoing (see also p. 44)

Give your readers precise meaning, not this vague buzzword. Sometimes, as in the last example, *ongoing* simply fills space—in this case by being redundant to *for years.*

NO   We have an <u>ongoing</u> agreement.

Employees were reprimanded on an <u>ongoing</u> basis.

She hated the traffic's <u>ongoing</u> din.

For years she has been faithful about her <u>ongoing</u> morning walks.

ES   We have an <u>open-ended</u> agreement.

Employees were reprimanded <u>continually</u>.

See *continual* ≠ continuous on p. 166.

She hated the traffic's <u>continuous</u> din.

For years she has been faithful about her morning walks.

only (see also pp. 49–50)

This may be the most frequently misplaced word in our language, sometimes creating confusion (first example), and other times weakness (second and third examples).

<u>**NO**</u> Motorists can <u>only</u> use the south road for the next five days.

<u>**YES**</u> Motorists can use <u>only</u> the south road for the next five days.

Motorists can use the south road <u>only</u> for the next five days.

As a student here, you will <u>only</u> succeed if you try.

As a student here, you will succeed <u>only</u> if you try.

It <u>only</u> happens once a year.

It happens <u>only</u> once a year.

Note: An early *only* is much more common than a well-placed *only*, even though the latter offers strength and clarity by sitting next to the word or phrase it modifies.

onset ≠ outset

Onset carries ominous overtones—if not the onset of disease, at least the onset of winter. Avoid using it where the more benign *outset* (meaning simply beginning) is appropriate. Probably the best advice is to use *beginning* or *start* rather than *outset*, and save *onset* to describe wars and plagues.

<u>**NO**</u> The researcher was careless about subject selection at the <u>onset</u> of her study.

<u>**YES**</u> The researcher was careless about subject selection at the

- <u>outset</u> of her study.

- <u>beginning</u> of her study.

optimum (see **maximum**)

option (see **alternative**)

over (see **above**)

pension ≠ penchant

Do not use the common term *pension* (an allowance, annuity, or subsidy) in place of the less common term *penchant* (a strong inclination)

<u>**NO**</u> Civilizations throughout history have had a <u>pension</u> for developing techniques of torture.

<u>**YES**</u> Civilizations throughout history have had a <u>penchant</u> for developing techniques of torture.

people ≠ persons

A group of ten *people*, if nine were to leave, would be reduced to one people; therefore, the original should be ten *persons*. Use *persons* when the number is known or conceivably could be known; use *people* when the number is indefinite, and when referring to a classification, as in "the Chinese people."

NO Michigan stadium seats more than 110,000 <u>people</u>.	**YES** Michigan stadium seats more than 110,000 <u>persons</u>.
During my travels there, I enjoyed being in the midst of warm, kind <u>persons</u>.	During my travels there, I enjoyed being in the midst of warm, kind <u>people</u>.

pinch-hit

Credit a substitute with pinch-hitting for you only if your intent is to have that person improve on your performance. Pinch-hitting, a term borrowed from the game of baseball, is exactly that—bringing to bear talent superior to that of the person replaced.

NO Elaine will <u>pinch-hit</u> for me while I am out of town.	**YES** Elaine will <u>attend to my daily business</u> while I am out of town.

> Here is a case in which *pinch-hit* would be an appropriate term. →

Elaine is more familiar with the case than I, so she will <u>pinch-hit</u> for me at next week's meeting.

plus

Use this term only within the context of a mathematical description, not as a bridge between two parts of a loosely crafted sentence.

NO The DSS case worker was frustrated by a heavy case load and an immovable bureaucratic structure, <u>plus</u> the emotional drain of helpless, demanding clients.	**YES** The DSS case worker was frustrated by a heavy case load and an immovable bureaucratic structure, <u>and</u> by the emotional drain of helpless, demanding clients.

possess

To *possess* is to have control of a tangible possession. The word rings hollow in reference to traits or feelings.

NO He <u>possesses</u> a cheerful demeanor.	**YES** He <u>has</u> a cheerful demeanor.
	He is cheerful.
I take comfort from the confidence he <u>possesses</u>.	I take comfort from the confidence he <u>exudes</u>.

potentially

Do not let the allure of *potentially* tempt you to insert it where it doubles the function of *could* or *possible* (*possibly; possibility*).

NO	He could <u>potentially</u> lose the job altogether if he insists on defying her.	**YES**	He could lose the job altogether if he insists on defying her.
	I see a <u>possible potential</u> for advancement.		I see <u>potential</u> for advancement.
			I see the <u>possibility</u> of advancement.

presently (see **currently**)

principle ≠ principal

A *principle* is a "rule, law, doctrine, or basic truth." *Principal* used as a noun means "chief" or "head," and used as an adjective means "highest" or "foremost."

NO	He accused his detractors of adhering to a <u>principal</u> he called "voodoo economics."	**YES**	He accused his detractors of adhering to a <u>principle</u> he called "voodoo economics."
	Two teachers were praised by the school's <u>principle</u>.		Two teachers were praised by the school's <u>principal</u>.
	The <u>principle</u> problem now is raising enough money to support it.		The <u>principal</u> problem now is raising enough money to support it.

problem (see **dilemma**)

process

Use the term *process* only to emphasize that you are referring to a systematic series of actions directed to some end. Do not let it become purposeless babble.

NO	Our vice president has a great amount to learn about <u>the mentoring process</u>.	**YES**	Our vice president has a great amount to learn about <u>mentoring</u>.
	Children should learn to apply <u>the process of critical thinking</u> to important problems.		Children should learn to apply <u>critical thinking</u> to important problems.

Here is a case in which *process* is an appropriate term.	⟶	Voting will remain the staple of our democracy so long as we maintain a fair, thorough, and transparent <u>process</u>.

186

proximity

Proximity means *closeness*. Avoid the common practice of preceding *proximity* with *close*, producing the oddly redundant message *close closeness*.

NO The researchers chose the testing room for its <u>close proximity</u> to the subjects' offices.

> The principle of simplicity dictates that *close to* is preferrable to *proximity to*.

YES The researchers chose the testing room

- for its <u>proximity to</u> the subjects' offices.

- because it was <u>close to</u> the subjects' offices.

reason, because

Use these words separately. Because their function overlaps, pairing them creates awkwardness.

NO One <u>reason</u> he found no significant differences between groups is <u>because</u> treatment ended after only twelve weeks.

YES One <u>reason</u> he found no significant differences between groups was <u>that</u> treatment ended after only twelve weeks.

<u>He found</u> no significant differences between groups, in part <u>because</u> treatment ended after only twelve weeks.

reason why

Do not insert *why* as baggage following *reason*. Use one term or the other.

NO I have no interest in when he did it or how he did it; I just want to know <u>the reason why</u>.

That is <u>the reason why</u> he resigned.

YES I have no interest in when he did it or how he did it; I just want to know

- <u>the reason</u>.
- <u>why</u>.

That is

- <u>the reason</u> he resigned.
- <u>why</u> he resigned.

relatively

Use *relatively* only when the relationship to which it refers is evident.

NO I am progressing <u>relatively well</u> with the writing of my dissertation.

> Another option is to precede *well* with an adverb other than *relatively*, e.g., *fairly* or *reasonably*.

YES I am progressing <u>well</u> with the writing of my dissertation.

Considering how I struggled with my masters thesis, I am progressing <u>relatively well</u> with my dissertation.

resiliency

Resiliency is only a variation of the preferred term, *resilience*.

NO That team is known for its <u>resiliency</u>.　　　**YES** That team is known for its <u>resilience</u>.

resources

Resources are sources of supplies, support, or aid. That describes everything and everyone who contributes anything to anyone in any way for any purpose. Realize how little you are saying when you refer simply to *resources*.

NO This change will supply us with <u>additional resources</u>.

YES This change will supply us with
- <u>millions of dollars of revenue</u>.
- <u>an abundant source of raw material</u>.
- <u>dozens of bright new personnel</u>.

She lacks the <u>resources</u> she needs.

She lacks the <u>money</u> she needs.

She lacks the <u>support</u> she needs <u>from family and friends</u>.

result in

To use *result in* or *resulted in* as a verb is to describe the end point of an action rather than the action itself. Replace the bland, all-purpose *resulted in* (past tense is most common) with an active verb that describes how, specifically, the subject affected the object. Samples follow:

accomplished	consummated	evoked	inspired	produced
achieved	contributed to	fomented	instigated	prompted
activated	created	forced	involved	provoked
aroused	derived	formulated	kindled	roused
bred	developed	generated	launched	sparked
brought about	discharged	incited	led to	spawned
built	elicited	induced	made	started
caused	enabled	inflicted	performed	stimulated
coerced	encompassed	influenced	persuaded	transacted
compelled	engendered	initiated	precipitated	triggered

I have gone to unusual lengths here because I see pervasive use of *resulted in* at the expense of rich, specific verbs.

NO Her quizzical note <u>resulted in</u> his inquiry.

YES Her quizzical note <u>prompted</u> his inquiry.

The cutting of fences <u>resulted in</u> a range war.

The cutting of fences <u>triggered</u> a range war.

His attention <u>resulted in</u> a romance that grew rapidly.

His attention <u>kindled</u> a romance that grew rapidly.

188

revisit (see also p. 48)

If your father is not well when you stop for a visit, you may decide to revisit him soon thereafter. To write about revisiting issues, on the other hand, is to use an odd, distracting colloquialism at the expense of specific information.

NO At our next seminar, I would like to revisit the issue of confidentiality.	**YES** At our next seminar, I would like to expand our debate about the issue of confidentiality.
When data collection flagged, the researcher and her associates revisited the plans they had made two weeks earlier.	When data collection flagged, the researcher and her associates reworked the plans they had made two weeks earlier.

separate (see **different**)

share in common

Whatever is shared is necessarily common ground, so pairing these words creates redundancy.

NO The length of the class session is the only variable the two treatment groups shared in common.	**YES** The length of the class session is the only variable the two treatment groups shared.
	The length of the class session is the only variable common to both treatment groups.

significance, significant

Like *correlation*, the term *significant* has specific meaning in statistical reporting. You can avoid confusion in scientific reports by avoiding its use in nonstatistical statements. (This issue applies primarily to writing that involves statistical language.)

NO None of today's changes seemed as significant as what we saw yesterday.	**YES** None of today's changes seemed as important as what we saw yesterday.
Here is an example of statistical use. ⟶	Differences were statistically significant ($p < .001$).

since ≠ because

Since is strongest when used in relation to a time frame (She had not seen him since his wife died.). *Since* means *because* only in a distant sense. For clarity and strength, use *because* when you mean *because*.

NO Since the graduate assistants had administered the tests, they were asked also to score them and interpret them.	**YES** Because the graduate assistants had administered the tests, they were asked also to score them and interpret them.

site

Site implies a particular location, with no direct relationship to structures.

NO The third-floor laboratories in the Jefferson <u>site</u> are inadequate.

YES The third-floor laboratories in the Jefferson <u>building</u> are inadequate.

Here is a precise use of *site*. ⟶ The roads to the Northridge <u>site</u> are poor.

some time ≠ sometime

Use *some time* when you mean "a quantity of time."

NO I need <u>sometime</u> to work if I am to finish it this week.

YES I need <u>some time</u> to work if I am to finish it this week.

Use *sometime* when you mean "at a time yet undetermined."

NO <u>Some time</u> he will have to face the truth.

YES <u>Sometime</u> he will have to face the truth.

We need to meet <u>some time</u> soon.

We need to meet <u>sometime</u> soon.

The plural, *sometimes*, means "on some occasions." (Sometimes he faces the truth, but sometimes he does not.)

stationery ≠ stationary

You write on *stationery*. That which is immovable is *stationary*.

NO E-mail has nearly replaced what was once a household commodity: <u>stationary</u>.

YES E-mail has nearly replaced what was once a household commodity: <u>stationery</u>.

I exercise daily on a <u>stationery</u> bike.

I exercise daily on a <u>stationary</u> bike.

statue ≠ statute ≠ stature

Do not misuse the word *statue*, which refers only to a three-dimensional sculpture, when you mean to refer to a *statute* (a law or decree) or to *stature* (height or status).

NO He violated the <u>statue</u> of limitations.

YES He violated the <u>statute</u> of limitations.

Decades of diligence finally brought him the <u>statue</u> he deserved.

Decades of diligence finally brought him the <u>stature</u> he deserved.

subsequently (see **consequently, subsequently, therefore**)

taunt ≠ taut

Do not use the common term *taunt* (to reproach in a sarcastic, insulting, or jeering manner) in place of the less common term *taut* (tightly drawn; not slack).

NO Unless the canvas is <u>taunt</u>, air is likely to lift it and loosen the ropes.

YES Unless the canvas is <u>taut</u>, air is likely to lift it and loosen the ropes.

tenant ≠ tenet

A *tenant* pays rent in exchange for occupying a dwelling. When you write about a principle or doctrine held by an organization or a group of persons, be sure to refer to it as a *tenet*.

NO Our Board of Governors subscribes to the <u>tenant</u> that cream should be allowed to rise to the top.

YES Our Board of Governors subscribes to the <u>tenet</u> that cream should be allowed to rise to the top.

that (see also p. 30)

Avoid inserting *that* where it is not needed, but use it where it gives help or comfort to the reader. Note my decision to leave one *that* in the sentence below. You need to acquire a sense for when *that* functions to the betterment of the sentence and when it is simply an irritating bump in the road. Reading aloud may help you make that judgment.

NO John teaches in the same way <u>that</u> Charles teaches, except <u>that</u> Charles knows <u>that</u> tact is important.

YES John teaches in the same way Charles teaches, except <u>that</u> Charles knows tact is important.

that, which (see also p. 97)

Eliminate ambiguity by choosing between *that* and *which* as your relative pronoun according to sentence function. To introduce restrictive clauses, use *that*, with no preceding comma (first example), or omit the relative pronoun altogether (second example). To introduce nonrestrictive clauses, use *which*, preceded by a comma (third example).

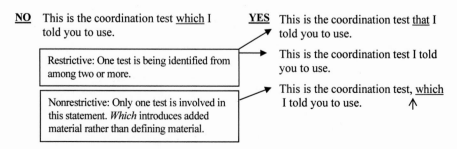

NO This is the coordination test <u>which</u> I told you to use.

Restrictive: One test is being identified from among two or more.

Nonrestrictive: Only one test is involved in this statement. *Which* introduces added material rather than defining material.

YES This is the coordination test <u>that</u> I told you to use.

This is the coordination test I told you to use.

This is the coordination test, <u>which</u> I told you to use.

the (see also p. 30)

The can become baggage in the same way *that* becomes baggage. Hunt through your writing and remove each extraneous *the*.

NO The books he read and the ideas he exchanged with others helped fulfill the dreams of a lifetime for this boy from a blue-collar neighborhood.	**YES** Books he read and ideas he exchanged with others helped fulfill dreams of a lifetime for this boy from a blue-collar neighborhood.

The next entry shows that *the,* used as underlined above, can be misleading

the ≠ a, an

Using *the* (specific) in place of *a* or *an* (non-specific) may mislead readers into inferring that *the* means "the one and only." The careless approach to data collection (first example) and the superintendent's abrasiveness (second example) probably led to more than one specific result.

NO Unreliable test scores were the result of his careless approach to data collection.

YES Unreliable test scores were a result of his careless approach to data collection.

> A logical progression from cause to effect by use of an active verb (*caused*) makes this revision stronger than the first.

His careless approach to data collection caused test scores to be unreliable.

The superintendent was generally abrasive, and the result was a revolt from building principals.

One result of the superintendent's abrasiveness was that building principals revolted.

therefore (see **consequently, subsequently, therefore**)

this, these

You risk making your writing difficult to understand—sometimes impossible to understand—when you use *this* or *these* rather than provide the information to which *this* or *these* refers.

NO He graduated from a highly rated school, but with marginal grades, and one of his letters of recommendation was strong. The personnel director took this into consideration.

YES He graduated from a highly rated school, but with marginal grades, and one of his letters of recommendation was strong. The personnel director

- took the inconsistency of his portfolio into consideration.

- took the reputation of the school and the strong letter into consideration.

torturous ≠ tortuous

Torturous means *painful*; *tortuous* means *indirect* or *winding*.

<u>NO</u> We spent a full day traveling one mile along the <u>torturous</u> path of the river.

<u>YES</u> We spent a full day traveling one mile along the <u>tortuous</u> path of the river.

Three of the seven hostages were hospitalized after their <u>tortuous</u> ordeal.

Three of the seven hostages were hospitalized after their <u>torturous</u> ordeal.

under (see **above**)

uninterested (see **disinterested**)

unknown

What is unknown to you is not necessarily unknown altogether. The subjects in this sentence, and probably their family and friends, knew the "unknown" addresses.

<u>NO</u> I could see that a follow-up study would be valuable, but the addresses of the subjects were <u>unknown</u>.

<u>YES</u> I could see that a follow-up study would be valuable, but

- I had no access to the subjects' addresses.

- the addresses of the subjects had been lost.

- the subjects had moved and left no forwarding addresses.

upcoming (see also p. 44)

This buzzword, devoid of informational value, apparently is designed to titillate. In the first example it replaces a more precise word, and in the second it is redundant to *will be held*. I have yet to find a use for this word.

<u>NO</u> We are encouraging employees to attend the <u>upcoming</u> conference.

<u>YES</u> We are encouraging employees to attend <u>Saturday's</u> conference.

The <u>upcoming</u> University Lecture Series will be held in Barronson Hall.

The University Lecture Series will be held in Barronson Hall.

update (see also p. 44)

Give your readers precise meaning, not this vague buzzword.

NO   The aide gave the teacher an <u>update</u>.

YES   The aide

- <u>reported</u> the day's events to the teacher.

- <u>oriented</u> the teacher to the new procedures.

🐝 utilize, utilization (see also pp. 14 and 153)

Do not use *utilize* as a synonym for *use*. First, it sounds pretentious. Second, it is imprecise. To utilize is not to use, but rather to convert a thing to usefulness in some particular way. One may utilize without using. Decades of widespread misuse have dulled most readers' sensitivity to the word's meaning as originally defined, and have caused revisers of recent dictionaries to relent and enter "synonym for use" as a secondary definition. Some words become so badly abused over time that the best practice is to abandon them altogether. *Utilize* may be such a word.

NO   We try to <u>utilize</u> everything we receive to good advantage.

YES   We try to <u>use</u> everything we receive to good advantage.

Is he <u>utilizing</u> all his talents in that job?

Is he <u>using</u> all his talents in that job?

Optimal <u>utilization</u> requires optimal skill.

Optimal <u>use</u> requires optimal skill.

veritable

This word almost always carries more decoration value than meaning.

NO   Even as a graduate student, she was a <u>veritable</u> model of scientific thought.

YES   Even as a graduate student, she was a model of scientific thought.

very

This word becomes tiresome and weak with overuse.

NO   I believe <u>very</u> strongly that she is a <u>very</u> competent doctor.

YES   I am sure she is a competent doctor.

virtually (see **literally**)

where ≠ in which, for which, to which, by which, through which

Where is a place—a matter of location. Inappropriate uses create odd statements.

NO The best photographs were those <u>where</u> everyone was standing.

YES The best photographs were those <u>in which</u> everyone was standing.

(*Where* everyone was standing may have been on the porch.)

Students can afford to take only those classes <u>where</u> they receive degree credit.

Students can afford to take only those classes <u>for which</u> they receive degree credit.

(*Where* they receive credit is likely to be on their transcripts, or at a particular university.)

The only statements to be published are those <u>where</u> we all agree.

The only statements to be published are those <u>to which</u> we all agree.

(*Where* we all agree may be in a conference room.)

whether or not

This phrase is useful when two conditions need to be given equal weight (The test will be given whether students are prepared or not.). More often, *or not* is baggage.

NO <u>Whether or not</u> the files would be available for a sufficient time was still to be determined.

YES <u>Whether</u> the files would be available for a sufficient time was still to be determined.

which (see **that, which**)

would

Do not use *would* without an accompanying *if, but,* or *except.*

NO Students <u>would be</u> tested in Room 324.

YES Students <u>will be</u> tested in Room 324.

Students <u>would be</u> tested in Room 324 <u>if</u> we were to schedule the test for a Tuesday or a Thursday.

would have ≠ had

The second *would have* in the example below is correct, but the first is a strangely common grammatical perversion of past perfect tense. *Would have,* being conditional, needs to be attached to a condition. This grammar error is more common in speech than in writing, but it has been known to mar a few pages.

NO If you <u>would have</u> let me know about last night's meeting, I would have gone with you.

YES If you <u>had</u> let me know about last night's meeting, I would have gone with you.

<u>Had you</u> let me know about last night's meeting, I would have gone with you.

FOUR BUSINESS BUZZWORDS ELABORATED UPON

No one seems to know for sure why or how buzzwords take root in the business community, but they do. Business professionals by the thousands embrace them, enabling those buzzwords to blunt communication for decades until they are replaced by their successors—which proceed to wreak the same kind of havoc.

Buzzwords highjack thought so surreptitiously that habituated users begin to perceive them as products of thought rather than as the anti-thought that they actually are. The primary reason to avoid using buzzwords is that they stop you short of saying everything you have to say. To highlight that problem, I've chosen four current buzzwords for elaboration in this appendix beyond the treatment given them elsewhere in the book. I'll leave still others (ongoing, updating, inputting, upcoming, accessing, addressing, looking at . . .) to be described in Appendix B and elsewhere.

impact (see also pp.18 and 175)

Impact used as a noun describes a forceful coming together that could be physical, psychological, or emotional. Used responsibly, impact is a strong and useful word:

> The impact of the meteor destroyed animal life for miles around.
> The serial killer's impact on the neighborhood psyche was shattering.
> The impact of his generosity will be felt for generations to come.

As a verb, *impact* has no such strength. It appears to describe a relationship, but in reality it requires readers to infer meaning from context clues. Read these two sentences:

During World War II, Hitler impacted the lives of the British people.

During World War II, Churchill impacted the lives of the British people.

The disparity between Hitler's and Churchill's relationship to the British people exposes *impact*'s impotence. Only readers in the know will be able to take meaning from those sentences. A re-casting of the sentences, leaning this time on thought rather than on a buzzword, would empower a larger audience to understand the message.

During World War II, Hitler rained terror on the lives of the British people.

During World War II, Churchill brought hope to the lives of the British people.

Specific, descriptive verbs used in place of the all-purpose verb *impact* will enlarge your audience for any number of statements. Look at the level of communication attained in these sentences by inserting verbs that truly characterize a relationship.

Her speech did little to ~~impact~~ influence voters.

How would your absence ~~impact~~ affect the others in the group?

Our corrective actions ~~impacted~~ improved both our relationships with clients and the morale of employees.

I intend to make decisions that ~~impact~~ enhance not only my business, but also the industry as a whole.

His help was both meaningful and ~~impactful~~ effective.

The oppressive environment ~~impacted workers~~ demoralized workers.

In short, by using *impact* rather than one from an enormous array of specific verbs—rich in shades of meaning—you squander an opportunity to describe the precise nature of a cause-and-effect relationship.

implement (see also pp.44 and 175)

Like *impact*, *implement* used as a noun is a useful word:

Of all these writing implements, the fountain pen is my favorite.

From tractor to hoe, our farm implements are the best you'll find.

As a strong leader, he was the key implement for healthy change.

And as with *impact*, *implement* as a verb only gives the impression that you're saying something specific. Look at the words inserted into these sentences in place of *implement*. You'll see that they represent specific thought as compared to simply plugging in a buzzword.

introduce
We should prepare employees carefully before we implement even the fairest of assessment systems.

initiate
If you are so sure of the proposed accounting system, implement it in your department as a trial.

install
We know exactly which system we need. All that is left is to implement it.

impose
If you implement a system as cumbersome as that, the clerical staff will revolt.

start
What sense will it make to implement a new training program 60 days before a major hiring?

make it work.
If your idea is so good, implement it.

establish
We need to implement parameters for the debate.

Readers will absorb immediately the specific meaning behind richly descriptive verbs, and they'll retain that meaning over time. In contrast, they'll tend to gloss over such one-term-fits-all buzzwords as *implement*. Over time, the word becomes a kind of repetitious sound effect that impairs the attention, comprehension, and recall of readers.

leverage (see also pp. 44 and 180)

Like *impact* and *implement*, *leverage* is strong when used as a noun. It represents power or advantage (mechanical or otherwise).

This crowbar isn't long enough to give me the leverage I need.
Using salary as leverage, he induced the workers to do his bidding.
He had enough leverage with Democrats to get the votes he needed.

When used as a verb, *leverage* becomes another all-purpose buzzword lacking in specificity—sounding strong but performing weakly. It implies that the leverager will gain an upper hand, and thus win a decided advantage over competitors. *Leverage* may have been used as a verb for the first time to describe a powerful action. Perhaps someone saw an overwhelming advantage waiting to be taken, and instead of saying "Use your millions as leverage against his indebtedness," the person tried to create a dramatic effect by inventing a new verb: "Leverage your millions against his indebtedness."

The implication of power causes *leverage* as a verb to disorient readers by overstatement when used in place of such everyday verbs as *use, apply, adopt, refer to,* or *take advantage of.*

Use
~~Leverage~~ exit interviews to gain insight into employee morale.

Make good use of
Many search engines are available. ~~Leverage~~ them.

Apply   to
~~Leverage~~ this information ~~in~~ your daily responsibilities.

refer to
If you lack expertise, ~~leverage~~ the Hanson guide.

adopt
It's wise to ~~leverage~~ good listening skills if you want to make inroads.

Take advantage of
~~Leverage~~ the useful information shown in Figure 7.

Leverage used as a verb disorients readers by imprecision when used in place of such colorfully descriptive, specific verbs as *exploit, cultivate, wield, manipulate,* or *seize.*

> exploit
> If he backs down, ~~leverage~~ the opportunity for all it's worth.

> cultivate
> You might ~~leverage~~ personal meetings to gain support down the road.

> wields
> He ~~leverages~~ threats to keep everyone in line.

> manipulate
> It takes practice to ~~leverage~~ all the aspects of the job.

> Seize
> ~~Leverage~~ the opportunity to rally your people around one goal.

When you reuse a single word such as *leverage* frequently in reference to a wide variety of circumstances, you mesmerize readers. It's a sign that you were thinking perfunctorily as you wrote. That encourages readers to think perfunctorily as they read. Consequently, your communication with them becomes less penetrating, less vivid, and less memorable than it might have been.

metrics (see also pp. 44 and 182)

The three previous buzzwords are nouns used ineffectively as verbs. In contrast, *metrics* is a noun used as a noun, but with such a variety of possible meanings that readers will need to interpret the word through context clues.

> Neither revenue nor profits are
> ~~The metrics aren't~~ what we had hoped they would be.

> estimates.
> We need to recalculate the outdated ~~metrics~~.

> scores
> The assessment ~~metrics~~ are shown in Figure 2.

measurements.
Those tools aren't going to give us the ~~metrics~~ we need.

expenses,
With those kinds of ~~metrics,~~ how can we not consider cutting costs?

criteria for success.
I think we need to review our ~~success metrics.~~

To refer to *revenue, profits, estimates, scores, measurements, expenses,* and *criteria* all with the single buzzword *metrics* is to tax all of your readers, and you'll shut some of them out from your meaning altogether.

A careless use of *metrics* is particularly destructive in the absence of context clues. The four sentences below challenge readers to be familiar with auxiliary information, be willing to dig for auxiliary information, or guess at meaning from among multiple possibilities.

We need to have metrics that are clearly understood.

We have to identify and finalize the metrics.

Metrics are essential to what we are trying to accomplish.

The metrics should allow for flexibility in setting our goals.

You'll not want to give your readers work assignments or guessing games when you are trying to impart information. Using language to intentionally hide meaning has become all too common in today's world of spin and politics, but generally the use of buzzwords amounts to an unintentional hiding of meaning. That puts damaging leaks in the communication pipeline.

Commit yourself to using specific, descriptive, meaningful words. Both you and your readers will reap the rewards of your doing so. You'll know you've actually said what you intended to say, and your readers will receive the clear, precise meaning they crave.

APPENDIX D

A WORKBOOK FOR EXERCISES COORDINATED WITH THE CHAPTERS AND SECTIONS OF THIS BOOK

PLEASE READ THIS

This appendix contains thirty writing exercises (pages 204–214) and thirty corresponding solutions (pages 215-244), along with commentary to help you understand the thinking behind the changes. In thirty places throughout this book you will be asked to examine one of the exercises. You may take a run at revising a given exercise before studying its corresponding solution if you like, but know that many are difficult to revise due to having multiple subjective solutions. In nearly every case you will gain substantial value from an exercise if you simply (1) read the original, (2) think a bit about potential revisions, (3) examine the given solutions, (4) read the comments that illuminate thought behind those solutions, and (5) read the clean revision in comparison to the original exercise.

Workbook Contents

Exercise/Solution

Writing Exercises

Coordinated with the Chapters and Sections of this book.

Exercise #1: Chapter 2, Let Simple Words Dominate. Examine this paragraph, the aim being to replace unnecessarily complex words with simpler words that improve clarity and precision (solution on page 215).

The package arrived about noon, several hours later than anticipated. More importantly, our technicians were unable to complete the installation for three reasons. Firstly, they were without a tool that would have facilitated holding the parts more accurately into place while the resin set. Secondly, the language barrier kept them from maximizing their collective experience. And thirdly, they utilized cotter pins that were too small, because that is all we had. I should add that I need someone here to assist me by relieving me of mundane daily tasks.

Exercise #2: Chapter 3, Use Active Verbs. Energize these paragraphs by replacing weak verbs and nominalized clauses with strong verbs that reveal the action in specific terms (solution on page 216). Expect word reduction as a byproduct.

The community had experienced a long, painful teachers' strike just four years earlier, and the resolve of the president of the Board of Education was that a reoccurrence must be avoided. A meeting with each member of the Board allowed individual opinions to be assessed. Next was a meeting of the superintendent with the Board. That meeting resulted in a strategy considered by all to be savvy and fair-minded.

Meanwhile, the opinion of the teachers was that members of the Board of Education had perpetrated an intentional delay in negotiations—that the Board had taken its action in the hope that time would negatively impact the teachers' position. Clearly, an atmosphere of mutual trust was not in place. The result was likely to be another rancorous and chaotic September.

Ultimately, a surprise tactic by parents was the difference. After a demonstration surrounding the Board of Education building during an eleventh-hour negotiation session, the parents' demand for a contract announcement from the superintendent and the teacher's union representative was successful. With no one allowed to leave until such an announcement had been made, a contract was produced—whether out of fear or shame.

Exercise #3: Chapter 3, Use Active Voice. Examine these paragraphs with thoughts of turning unwarranted passive-voice writing into stronger, more reader-friendly, active-voice writing (solution on page 217). (Note: In the previous exercise you will have jettisoned some passive voice writing as a byproduct of infusing it with active verbs.)

New patterns have been ordered. The efficiency of the cutters should be increased by those patterns after a week or two. That much time is needed before a feeling for the new approach is acquired and before old habits are broken and new habits formed.

The impending change has been a topic of conversation around here for more than two months. Resistance has been voiced by some, but support is strong from others. Only after a period of time has passed and everyone has had a chance to adjust will the verdict be in. Expectations are that a firm choice between the old and the new can be made wisely about six months after the new approach has been introduced.

Exercise #4: Chapter 3, Keep People Visible (Personification). Examine this paragraph with thoughts of making the actors apparent. Because you will have to manufacture actors, expect wide variances between your solution and the solution shown, both for this exercise and for exercise #5 (solution on page 218).

Literature on the relationship between academic aptitude and music aptitude disputes the thought that one factor can be predicted by the other. Most research has found a correlation of .20 to .30. That fact shows that schools need to be concerned about the questionable practice of using the Wechsler Intelligence Scale for Children (WISC) as a gatekeeper for non-academic gifted and talented classes. A WISC score of 130 may indicate that a child is academically bright in spite of a music aptitude at perhaps the 50th percentile. Conversely, a WISC score of 110, well below the criterion for admission to the gifted program, might belong to a student whose music aptitude is at the 98th percentile. A responsible educational system will strive to match students with enrichment opportunities according to their aptitude for the content of the enrichment.

Exercise #5: Chapter 3, Keep People Visible (Personal References). Examine this paragraph with thoughts of infusing it with personal references that remove some of its blandness. Changes will be too extensive and require too much invention to compare with revisions shown (solution on page 219).

During the past three years, experiments by research personnel have shown promising results. Subjects to whom the new drug was administered have shown remarkable resilience to the infection. These results have encouraged the planning of a second wave of studies scheduled to begin in September. Administrative support is at an all-time high, and confidence is apparent among scientists who only a few years ago felt defeated.

Exercise #6: Chapter 4, Be Consistent. Examine these paragraphs with thoughts of making terms consistent (solution on page 220).

Subjects for this study were male and female English students in grades six and eight, with 30 of each sex from each grade ($N = 120$). All the children were taught by the same teacher in four randomly selected groups balanced for both gender and grade level. Groups 6M (sixth grade, male) and 8M (eighth grade male) were taught by a structured approach. Groups 6F (sixth grade, female) and 8F (eighth grade, female) were taught by a self-discovery approach.

The methods were chosen specifically to observe boys' reactions to a structured method and girls' reactions to a self-discovery method, with no intention to compare the two approaches across genders. Each group met twice weekly for 50 minutes per session. The boys' classes met at 9:00 a.m. and the girls' classes at 10:00 a.m. to eliminate divergent times of day as a contaminating factor. Content was identical for males and females. Only the approach to teaching varied.

Exercise #7: Chapter 4, Avoid Overstatement. Examine this paragraph with thoughts of eliminating overstatements that might undermine the writer's credibility (solution on page 221).

The children's behavior during the field trip was unbelievable. We learned that the planning we did was necessary to having the day run smoothly. The older children were really cooperative, and the younger children listened well. I decided that Mrs. McDougle was very right about two things. First, the Grand Canyon is amazingly gorgeous and breathtaking beyond all expectations. Second, her approach to organizing such an excursion is very unique.

Exercise #8: Chapter 4, Avoid Understatement. Examine this paragraph with thoughts of eliminating overly cautious statements and vague word choices that veil the message and undermine the credibility of the writer. Your solution will necessarily vary greatly from the revision shown, because lack of information in the original requires extensive invention (solution on page 222).

An experienced detective might predict some of the possible scenarios that could develop in the wake of a murder investigation. Ulterior motives will exist in anyone with a reason for hiding the killer's identity, with a danger of those motives impeding the investigation. Even persons in the dark about the identity of the murderer might suspect a friend, and could decide to thwart possible investigative efforts. The Commissioner is trying to move a new initiative forward to clear the way for more productive investigations. He has appointed Lieutenant Cooper to spearhead the effort and to create whatever training programs may be needed.

Exercise #9: Chapter 4, Avoid Jargon. Jargon, because it is personal, varies greatly. Make two lists of jargon that you might be tempted to use, one of professional jargon (shop talk) and one of social jargon (colloquialisms). Incorporate terms from each list into a few sentences, and then search for alternate, more widely known terms with which to replace your narrow terms. By creating your own original examples and revisions for this exercise, you will (1) become conscious of the kinds of jargon you are in danger of using, and (2) develop a feel for how to write alternative expressions that will communicate effectively with a wide audience (solution is personal).

Exercise #10: Chapter 4, Use Positive Form. Examine these paragraphs with thoughts of turning unwarranted negative-form statements into stronger, reader-friendly positive forms (solution on page 223).

The cost of the addition will not be close to the amount budgeted. Still, we do not have any choice but to proceed. We need the space desperately. Laboratory space is not adequate.

I have not heard very many complaints from our researchers about their working conditions, but I know they do not have much of what they need to conduct first-rate studies. I will submit a proposal next week for about $50,000 in additional equipment. I am writing now to give you time to think about where to get the money. I am sure that when you see the details of my proposal you will not disagree about the need. Not very often have I been so sure of my position.

Exercise #11: Chapter 4, Use Parallel Form. Examine these paragraphs in a way that makes good use of parallel form (solution on page 224).

If your business is exclusively an indoor enterprise, probably you give little or no consideration to the effects of season changes on your workers. You may want to reconsider that practice. A nearly universal fact is that season changes alter levels of productivity. Research has shown this to be true for administration, clerical staff, service providers, and assembly-line workers.

If you manage large numbers of workers,

a. research about the effects of season changes may be useful to you,

b. you may want to distill what you learn into an informational pamphlet for your workers

c. production figures from one season to another should be compared, and

d. you could benefit by designing specific countermeasures.

Whatever your business, you have problems and you are looking for answers. But some of the problems themselves may be hidden from view in so simple an issue as the time of year. Be careful not to be so attentive to the obvious that you open yourself to damage that can be inflicted by the inconsequential.

Exercise #12: Chapter 5, Avoid Filler. Examine these paragraphs with thoughts of removing filler words and phrases (solution on page 225).

The investigator's job was to identify the people who were responsible, and to do so in the process of safeguarding the company's public image. He met with the CEO on a daily basis to monitor the fallout. The kind of work that he was doing and the people who he met were unusual compared with any of the work that he had done in any of his previous positions.

The first week of the investigator's work passed, and he made plans for his second week on the case. At the beginning of his second week he introduced himself to two key players—Lance Atwood and Theresa Kestler—and began spending time with them for the purpose of winning their trust and confidence. It was less than a week later that they introduced him to the mastermind of the scheme. Soon he had exposed all the culprits, and by means of his brilliant interrogation techniques extracted confessions from everyone.

Exercise #13: Chapter 5, Avoid Redundancy. Examine these paragraphs with thoughts of removing redundancies to information written or implied elsewhere in the piece, or to anything universally known (solution on page 226).

Having now tried four different employees in that position in less than a year, I feel obligated to offer my personal opinion: we have the job configured in a way that no one can manage it. If we expect success there in the future, we need to make changes. I think we should both redistribute the work among the four persons working in that department as well as redesign the workstation for this unique position that has given us so much trouble in the past.

I visited a company in Chicago last week, where I spent approximately an hour to an hour and a half touring facilities. Where they once had four persons sharing the same space, they installed small, separate offices. That kind of change here might possibly improve concentration, morale, and productivity.

Exercise #14: Chapter 6, Make Smaller Sentences. Examine this three-sentence paragraph with thoughts of creating two paragraphs that contain multiple sentences. The average number of words per sentence in the original is 43. An infinite number of revisions is possible: be flexible in evaluating your work (solution on page 227).

Personnel issues have become complex as compared with decades ago—when the boss gave orders and employees expected to follow them—now that well-meaning protections installed to guard against employer abuses based on gender, race, and age have created loopholes that too many workers now seem willing to exploit in unprincipled ways. Now that the abusive hand has been passed from employer to worker, we may well be heading toward an exodus of good leaders from management roles, followed by a crisis in the quality of leadership, followed by a new round of abusive behavior stemming from the desperation of weak leaders trying to coax productivity from self-serving, game-playing employees. Unless we find a way to right this ship, we are likely to be left with a disastrous future.

Exercise #15: Chapter 6, Use Markers. Insert "markers," (1, 2, . . . or a, b . . .) at appropriate points within this sentence to make it easily digested without dividing it into multiple sentences (solution on page 228).

The issues discussed at the last board meeting were the prospect of closing two of the seven East Coast plants and distributing the production of those two among the other five in the most geographically sensible way, hiring a consulting firm to assume all responsibility for marketing, which has been a high-cost, low-yield endeavor as currently carried out within the corporate structure, abandoning product lines that have either lost money in recent years or shown marginal profits during the last decade, and reducing the workforce across the entire company by as much as 20 percent.

Exercise #16: Chapter 6, Use Punctuation. Use tools of punctuation to make this sentence easily digested as a single sentence (solution on page 229).

Adjudication of the local ethnic dance competition, begun here in 1927, involves a system of points awarded for the quality of the material, referred to as "selection," the uniqueness of the performance, referred to as "originality," the style of the performer, referred to as "form," and the category that is worth perhaps more than the other three categories combined, that being the level of overall competence exhibited, referred to as "skill."

Exercise #17: Chapter 6, Draw a Picture. Display the burdensome details of this unreadable sentence in a table or figure that makes those details more digestible for readers (solution on page 229).

Over the last quarter, the number of new accounts signed was 512 in Region I (215 at Ridley, 161 at Harriman, and 136 at Prospect), 468 in Region II (175 at Logan, 147 at Washington, and 146 at Hawthorne), and only 278 in Region III (103 at Simpson, 97 at Scott, and 78 at Littman).

Exercise #18: Chapter 7, Choose Specific Terms Over General. Find general terms that weaken these paragraphs—terms referred to variously as buzzwords or vocabulary eaters—and replace those terms with stronger, more specific terms. You will need to make some interpretations and exercise creativity (solution on page 230).

We acknowledge the problem. It is real, and we are committed to addressing it. We will look at several approaches. As experienced supervisors, probably you have valuable input to offer.

Because of the quantity of data we have to deal with, we are unlikely to have concrete answers for the upcoming meeting. Probably we are looking at at least two weeks to understand how to deal with all areas of the problem. I will update everyone on progress along the way.

I plan to implement my search for solutions the minute I enter my office tomorrow morning. Because I expect an ongoing process to be necessary, I am looking to implement weekly meetings beginning two weeks from tomorrow. At that time we will include employees from both areas. Whatever it takes, we are looking to put all of this last quarter's organizational problems behind us so you can implement your programs free of the chaos you have had to deal with recently.

Exercise #19: Chapter 7, Respect Shades of Meaning. Consider alternatives to the underlined words (solution on page 231).

I believe you are as <u>anxious</u> as I to launch this exciting project. I want you to interview <u>both</u> candidates. Because of your background, I <u>feel</u> that will be important to our making the best selection.

Once I have <u>determined</u> the costs to be incurred between here and completion, we will be ready to <u>solve</u> some of the more difficult questions. I know already that one of the chief <u>dilemmas</u> will be storage space for all the equipment involved.

Exercise #20: Chapter 8, Keep the Modifier and the Modified Together. Circle misplaced modifiers in this paragraph and draw an arrow from each to show its correct location (solution on page 232).

Our appointment with the WestMax team was set for 9:00 a.m. After we had almost waited for an hour, three of their five arrived. Sanderson announced without apology that there would only be four of them, and that the fourth was on his way. They never specifically told us what their problems had been that morning, but rather proceeded with the conversation as if they just wanted to get it finished and leave. By the time their fourth arrived, our team was not talking at all. Any company that brings that much rudeness and inconsideration to the table has to bring an enormous load of good business as compensation, and they had not even brought anything above average.

Exercise #21: Chapter 8, Follow an Action Phrase with the Action's Subject. Examine these paragraphs to correct misplaced subjects (solution on page 233).

After planning on the promotion for more than a year, Gail Fraley's supervisor disappointed her by giving the position to an outside applicant. She was bitter. With twenty years of diligent and faithful service on record, the company owed her more.

Gail was even more bitter when she learned of the nepotism behind the appointment of Karen Shield. Having married the boss's son two years earlier, her appointment was assured from the moment she applied.

Exercise #22: Chapter 8, Orient Readers with Word Placement. Examine this paragraph with thoughts of improving reader orientation (solution on page 234).

<u>All Directors and Managers of the Protocarcsic Division</u>

The fall marketing campaign is about to begin. Priority marketing will be given to our product, according to what Mr. Duncan said this morning. Let me remind you that a division other than ours has been given priority in the fall campaign every year since 2015. This is an opportunity. We will meet to explore ways we can help the marketing department Monday morning at 9:30. Information and ideas that you think will be of use should be brought to the meeting.

Exercise #23: Chapter 8, Emphasize Material with Word Placement. Examine this paragraph with thoughts of emphasizing points that seem most important. Be conservative. I believe only two sentences need changes (solution on page 235).

Some service companies pride themselves on the number of services they offer. Others pride themselves on offering only a few services, but at an exceptionally high level of performance. We have not made a conscious decision about our place on that breadth/depth continuum in the midst of our growth. If we continue to "let it ride," we risk making ourselves victims of circumstance—a conglomeration of workers with no firm identity drifting down paths of least resistance in the hope that everything will turn out for the best. Few, if any, successful companies have wandered into their success with neither identity nor design, judging by what I have learned by reading their history.

Exercise #24: Chapter 9, Incorrect Word Choice, Subject/Verb Disagreement, Dangling Participle, Split Infinitive. Examine these paragraphs to remove the nine grammatical errors they contain (solution on page 236).

Observing her performance for the team from an outsider's view, she handles less clients than the others, writes a smaller amount of contracts, and—like I wrote in my first report—backs off from group projects where she should contribute. The latter is most disconcerting to her colleagues. Some have openly accused her of laying down on the job.

If the CEO hopes to dramatically improve on last year's performance, he will need to make important personnel decisions soon. A series of recent personnel losses, troubling inquiries, and large, puzzling mistakes have put him in a very difficult position.

Exercise #25: Chapter 9, Wrong Verb Tense, Careless Use of Prepositions, Wrong Pronoun Case, and Antecedent/Pronoun Disagreement. Examine this paragraph to remove the five grammatical errors it contains (solution on page 237).

Yesterday he told me that he saw nothing over the previous few weeks to make him suspicious. Seeing he had just come off of vacation, I appreciated him offering to talk to me. Both of us knew our collaboration could lead to others resenting him and I. Too often, when a person tries to do what is right, they find themselves giving credence to Clare Booth Luce's cynical observation that "no good deed goes unpunished."

Exercise #26: Chapter 11, Accommodate Gender Elegantly. Examine this paragraph with thoughts of using elegant non-sexist language (solution on page 238).

When an employee is chronically late, they will be counseled for three occurrences before being written up. After a fifth occurrence in less than six months, s/he will be put on probation. A sixth occurrence within a year will be considered cause for his/her termination.

A supervisor will have some room for discretion, but he must make a strong case for retaining any chronically late employee. Failure to appear for work on time is irresponsible, and it reflects poorly on both the employee and her department.

Note: These last four exercises involve all the punctuation described in Chapters 11 and 12 except sentence enders (periods, question marks, exclamation points) and contractions. The order of the content is not in absolute correspondence with the order presented in the book.

Exercise #27: apostrophes, quotation marks, and hyphens. Examine this paragraph for flaws in the use of or failure to use these three punctuation marks (solution on page 239).

I read in the manager's report that each manager gave a deep dive answer to the question "What do I see as the greatest impediment to this companys' being managed efficiently"? Apparently the same question had been asked of managers in the 1990's, and the CEOs purpose in asking again was "to see changes, both in the opinions of the managers and in what we refer to as "glaring gaps" between what we need and what we have".

213

Exercise #28: commas. Add and delete commas in these paragraphs to arrive at a use of commas that you believe is optimal (solution on page 240).

Gerald Wheeler came to us with a series of complaints and we gave our full attention to every item on his list. He talked, and we listened. Showing admirable patience and stamina Jeff typed furiously for nearly an hour to record all the proceedings. Gerald, appearing desperate to make his points spoke rapidly and loudly. Sarah who had an important appointment after work, left at 5:00 p.m. The rest of us, stayed another hour.

Gerald's most passionate wish was to talk directly to the Director of Human Resources who had fired him. We told him we would be unwise to promise him a resolution, which we had no authority to carry out. Eventually, he left with none of the answers, consolation or satisfaction he had been seeking.

Exercise #29: semicolons and colons. Examine this paragraph for appropriate use of semicolons and colons (solution on page 242).

Several noted scientists agree (Bronson, 1997) (Mason, 2003) (Shepherd, 2005) (Zendler, 2007). That makes his argument more convincing, helps sway board members, who tend to be conservative, and improves his chances, lean as they still are, of fending off challenges. One large hurdle still remains; convincing the stockholders that the investment is sound. The steps I recommend are to:

    1. solicit strong statements of support from leading scientists.

    2. write a convincing piece for the stockholder newsletter.

    3. meet individually with key players.

Exercise #30: hyphens, dashes, parentheses, slashes, brackets, and ellipses.
Examine this paragraph for appropriate use of these six punctuation marks (solution on page 243).

The rough hewn wood trim, the faded/peeling paint, and the dingy tile floors, with particularly dirty grout, made the old warehouse a challenge to convert quickly into usable office space. Bob Ferris studied the space thoroughly, all the while envisioning what he could do-working with no help from the others-to meet the deadline. He remembered the advice his father had given him years earlier: "Focus on the basic problems. Details, if you get too caught up in them, will eat you alive and keep you from the necessities that you need to take care of."

Solutions to Writing Exercises

Coordinated with the Chapters and Sections of this book.

Exercise #1: Chapter 2, Let Simple Words Dominate.

(1.) expected

The package arrived about noon, several hours later than ~~anticipated.~~ More

(2.) important,

~~importantly,~~ our technicians were unable to complete the installation for three reasons.

(3.) First,   (4.) held

~~Firstly,~~ they were without a tool that would have ~~facilitated holding~~ the parts more

(3.) Second,

accurately into place while the resin set. ~~Secondly,~~ the language barrier kept them from

(5.) making the most of   (3.) third,   (6.) used

~~maximizing~~ their collective experience. And ~~thirdly,~~ they ~~utilized~~ cotter pins that were

(7.) help

too small, because that is all we had. I should add that I need someone here to ~~assist~~ me

by relieving me of mundane daily tasks.

Comments

Down-to-earth word choices help readers read freely, feel less intimidated, and assimilate information more quickly. Also, the revision gives readers a more honest (precise) account of the writer's thoughts.

1. Was the arrival of the package an event anticipated with some kind of preparation? More likely it was merely an expectation.

2. The point is that installation problems were a more *important* issue than was the late arrival of the package.

3. The order of the points made was *first*, *second*, and *third*. The issue is sequence.

4, 5, 6. These choices are just a matter of a writer shedding pretentious affectations.

7. The writer's plans are not to do mundane tasks with *assistance*, but rather to have another person *help* the total effort by doing many of those tasks independently.

Clean Revision

The package arrived about noon, several hours later than expected. More important, our technicians were unable to complete the installation for three reasons. First, they were without a tool that would have held the parts more accurately into place while the resin set. Second, the language barrier kept them from making the most of their collective experience. And third, they used cotter pins that were too small, because that is all we had. I should add that I need someone here to help me by relieving me of mundane daily tasks.

Exercise #2: Chapter 3, Use Active Verbs.

The community had *suffered* ~~experienced~~ a long, painful teachers' strike just four years earlier, and ~~the resolve of~~ *resolved to avoid a* the president of the Board of Education ~~was that a~~ reoccurrence. *She met* ~~must be avoided. A meeting~~ with each member of the Board ~~allowed~~ *to assess* individual opinions. *Then she asked* ~~to be assessed. Next was a meeting of~~ the superintendent *to meet* with the Board. ~~That meeting~~ *Together they designed a strategy that all deemed* ~~resulted in a strategy considered by all to be~~ savvy and fair-minded.

Meanwhile, ~~the opinion of the~~ teachers ~~was that~~ *thought* members of the Board of Education had ~~perpetrated an intentional delay in~~ *delayed* negotiations *intentionally* ~~that the Board had taken its action in~~ ~~the hope that time would negatively impact~~ *to weaken* the teachers' position. Clearly, ~~an atmosphere of~~ *neither side trusted the other.* ~~mutual trust was not in place. The result was likely to be~~ *The table had been set for* another rancorous and chaotic

September.

Ultimately, *parents made the difference with* a surprise tactic. ~~by parents was the difference. After a demonstration~~ *Several hundred of them* ~~surrounding~~ *surrounded* the Board of Education building during an eleventh-hour negotiation session, ~~the~~. *They demanded* ~~parents' demand for~~ a contract announcement from the superintendent and the teacher's union representative ~~was successful. With no one allowed to~~ *, refusing to let anyone* leave until ~~such an~~ *that was accomplished.* ~~announcement had been made, a contract was produced~~—Whether out of fear or shame, *the two parties agreed on a contract.*

Comments

The strength of the revision is in its vigor, and that vigor is generated by action words: *suffered, resolved, met, asked, designed, deemed, thought, delayed, weaken, made, surrounded, demanded, refusing, agreed.* Notice also that the revision features active voice over passive (more in the next exercise), and that it is more concise. To write around verbs requires more words than to use the verbs themselves. So, avoiding strong verbs does more than stultify writing: it requires readers to read more pages. Which style would you prefer to read—particularly in a long document?

Clean Revision

The community had suffered a long, painful teachers' strike just four years earlier, and the president of the Board of Education resolved to avoid a reoccurrence. She met with each member of the Board to assess individual opinions. Then she asked the superintendent to meet with the Board. Together they designed a strategy that all deemed both savvy and fair-minded.

Meanwhile, teachers thought members of the Board of Education had delayed negotiations intentionally to weaken the teachers' position. Clearly, neither side trusted the other. The table was set for another rancorous and chaotic September.

Ultimately, parents made the difference with a surprise tactic. Several hundred of them surrounded the Board of Education building during an eleventh-hour negotiation session. They demanded a contract announcement from the superintendent and the teacher's union representative, refusing to let anyone leave until that was accomplished. Whether out of fear or shame, the two parties agreed on a contract.

Exercise #3: Chapter 3, Use Active Voice.

We have ordered new patterns that should increase the
~~New patterns have been ordered. The~~ efficiency of the cutters ~~should be increased~~
They will need that   to acquire
~~by those patterns~~ after a week or two. ~~That~~ much time ~~is needed before~~ a feeling for the new
and to replace old habits with new.
approach ~~is acquired and before old habits are broken and new habits formed.~~
Everyone in the plant has been talking about the impending change
~~The impending change has been a topic of conversation around here~~ for more than
Some are resisting it, but others support it strongly. We will have a verdict only
two months. ~~Resistance has been voiced by some, but support is strong from others. Only~~
after a period of time has passed and everyone has had a chance to adjust. ~~will the verdict be~~
The manager believes we will be prepared to make a wise
~~in. Expectations are that a firm~~ choice between the old and the new ~~can be made wisely~~ about
six months after introducing the new approach.

Comments

Notice the absence of people taking action or offering thoughts in the passive-voice original. You'll find those people in the revision: we, the cutters, the manager, everyone in the plant. As heavily laced as this example is with passive voice, it's not far-fetched. Passive voice is a kind of snare. Once you step into it, it's likely to capture you and sap your writing of vigor. Beware!

Clean Revision

We have ordered new patterns that should increase the efficiency of the cutters after a week or two. They will need that much time to acquire a feeling for the new approach and to replace old habits with new.

Everyone in the plant has been talking about the impending change for more than two months. Some are resisting it, but others support it strongly. We will have a verdict only after a period of time has passed and everyone has had a chance to adjust. The manager believes we will be prepared to make a wise choice between the old and the new about six months after introducing the new approach.

Exercise #4: Chapter 3, Keep People Visible (Personification).

Literature on the relationship between academic aptitude and music aptitude
reveals   cannot   researchers have
~~disputes the thought~~ that one factor ~~can~~ be predicted from the other. Most ~~research has~~ found
school personnel
a correlation of .20 to .30. That fact shows that ~~schools~~ need to be concerned about

the questionable practice of using the Wechsler Intelligence Scale for Children (WISC) as a

gatekeeper for non-academic gifted and talented classes. A WISC score of 130 may indicate

that a child is academically bright in spite of a music aptitude at perhaps the 50th percentile.

Conversely, a WISC score of 110, well below the criterion for admission to the gifted

program, might belong to a student whose music aptitude is at the 98th percentile. ~~A~~
Responsible educators
~~responsible educational system~~ will strive to match students with enrichment opportunities

according to their aptitude for the content of the enrichment.

Comments

Note that in the first sentence my judgment allows for "Literature…reveals," but not "Literature…disputes." Where you draw the line for personification is a judgment call. If you have any doubt about how to attribute a given action, write the sentence twice, once with a non-human as the subject and once with a human as the subject. After reading the two next to each other, you'll know which version your mind receives most comfortably.

Clean Revision

Literature on the relationship between academic aptitude and music aptitude reveals that one factor cannot be predicted from the other. Most researchers have found a correlation of .20 to .30. That fact shows that school personnel need to be concerned about the questionable practice of using the Wechsler Intelligence Scale for Children (WISC) as a gatekeeper for non-academic gifted and talented classes. A WISC score of 130 may indicate that a child is academically bright in spite of a music aptitude at perhaps the 50th percentile. Conversely, a WISC score of 110, well below the criterion for admission to the gifted program, might belong to a student whose music aptitude is at the 98th percentile. Responsible educators will strive to match students with enrichment opportunities according to their aptitude for the content of the enrichment.

Exercise #5: Chapter 3, Keep People Visible (Personal References). Note: an overlay of revisions is impractical: see "clean revision."

Original

During the past three years, experiments by research personnel have shown promising results. Subjects to whom the new drug was administered have shown remarkable resilience to the infection. These results have encouraged the planning of a second wave of studies scheduled to begin in September. Administrative support is at an all-time high, and confidence is apparent among scientists who only a few years ago felt defeated.

Clean Revision

After three years of experiments, team leader Glenda Taylor says "results are promising. Nearly all subjects who've received the new drug are remarkably resilient to the infection." Taylor's team of seven will begin a second wave of studies in September. Asked about administrative commitment, COO Brent Harwood declared "They've earned whatever support we can give." In contrast to a few years ago, confidence shone brightly today in the faces of Dr. Taylor's staff.

Comments

The clean revision is not so much a revision as a rewritten version, so any solution you attempted is likely to bear little resemblance to it. Your only measure will be the extent to which you found ways to bring life to the text. That being said, I should point out that the original is perfectly acceptable as it stands. The purpose here is not to correct errors, but simply to show ways in which personal references can enliven a piece of writing. In the end, your choice of style will depend very much on the nature of your document and on your intentions for its use. The same information might look quite different in a newsletter than it does in a report.

One way I gave a personal feeling to the revision was to name and quote individual persons, but there is more to it than that. By referring to the scientists as

"Taylor's team of seven," and by saying that confidence shone brightly in their faces, I put readers in the midst of a crowd of real, expressive people. Only two became known by name, but the reader can imagine all of them at work more so than when they were known simply as "administrative support" or "research personnel."

Exercise #6: Chapter 4, Be Consistent.

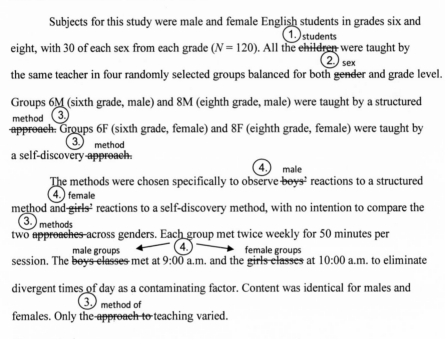

Subjects for this study were male and female English students in grades six and eight, with 30 of each sex from each grade ($N = 120$). All the ~~children~~ students were taught by the same teacher in four randomly selected groups balanced for both ~~gender~~ sex and grade level.

Groups 6M (sixth grade, male) and 8M (eighth grade, male) were taught by a structured ~~approach.~~ method Groups 6F (sixth grade, female) and 8F (eighth grade, female) were taught by a self-discovery ~~approach.~~ method

The methods were chosen specifically to observe ~~boys'~~ male reactions to a structured method and ~~girls'~~ female reactions to a self-discovery method, with no intention to compare the two ~~approaches~~ methods across genders. Each group met twice weekly for 50 minutes per session. The ~~boys classes~~ male groups met at 9:00 a.m. and the ~~girls classes~~ female groups at 10:00 a.m. to eliminate divergent times of day as a contaminating factor. Content was identical for males and females. Only the ~~approach to~~ method of teaching varied.

Comments

1. I changed *children* to *students* for consistency with the preceding sentence.

2. I changed *gender* to *sex* for consistency with the preceding sentence.

3. I changed *approach* to *method* for consistency with the next paragraph. Note that where terms are inconsistent, the first term used is not necessarily the best. In this context, *method* is more precise than *approach*. The two ways of teaching used in the study were designed in detail and used in multiple locations, so they became *methods* rather than mere *approaches*.

4. Sometimes you'll find yourself forced to choose between conflicting principles. *Boys' reactions* and *girls' reactions*, for example, may be more specific terms than *male reactions* and *female reactions*, but the opening

description of the subjects refers to them as *male* and *female*—common in scientific studies. In research writing, faced with the choice between consistency of terms and such a slight gain in specificity, you need to choose consistency. Alleviation of confusion is the higher value.

Clean Revision

Subjects for this study were male and female English students in grades six and eight, with 30 of each sex from each grade ($N = 120$). All the students were taught by the same teacher in four randomly-selected groups balanced for both sex and grade level. Groups 6M (sixth grade, male) and 8M (eighth grade, male) were taught by a structured method. Groups 6F (sixth grade, female) and 8F (eighth grade, female) were taught by a self-discovery method.

The methods were chosen specifically to observe male reactions to a structured method and female reactions to a self-discovery method, with no intention to compare the two methods across genders. Each group met twice weekly for 50 minutes per session. The male groups met at 9:00 a.m. and the female groups at 10:00 a.m. to eliminate time of day as a contaminating factor. Content was identical for males and females. Only the method of teaching varied.

Exercise #7: Chapter 4, Avoid Overstatement.

The children's behavior during the field trip was ~~unbelievable.~~ ① outstanding We learned that the planning we did was ~~necessary~~ ② important to having the day run smoothly. The older children were ~~really~~ ③ cooperative, and the younger children listened well. I decided that Mrs. McDougle was ~~very~~ ③ right about two things. First, the Grand Canyon is ~~amazingly~~ ④ gorgeous and breathtaking beyond all expectations. Second, her approach to organizing such an excursion is ~~very~~ ③ unique.

Comments

1. *Unbelievable* is a common overstatement. Probably a witness would have found the children's behavior impressive, but not beyond believability.

2. As important as the planning was, can the writer be certain that it was absolutely *necessary* to their having a smooth-running day?

3. Without the elevating modifiers *really* and *very,* readers know that the older children were cooperative (not uncooperative), that Mrs. McDougle was right (not wrong), and that Mrs. McDougle's approach is unique (not commonplace).

4. Though the issue of overstatement here is a judgment call, the awkward adverb *amazingly* makes the writer appear to be stretching for description.

Clean Revision

The children's behavior during the field trip was outstanding. We learned that the planning we did was important to having the day run smoothly. The older children were cooperative, and the younger children listened well. I decided that Mrs. McDougle was right about two things. First, the Grand Canyon is gorgeous and breathtaking beyond all expectations. Second, her approach to organizing such an excursion is unique.

Exercise #8: Chapter 4, Avoid Understatement.

An experienced detective might predict some of the ~~possible~~ scenarios that ~~could~~ ①

develop in the wake of a murder investigation. Ulterior motives ~~will exist in anyone~~ ②

threaten to impede
~~with a reason~~ for hiding the killer's identity, ~~with a danger of those motives impeding~~ the

③ , but suspecting
investigation. Even persons in the dark about the identity of the murderer ~~might suspect~~

④
a friend, ~~and~~ could decide to thwart ~~possible~~ investigative efforts. The Commissioner is ⑤

reduce such problems by training new detectives to be more skillful at spotting subterfuge,
trying to ▲ ~~move a new initiative forward to clear the way for more productive investigations.~~
and by creating ways to isolate informants from each other earlier in the investigation.
He has appointed Lieutenant Cooper to spearhead the effort and to create whatever training

are ⑥
programs ~~may be~~ needed.

Comments

1. *Might predict* leaves plenty of latitude for an experienced detective without the help of *possible* and *could* (which, even if one were needed, duplicate each other).

2. The source of ulterior motives would necessarily be someone who has a reason for hiding the killer's identity.

3. The actions described would come not from one who *might* suspect, but from one who *does* suspect a particular person.

4. *Could* leaves enough latitude without the help of *possible*.

5. Most readers are frustrated and annoyed when such a mushy phrase as *move a new initiative forward* replaces specifics. Such a phrase, amounting to a string of words posing as information, leaves an

impression that the writer is hiding something. (Uncharacteristically, this revision increases rather reduces the number of words used.)

6. Lieutenant Cooper is likely to put his efforts into creating programs that *are* needed rather than into programs that simply *may be* (and therefore may not be) needed.

Clean Revision

An experienced detective might predict some of the scenarios that develop in the wake of a murder investigation. Ulterior motives for hiding the killer's identity threaten to impede the investigation. Even persons in the dark about the identity of the murderer, but suspecting a friend, could decide to thwart investigative efforts. The Commissioner is trying to lessen such problems by training new detectives to be more skillful at spotting subterfuge, and by creating better ways to isolate informants from each other earlier in the investigation. He has appointed Lieutenant Cooper to spearhead the effort and to create whatever training programs are needed.

Exercise #9: Chapter 4, Avoid Jargon. No solutions can be provided for this personal exercise.

Exercise #10: Chapter 4, Use Positive Form.

The cost of the addition will ~~not be close to~~ *be much greater than* the amount budgeted. Still, we ~~do not have any~~ *have no* choice but to proceed. We need the space desperately. Laboratory space is ~~not adequate.~~ *inadequate*

I have ~~not heard very many~~ *heard few* complaints from our researchers about their working conditions, but I know they ~~do not have~~ *lack* much of what they need to conduct first-rate studies.

I will submit a proposal next week for about $50,000 in additional equipment. I am writing now to give you time to think about where to get the money. I am sure that when you see the details of my proposal you will ~~not disagree~~ *agree* about the need. ~~Not very often~~ *Seldom* have I been so sure of my position.

Comments

Some decisions made here are subjective. (1) At the end of the first paragraph, *not adequate* may present the intended tone better than *inadequate.* (2) Sometimes intentional understatements, such as using *not disagree* in place of *agree* in the next-to-last sentence, serve a purpose, but I recommend against using that ploy frequently.

Most other revisions shown are clear improvements. Notice that the writing of a positive form sometimes is a simple matter of exercising a mature vocabulary, as in using *seldom* in the last sentence rather than *not very often*.

Clean Revision

The cost of the addition will be much greater than the amount budgeted. Still, we have no choice but to proceed. We need the space desperately. Laboratory space is inadequate.

I have heard few complaints from our researchers about their working conditions, but I know they lack much of what they need to conduct first-rate studies. I will submit a proposal next week for about $50,000 in additional equipment. I am writing now to give you time to think about where to get the money. I am sure that when you see the details of my proposal you will agree about the need. Seldom have I been so sure of my position.

Exercise #11: Chapter 4, Use Parallel Form.

If your business is exclusively an indoor enterprise, probably you give little or no consideration to the effects of season changes on your workers. You may want to reconsider that practice. A nearly universal fact is that season changes alter levels ~~of productivity~~ _{productivity}. Research has shown this to be true for ~~administration,~~ _{administrators} clerical staff, service providers, and assembly-line workers.

If you manage large numbers of workers, _{you may want to}
  a. _{read} research about the effects of season changes ~~may be useful to you~~,

  b. ~~you may want to~~ distill what you learn into an informational pamphlet for your workers,

  c. _{compare} production figures from one season to another ~~should be compared,~~ and

  d. ~~you could benefit by designing~~ _{design} specific countermeasures.

Whatever your business, you have problems and you are looking for ~~answers~~ _{solutions.} But some of the problems themselves may be hidden from view in so simple an issue as the time of year. Be careful not to be so attentive to the obvious that you ~~open yourself to damage that~~ _{lose sight of the subtle.} ~~can be inflicted by the inconsequential.~~

Comments

The nonparallel structures you are most likely to have repaired are the nonparallel series immediately prior to the list (*administrators*) and nonparallel entries in the list itself. Verbs work well as parallel leads into the list entries: *read*, *distill*, *compare*, and *design*. The first opportunity for parallel construction (third sentence) is less prominent: "Season changes alter productivity levels." So are the two word-pairings near the end: *problems* and *solutions*; *obvious* and *subtle*.

Clean Revision

If your business is exclusively an indoor enterprise, probably you give little or no consideration to the effects of season changes on your workers. You may want to reconsider that practice. A nearly universal fact is that season changes alter productivity levels. Research has shown this to be true for administrators, clerical staff, service providers, and assembly line workers.

If you manage large numbers of workers, you may want to

        a. read research about the effects of season changes,
        b. distill what you learn into an informational pamphlet for your workers,
        c. compare production figures from one season to another, and
        d. design specific countermeasures.

Whatever your business, you have problems and you are looking for solutions. But some of the problems themselves may be hidden from view in so simple an issue as the time of year. Be careful not to be so attentive to the obvious that you lose sight of the subtle.

Exercise #12: Chapter 5, Avoid Filler.

The investigator's job was to identify the people ~~who were~~ responsible, and to do so ~~in the process of~~ _{while} safeguarding the company's public image. He met with the CEO ~~on a~~ daily ~~basis~~ to monitor the fallout. The kind of work ~~that~~ he was doing and the people ~~who~~ he met were unusual compared with any of the work ~~that~~ he had done ~~in any of his previous~~ _{previously.} ~~positions.~~

~~The first week of the investigator's work passed, and he made plans for his second week on the case.~~ At the beginning of his second week ~~he~~ _{on the case, the investigator} introduced himself to two key players—Lance Atwood and Theresa Kestler—and began spending time with them ~~for the purpose of winning~~ _{to win} their trust and confidence. ~~It was~~ less than a week later ~~that~~ they introduced him to the mastermind of the scheme. Soon he had exposed all the culprits, and by means of his brilliant interrogation techniques extracted confessions from everyone.

Comments

When you look for filler, be sure to think outside the specific words and phrases shown in the examples and tables of Chapter 5. For example, at the end of the first paragraph of this exercise, to replace *in any of his previous positions* with *previously* works well. The slight change in precise meaning is innocuous. Possibilities for removing filler are endless, or at least seem to be.

When nearly an entire sentence is filler, as in the opening of the second paragraph, you are likely to find yourself salvaging material of value and transplanting it to another sentence. Keep sentence-combining in mind as a way to fight filler.

Clean Revision   (Word Reduction: 159 to 117)

The investigator's job was to identify the people responsible, and to do so while safeguarding the company's public image. He met with the CEO daily to monitor fallout. The kind of work he was doing and the people he met were unusual compared with any work he had done previously.

At the beginning of his second week on the case, the investigator introduced himself to two key players—Lance Atwood and Theresa Kestler—and began spending time with them to win their trust and confidence. Less than a week later they introduced him to the mastermind of the scheme. Soon he had exposed all the culprits, and by his brilliant interrogation techniques extracted confessions from everyone.

Exercise #13: Chapter 5, Avoid Redundancy.

Having now tried four ~~different~~ employees in that position in less than a year, I feel obligated to offer my ~~personal~~ opinion: we have the job configured in a way that no one can manage ~~it.~~ If we expect success there ~~in the future,~~ we need to make changes. I think we should ~~both~~ redistribute the work among the four persons working in that department as well as redesign the workstation for this one unique position that has given us so much trouble ~~in the past.~~

I visited a company in Chicago last week, where I spent ~~approximately~~ an hour to an hour and a half touring facilities. Where they once had four persons sharing ~~the same~~ space, they installed small, separate offices. That kind of change here might ~~possibly~~ improve concentration, morale, and productivity.

Comments

Without *different*, readers will not think the four employees are the same person; without *personal*, they will not think the opinion belongs to someone else; without *it* they will still know that the job is what needs managing; and without *in the future*, they will not be at a loss as to when success is expected. *Both* duplicates *as well as*, and without *in the past*, readers will know when previous problems occurred.

An hour to an hour and a half is an approximation, making *approximately* a redundancy, and a space shared is necessarily the *same* space. *Possibly* is commonly inserted as a redundancy to *might* or *could* (as is its first cousin, *potentially*).

Clean Revision   (Word Reduction: 132 to 119)

Having now tried four employees in that position in less than a year, I feel obligated to offer my opinion: we have the job configured in a way that no one can manage. If we expect success there, we need to make changes. I think we should redistribute the work among the four persons working in that department as well as redesign the workstation for this one unique position that has given us so much trouble.

I visited a company in Chicago last week, where I spent an hour to an hour and a half touring facilities. Where they once had four persons sharing space, they installed small, separate offices. That kind of change here might improve concentration, morale, and productivity.

Exercise #14: Chapter 6, Make Smaller Sentences.

Personnel issues have become complex ~~as compared with~~ decades ago, ~~when~~ the [D]
boss gave orders and employees expected to follow them. More recently, ~~now that~~ well-meaning

protections installed to guard against employer abuses based on gender, race, and age
have created loopholes. ~~that~~ T too many workers now seem willing to exploit those loopholes in unprincipled

ways. ¶ So ~~Now that~~ the abusive hand has been passed from employer to worker, ~~we may well~~ a circumstance
~~be heading toward~~ that could spark an exodus of good leaders from management roles. That could lead to ~~followed by~~ a crisis

in the quality of leadership, followed by a new round of abusive behavior stemming from

the desperation of weak leaders trying to coax productivity from self-serving, game-playing
employees. We must ~~Unless we~~ find a way to right this ship, to avoid ~~we are likely to be left with~~ a disastrous

future. (*For greater strength, reverse this last sentence: "To avoid...right this ship."*)

227

Comments

You can see that total word reduction (just 129 to 121) is not the primary objective in repairing over-stuffed writing. The primary objective is to avoid filler and redundancies that generate too many words in each sentence—not necessarily too many words overall. You might even find yourself increasing the total word count a bit in the course of repairing overstuffed writing. The following statistics illuminate this revision:

	Paragraphs	Sentences	Words	Words per Sentence	Average Words per Sentence
Original	1	3	129	52, 58, 19	43
Revision	2	7	121	5, 12, 19, 13, 24, 34, 14	17

Notice particularly the variability in sentence length and the average sentence length. (To find average sentence length for a paragraph or section in Microsoft® Word, use Word Count, and then divide by the number of sentences.) Good writing generally conforms to Rudolph Flesch's advice about those matters (see p. 36).

Clean Revision

Personnel issues have become complex. Decades ago, the boss gave orders and employees expected to follow them. More recently, well-meaning protections installed to guard against employer abuses based on gender, race, and age have created loopholes. Too many workers now seem willing to exploit those loopholes in unprincipled ways.

So the abusive hand has been passed from employer to worker, a circumstance that could spark an exodus of good leaders from management roles. That could lead to a crisis in the quality of leadership, followed by a new round of abusive behavior stemming from the desperation of weak leaders trying to coax productivity from self-serving, game-playing employees. To avoid a disastrous future, we must find a way to right this ship.

Exercise #15: Chapter 6, Use Markers. Note: an overlay of revisions is impractical: see "clean revision."

The issues discussed at the last board meeting were the prospect of closing two of the seven East Coast plants and distributing the production of those two among the other five in the most geographically sensible way, hiring a consulting firm to assume all responsibility for marketing, which has been a high-cost, low-yield endeavor as currently carried out within the corporate structure, abandoning product lines that have either lost money in recent years or shown marginal profits during the last decade, and reducing the workforce across the entire company by as much as 20 percent.

Clean Revision

The issues discussed at the last board meeting were the prospects of (1) closing two of the seven East Coast plants and distributing the production of those two among the other five in the most geographically sensible way; (2) hiring a consulting firm to assume all responsibility for marketing, which has been a high-cost, low-yield endeavor as currently carried out within the corporate structure; (3) abandoning product lines that have either lost money in recent years or shown marginal profits during the last decade; and (4) reducing the workforce across the entire company by as much as 20 percent.

Comments

You can help readers maintain concentration through long sentences having several discrete pieces of information by using either letters or numbers to flag changes in content. A secondary advantage of markers is that they enable readers to refer back to a particular point without searching for the seams in the sentence. Notice the parallel terms that begin each segment: *closing*, *hiring*, *abandoning*, *reducing*.

Exercise #16: Chapter 6, Use Punctuation. Note: an overlay of revisions is impractical: see "clean revision."

Original

Adjudication of the local ethnic dance competition, begun here in 1927, involves a system of points awarded for the quality of the material, referred to as "selection," the uniqueness of the performance, referred to as "originality," the style of the performer, referred to as "form," and the category that is worth perhaps more than the other three categories combined, that being the level of overall competence exhibited, referred to as "skill."

Clean Revision

Adjudication of the local ethnic dance competition, begun here in 1927, involves a system of points awarded for the quality of the material (selection), the uniqueness of the performance (originality), the style of the performer (form), and—worth perhaps more than the other three categories combined—overall competence (skill).

Comments

As you become conversant with the full range of punctuation marks, you'll expand your arsenal of tools for clarifying long sentences.

Exercise #17: Chapter 6, Draw a Picture. Note: an overlay of revisions is impractical: see "clean revision."

Original

        Over the last quarter, the number of new accounts signed was 512 in Region I (215 at Ridley, 161 at Harriman, and 136 at Prospect), 468 in Region II (175 at Logan, 147 at Washington, and 146 at Hawthorne), and only 278 in Region III (103 at Simpson, 97 at Scott, and 78 at Littman).

Clean Revision

        The number of new accounts signed across our company over the last quarter is shown by Region and Site in Table 1.

TABLE 1: Number of New Accounts Signed Over the Last Quarter, by Region and Site

REGION I		REGION II		REGION III	
Ridley	215	Logan	175	Simpson	103
Harriman	161	Washington	147	Scott	97
Prospect	136	Hawthorne	146	Littman	78
TOTAL	512	TOTAL	468	TOTAL	278

Exercise #18: Chapter 7, Choose Specific Terms Over General.

        We acknowledge the problem. It is real, and we are committed to ~~addressing~~ (solving) it. We will ~~look at~~ (consider) several approaches. As experienced supervisors, probably you have valuable ~~input~~ (thoughts and ideas) to offer.

        Because of the quantity of data we have to ~~deal with,~~ (sort and analyze,) we are unlikely to have concrete answers for ~~the upcoming~~ (next week's) meeting. Probably we ~~are looking at~~ (will need) at least two weeks to understand how to ~~deal with all areas~~ (undertake all aspects) of the problem. I will ~~update~~ (inform) everyone ~~on~~ (of) progress along the way.

        I plan to ~~implement~~ (begin) my search for solutions the minute I enter my office tomorrow morning. Because I expect ~~an ongoing process~~ (a long-term effort) to be necessary, I ~~am looking to~~ (plan to) ~~implement~~ (resume) weekly meetings beginning two weeks from tomorrow. At that time, we will include employees from both ~~areas.~~ (departments) Whatever it takes, we ~~are looking~~ (expect) to put all of this last quarter's organizational problems behind us so you can ~~implement~~ (administer) your programs free of the ~~chaos~~ (overcome) you have had to deal with recently.

Comments

This excerpt, of course, comes from a larger context in which the company, its problems, the data, etc. are familiar to readers. Even without that information, you will see ways to apply more precise language. By touting the virtues of specificity and precision, I do not imply that you should avoid general terms altogether. Sometimes they are appropriate. My point is that the general terms you use should stem from your having thought about the effect you want rather than from having neglected to think deeply. Simply put, the revised version, as compared to the original, says more. My assumption is that one who decides to use language wants to say more within a given space rather than less.

Clean Revision

We acknowledge the problem. It is real, and we are committed to solving it. We will consider several approaches. As experienced supervisors, probably you have valuable thoughts and ideas to offer.

Because of the quantity of data we have to sort and analyze, we are unlikely to have concrete answers for next week's meeting. Probably we will need at least two weeks to understand how to undertake all aspects of the problem. I will inform everyone of progress along the way.

I plan to begin my search for solutions the minute I enter my office tomorrow morning. Because I expect a long-term effort to be necessary, I plan to resume weekly meetings beginning two weeks from tomorrow. At that time, we will include employees from both departments. Whatever it takes, we expect to put all of this last quarter's organizational problems behind us so you can administer your programs free of the chaos you have had to overcome recently.

Exercise #19: Chapter 7, Respect Shades of Meaning.

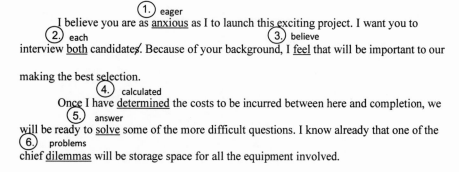

(1.) eager
I believe you are as <u>anxious</u> as I to launch this exciting project. I want you to
(2.) each   (3.) believe
interview <u>both</u> candidates. Because of your background, I <u>feel</u> that will be important to our

making the best selection.
(4.) calculated
Once I have <u>determined</u> the costs to be incurred between here and completion, we
(5.) answer
will be ready to <u>solve</u> some of the more difficult questions. I know already that one of the
(6.) problems
chief <u>dilemmas</u> will be storage space for all the equipment involved.

Comments

1. *Anxious* implies an element of fear (anxiety); to depict enthusiastic readiness without anxiety, use *eager*.

2. To write "both candidates" is to leave open the possibility of interviewing them together. Although that interpretation is unlikely, "each candidate" carries the precision needed to remove all doubt.

3. The writer's knowledge of the reader's background instills a belief (based on information) more so than a feeling (based on emotion).

4. The two connotations of *determine* leave readers to interpret meaning as either "identify" or "decide upon." Assuming the first connotation applies here, I have chosen the unambiguous *calculated*. (*Identified* would work, but it is less precise.)

5. We answer questions and solve problems.

6. A dilemma is a choice between two undesirable outcomes. Insufficient storage space is a problem, not a dilemma.

Clean Revision

I believe you are as eager as I to launch this exciting project. I want you to interview each candidate. Because of your background, I believe that will be important to our making the best selection.

Once I have calculated the costs to be incurred between here and completion, we will be ready to answer some of the larger questions. I know already that one of the chief problems will be storage space for all the equipment involved.

Exercise #20: Chapter 8, Keep the Modifier and the Modified Together.

Our appointment with the WestMax team was set for 9:00 a.m. After we had ①almost waited for an hour, three of their five arrived. Sanderson announced without apology that there would ②only be four of them, and that the fourth was on his way. They never ③specifically told us what their problems had been that morning, but rather proceeded with the conversation as if they ④just wanted to get it finished and leave. By the time their fourth arrived, our team was not talking at all. Any company that brings that much rudeness and inconsideration to the table has to bring an enormous load of good business as compensation, and they had not ⑤even brought anything above average.

Comments

1. To *almost wait* is to not wait. The group had in fact waited, and the wait amounted to *almost an hour.*

2. Misplacement of *only* disrupts *would be.*

3. This misplaced modifier is, more specifically, a misplaced adverb. Not only does the revision improve precision by having *specifically* modify *what* rather than *told*, but the change keeps *never told us* intact.

4. Misplacement of *just* disrupts *they wanted.*

5. Alternate wording might be preferable. Rather than the negative form "…had not brought anything even above average," the writer might use positive form: "…had brought nothing even above average."

Notice that misplaced modifiers commonly disrupt the connection between helping verb and verb (*had waited; would be*) or between subject and verb (*they wanted*). So pulling the trigger early on modifiers not only robs sentences of the good effect of modifier and modified next to each other, but it also inflicts damage on the heart of the sentence: the subject and verb.

Clean Revision

Our appointment with the WestMax team was set for 9:00 a.m. After we had waited for almost an hour, three of their five arrived. Sanderson announced without apology that there would be only four of them, and that the fourth was on his way. They never told us specifically what their problems had been that morning, but rather proceeded with the conversation as if they wanted to just get it finished and leave. By the time their fourth arrived, our team was not talking at all. Any company that brings that much rudeness and inconsideration to the table has to bring an enormous load of good business as compensation, and they had brought nothing even above average.

Exercise #21: Chapter 8, Follow an Action Phrase with the Action's Subject.

After planning on the promotion for more than a year, ~~Gail Fraley's supervisor~~ Gail Fraley was disappointed ~~her by giving~~ when her supervisor gave the position to an outside applicant. She was bitter. With twenty years of diligent and faithful service on record, ▲ she believed the company owed her more.

Gail was even more bitter when she learned of the nepotism behind the appointment of Karen Shield. Having married the boss's son two years earlier, ~~her~~ Karen ~~appointment~~ was assured ▲ of the appointment from the moment she applied.

- - -

233

Comments

Do not let possessives deceive you into thinking you have the correct subject in place. Following the opening phrase, Gail Fraley's name functions only as an adjective modifying the incorrect subject: *supervisor*. The rightful subject is *Gail Fraley*. The misplacement in the last sentence is similar: *her* is only a possessive pronoun that refers to *Karen* and modifies the erroneous subject: *appointment*. *Karen* is the rightful subject.

To correct the misplaced subject in the last sentence of the first paragraph, I altered the message slightly by adding *believed*. I felt confident that doing so did not alter meaning, because the context of the message implies strongly that Gail Fraley believed the company to be in her debt. Interpreting meaning is no issue when you edit your own work, but you must be careful to not alter meaning when you edit the work of others.

Clean Revision

After planning on the promotion for more than a year, Gail Fraley was disappointed when her supervisor gave the position to an outside applicant. She was bitter. With twenty years of diligent and faithful service on record, she believed the company owed her more.

Gail was even more bitter when she learned of the nepotism behind the appointment of Karen Shield. Having married the boss's son two years earlier, Karen was assured of the appointment from the moment she applied.

Exercise #22: Chapter 8, Orient Readers with Word Placement.

All Directors and Managers of the Protocarcsic Division

The fall marketing campaign is about to begin. Priority marketing will be given to our product, according to what Mr. Duncan said this morning. Let me remind you that a division other than ours has been given priority in the fall campaign every year since 2015. This is an opportunity. We will meet to explore ways we can help the marketing department, Monday morning at 9:30 Information and ideas that you think will be of use. should be You should bring brought to the meeting.

Comments

This example shows four types of orienting material that give readers a context for whatever follows: a source (Mr. Duncan), a year (2015), a time (Monday morning at 9:30), and a directive (You should bring...). A key to identifying orienting material in your writing and placing it wisely is to keep your readers ever in mind. Just as you keep your attention on listeners as you speak, you should keep your attention on readers as you write.

Clean Revision

All Directors and Managers of the Protocarcsic Division

The fall marketing campaign is about to begin. According to what Mr. Duncan said this morning, priority marketing will be given to our product. Let me remind you that every year since 2015 a division other than ours has been given priority in the fall campaign. This is an opportunity. We will meet Monday morning at 9:30 to explore ways we can help the marketing department. You should bring to the meeting information and ideas that you think will be of use.

Exercise #23: Chapter 8, Emphasize Material with Word Placement.

Some service companies pride themselves on the number of services they offer.

Others pride themselves on offering only a few services, but at an exceptionally high level of

performance. We have not made a conscious decision about our place on that breadth/depth

— (enclose between commas)

continuum in the midst of our growth If we continue to "let it ride," we risk making our-

selves victims of circumstance—a conglomeration of workers with no firm identity drifting

I have read enough

down paths of least resistance in the hope that everything will turn out for the best. Few, if

about   to know that few, if any,

any, successful companies have wandered into their success with neither identity nor design.

judging by what I have learned by reading their history.

Comments

Two phrases in this paragraph struck me as deserving to be placed at the end of a sentence for emphasis: "our place on that breadth/depth continuum" and "with neither identity nor design." To make room for those phrases in the desired positions of emphasis, I had to find new homes for material that had been occupying that prime real estate: "in the midst of our growth," and "judging by what I have learned by reading their history." To accomplish the second, I had to exercise a little creativity that altered the wording but preserved the meaning.

Clean Revision

Some service companies pride themselves on the number of services they offer. Others pride themselves on offering only a few services, but at an exceptionally high level of performance. We, in the midst of our growth, have not made a conscious decision about our place on that breadth/depth continuum. If we continue to "let it ride," we risk making ourselves victims of circumstance—a conglomeration of workers with no firm identity drifting down paths of least resistance in the hope that everything will turn out for the best. I have read enough about the history of successful companies to know that few, if any, have stumbled into their success with neither identity nor design.

Exercise #24: Chapter 9, Incorrect Word Choice, Subject/Verb Disagreement, Dangling Participle, Split Infinitive.

(1.) I see that
Observing her performance for the team from an outsider's view, she handles
(2.) fewer   (3.) number   (4.) as
~~less~~ clients than the others, writes a smaller ~~amount~~ of contracts, and—~~like~~ I wrote in my first
(5.) to which   (6.) last
report—backs off from group projects ~~where~~ she should contribute. The ~~latter~~ is most
(7.) lying
disconcerting to her colleagues. Some have openly accused her of ~~laying~~ down on the job.
(8.)
If the CEO hopes to (dramatically) improve on last year's performance, he will need

to make important personnel decisions soon. A series of recent personnel losses, troubling
(9.) has
inquiries, and large, puzzling mistakes ~~have~~ put him in a very difficult position.

Comments

1. The dangling participle (misplaced subject) in the first sentence erroneously places the object of the observation (she) in the position of observing herself from the outside.

2. *Less* refers to an uncountable noun, *fewer* to a countable noun.

3. *Amount* refers to an uncountable noun, *number* to a countable noun.

   Note that replacing *amount* with *number*, while correct, is not necessarily best. We could reduce the number of words and create parallel construction by replacing "a smaller number of contracts" with "fewer contracts."

4. *Like* should be followed only by a noun or a noun phrase.

5. *Where*, appropriate only for reference to a location, should not replace *to which, in which, for which, by which,* or *through which.*

6. *Latter* refers to the second of two; *last* refers to the last of more than two.

For more complete explanations of these word-choice errors (2–7), turn to Appendix B.

7. A person *lays* down objects, but in assuming a prone position, *lies* down.

8. There is no reason to split the infinitive *to improve*. *Dramatically* serves the sentence just as well in its new position.

9. The singular subject, *series*, calls for a singular verb. This is a case of the writer having been pulled to a plural verb by intervening plural terms.

Clean Revision

Observing her performance for the team from an outsider's view, I see that she handles fewer clients than the others, writes fewer contracts, and—as I wrote in my first report—backs off from group projects to which she should contribute. The last is most disconcerting to her colleagues. Some have openly accused her of lying down on the job.

If the CEO hopes to improve dramatically on last year's performance, he will need to make important personnel decisions soon. A series of recent personnel losses, troubling inquiries, and large, puzzling mistakes has put him in a very difficult position.

Exercise #25: Chapter 9, Wrong Verb Tense, Careless Use of Prepositions, Wrong Pronoun Case, and Antecedent/Pronoun Disagreement.

(1.) had seen
Yesterday he told me that he ~~saw~~ nothing over the previous few weeks to make him
(2.)   (3.) his
suspicious. Seeing he had just come off ~~of~~ vacation, I appreciated ~~him~~ offering to talk to me.
(4.) me
Both of us knew our collaboration could lead to others resenting him and ~~I.~~ Too often, ~~when a~~
those who try (5.)
~~person tries~~ to do what is right, ~~they~~ find themselves giving credence to Clare Booth Luce's

cynical observation that "no good deed goes unpunished."

Comments

1. Yesterday was the past; the seeing was in the past of the past. That calls for past perfect tense: *had seen*.

2. The double preposition *off of* needs to be pared down to simply *off*. (Probably an alternate wording altogether would improve the sentence.)

3. What is appreciated is not *him*, but the offering. Whose offering? *His* offering. Therefore, the possessive (not objective) pronoun case is needed.

4. Others will resent *me* (objective case) not *I* (subjective case).

5. The singular antecedent, *a person,* is matched with a plural pronoun, *they,* in deference to gender-neutral language. That aim can be achieved

elegantly by reconstructing the sentence to eliminate the offending pronoun. You will read more examples in the next exercise.

Clean Revision

Yesterday he told me that he had seen nothing over the previous few weeks to make him suspicious. Seeing he had just come off vacation, I appreciated his offering to talk to me. Both of us knew our collaboration could lead to others resenting him and me. Too often, those who try to do what is right find themselves giving credence to Clare Booth Luce's cynical observation that "no good deed goes unpunished."

Exercise #26: Chapter 11, Accommodate Gender Elegantly.

(1.) employees are
When ~~an employee is~~ chronically late, they will be counseled for three occurrences (2.) an employee
before being written up. After a fifth occurrence in less than six months, ~~s/he~~ will be put on (3.)
probation. A sixth occurrence within a year will be considered cause for ~~his/her~~ termination. (4.)
A supervisor will have some room for discretion, but ~~he~~ must make a strong case for

retaining any chronically late employee. Failure to appear for work on time is irresponsible, (5.) the
and it reflects poorly on both the employee and ~~her~~ department.

Comments

1. Changing the singular antecedent to plural (employees) creates agreement in number between it and the plural pronoun (they). To write still more efficiently, eliminate the pronoun: "Chronically late employees will be…."

2. To dispense with the unpronounceable "s/he," reuse "employee."

3. No pronoun is needed. The object of the termination is obvious.

4. The generic-masculine "he" can be eliminated. "Supervisor" will carry over as the understood subject of the second independent clause.

5. The generic feminine pronoun "her" can be replaced comfortably with "the."

Clean Revision

Chronically late employees will be counseled for three occurrences before being written up. After a fifth occurrence in less than six months, the employee will be put on probation. A sixth occurrence within a year will be considered cause for termination.

A supervisor will have some room for discretion, but must make a strong case for retaining any chronically late employee. Failure to appear for work on time is irresponsible, and it reflects poorly on both the employee and the department.

Exercise #27: apostrophes, quotation marks, and hyphens.

(1.) managers'   (2.) deep-dive

I read in the manager's report that each manager gave a deep dive answer to the

(3.) company's

question, "What do I see as the greatest impediment to this companys' being managed

(4.) efficiently?"   (5.) 1990s

efficiently"? Apparently the same question had been asked of managers in the 1990's, and

(6.) CEO's

the CEOs purpose in asking again was "to see changes, both in the opinions of the

(7.) 'glaring gaps'   (8.)   have."

managers and in what we refer to as "glaring gaps" between what we need and what we have".

Comments

1. The sentence makes clear that the meeting was not a single manager's meeting, but rather a meeting of managers. So the report was a managers' (plural possessive) report.

2. The two words have meaning only when combined as a compound word.

3. *Company* is singular, so the singular form of the possessive is needed: company's.

4. A question mark that is part of a quote should be enclosed within the quotation marks.

5. The term *1990s* in this sentence refers to a group of years. Nothing is possessed, so the term should be written as a simple plural, not a possessive.

6. The CEO, a singular person, possesses the purpose referred to, so the singular possessive form is needed.

7. Single quotation marks are used to signal a quotation within a quotation.

8. In the American form of written English, periods are enclosed within quotation marks.

Clean Revision

I read in the managers' report that each manager gave a deep-dive answer to the question "What do I see as the greatest impediment to this company's being managed efficiently?" Apparently the same question had been asked of managers in the 1990s, and the CEO's purpose in asking again was "to see changes, both in the opinions of the managers and in what we refer to as 'glaring gaps' between what we need and what we have."

<u>Exercise #28: commas.</u>

(1.) complaints,

Gerald Wheeler came to us with a series of complaints and we gave our full

(2.) talked and

attention to every item on his list. He talked, and we listened. Showing admirable patience

(3.) stamina,

and stamina Jeff typed furiously for nearly an hour to record all the proceedings. Gerald,

(4.) points, spoke   (5.) Sarah,

appearing desperate to make his points spoke rapidly and loudly. Sarah who had an

(6.) us stayed

important appointment after work, left at 5:00 p.m. The rest of us, stayed another hour.

Gerald's most passionate wish was to talk directly to the Director of Human

(7.) Resources, who

Resources who had fired him. We told him we would be unwise to promise him a

(8.) resolution that   (9.) Eventually he left,

resolution, which we had no authority to carry out. Eventually, he left with none of the

(10.) consolation,

answers, consolation or satisfaction he had been seeking.

<u>Comments</u>

1. Use a comma before a conjunction that joins two independent clauses. The comma alerts readers to *and*'s function as a subordinating conjunction (connecting grammatically unequal material) rather than a coordinating conjunction (connecting grammatically equal material). A coordinating conjunction would connect, for example, "a series of complaints and questions."

2. An exception may be made to the rule described in comment #1 if the independent clauses are short enough to avoid even a momentary distraction for readers. These two-word independent clauses qualify, so the comma is a matter of choice.

3. The meat of this sentence begins with the subject and verb: *Jeff typed*. Set off the introductory phrase preceding the subject and verb with a comma.

4. Enclose parenthetical material (*appearing desperate to make his points*) between commas. The comma following the parenthetical material is missing in the original.

5. Enclose parenthetical material (*who had an important appointment after work*) between commas. The comma preceding the parenthetical material is missing.

6. The comma separating subject from verb appears random.

7. Assuming only one Director of Human Resources, "who fired him" must be a nonrestrictive clause (added information). Without the comma, the clause restricts the comment to the specific Director of Human Resources who fired him, in contrast to another Director of Human Resources (or maybe several) who had not fired him.

8. This problem is the reverse of #7. The group might have resolved the issue within the boundaries of their authority. So "which we had no authority to carry out" is a restrictive clause—one whose meaning is restricted to a resolution for which they had no authority. In keeping with the advice of Strunk & White, among others, I have used *that* as the relative pronoun of choice for introducing a restrictive clause.

9. The choice of comma placement here depends on intended meaning. The original works if the purpose is to emphasize his leaving without answers rather than with answers (restrictive). The revision reflects an assumption that the primary message is "eventually he left," with the remainder functioning as added information (nonrestrictive). Assuming the latter meaning, you could emphasize the added information by replacing the comma with a dash.

10. Controversy still reigns over the use of a final comma in a series. To my eye, a final comma clarifies the independence of the entries. Here, the lack of a comma creates a visual relationship between *consolation* and *satisfaction* that is closer than either of their relationships to *answers*. As series become longer and more complex, especially if some of the entries themselves contain correlating conjunctions, lack of the final comma can cause confusion and force rereading. Habitual use of the final comma in a series guarantees clarity and consistency, two qualities of writing that readers universally appreciate.

Clean Revision

Gerald Wheeler came to us with a series of complaints, and we gave our full attention to every item on his list. He talked and we listened. Showing admirable patience and stamina, Jeff typed furiously for nearly an hour to record all the proceedings. Gerald, appearing desperate to make his points, spoke rapidly and loudly. Sarah, who had an important appointment after work, left at 5:00 p.m. The rest of us stayed another hour.

Gerald's most passionate wish was to talk directly to the Director of Human Resources, who had fired him. We told him we would be unwise to promise him a resolution that we had no authority to carry out. Eventually he left—with none of the answers, consolation, or satisfaction he had been seeking.

Exercise #29: semicolons and colons.

          (1.) (Bronson, 1997; Mason, 2003; Shepherd, 2005; Zendler, 2007).
Several noted scientists agree (Bronson, 1997) (Mason, 2003) (Shepherd, 2005)
          (2.) convincing; helps
(Zendler, 2007). That makes his argument more convincing, helps sway board members,
    (2.) conservative; and
who tend to be conservative, and improves his chances, lean as they still are, of fending off
      (3.) remains: convincing
challenges. One large hurdle still remains; convincing the stockholders that the investment
      (4.) to
is sound. The steps I recommend are to:

    1. solicit strong statements of support from leading scientists,

    2. write a convincing piece for the stockholder newsletter, and

    3. meet individually with key players.

Comments

1. You can put a series of citations into one list by separating the larger elements with semicolons, leaving commas to separate information within the elements.

2. The same principle at work in #1 can be applied to a series of information within a complex sentence, with semicolons functioning as hard pauses to separate the larger elements and commas functioning as softer pauses to separate material within the elements.

3. Whereas a semicolon simply helps you organize and separate material, a colon signals a specific relationship between the material preceding it and the material following it. A colon says, "let me give you detail." A colon is appropriate to introduce an explanation, amplification, or illustration, as is the case here.

4. Like a period, a colon signifies a full stop. A colon would work for a list introduced by "The steps I recommend are as follows:" You can test how well a colon works by converting the list to a sentence format. For example, you would not write, "The steps I recommend are to: solicit…".

Clean Revision

Several noted scientists agree (Bronson, 1997; Mason, 2003; Shepherd, 2005; Zendler, 2007). That makes his argument more convincing; helps sway board members, who tend to be conservative; and improves his chances, lean as they still are, of fending off challenges. One large hurdle still remains: convincing the stockholders that the investment is sound. The steps I recommend are to

1. solicit strong statements of support from leading scientists,

2. write a convincing piece for the stockholder newsletter, and

3. meet individually with key players.

Exercise #30: hyphens, dashes, parentheses, slashes, brackets, and ellipses

① rough-hewn   ② faded and peeling
The rough hewn wood trim, the faded/peeling paint, and the dingy tile floors,
③ (with particularly dirty grout)
with particularly dirty grout, made the old warehouse a challenge to convert quickly into

usable office space. Bob Ferris studied the space thoroughly, all the while envisioning what
        do—working   ④   others—to
he could do-working with no help from the others-to meet the deadline. He remembered
                                                        Details...
the advice his father had given him years earlier: "Focus on the basic problems. ~~Details, if~~
⑤ will...keep you from [taking care of] the necessities."
~~you get too caught up in them, will eat you alive and keep you from the necessities that you~~

~~need to take care of.~~"

Comments

1. When two or more words work in combination to form a single term, help the reader see that term instantly by joining the words with a hyphen.

2. Rather than place a careless slash between two terms, decide your exact meaning and express it in full. Careless slashes assign the reader a job that is rightfully yours as writer.

3. This use of parentheses is subjective. Keep in mind that when a sentence becomes crowded with more thoughts than fit comfortably, punctuation options can be helpful. If the phrase "particularly dirty grout" deserves less prominence than the other information in the sentence, you can indicate that by enclosing the material in parentheses, as I have here. If the extra information is worthy of greater emphasis, you can show that by using the mark of self-interruption: dashes.

4. Never use hyphens (designed to join) where you intend dashes (designed to separate). To emphasize material by use of the mark of self-interruption, use the long dash (em dash). Any other form of dash is less effective, and the hyphen is counterproductive.

5. If you wanted to reduce the length of the quotation while retaining its essence, you could do so by using an ellipsis and a set of brackets as shown.

<u>Clean Revision</u>

The rough-hewn wood trim, the faded and peeling paint, and the dingy tile floors (with particularly dirty grout) made the old warehouse a challenge to convert quickly into useable office space. Bob Ferris studied the space thoroughly, all the while envisioning what he could do—working with no help from the others—to meet the deadline. He remembered the advice his father had given him years earlier: "Focus on the basic problems. Details…will keep you from [taking care of] the necessities."

Personal Dictionary

Periodically you'll encounter other words that you find troublesome, or words that seem useful to you but are unfamiliar. This page and the next offer a convenient place to enter and store those words.

Word	Definition and Example

Personal Dictionary

Word   Definition and Example

INDEX

An asterisk (*) indicates that the word itself is the issue.